JESUS CHRIST

The Jesus of History,
the Christ of Faith

J. R. PORTER

New York   Oxford
Oxford University Press
1999

Oxford University Press

Oxford   New York
Athens   Auckland   Bangkok   Bogotá   Buenos Aires
Calcutta   Cape Town   Chennai   Dar es Salaam   Delhi
Florence   Hong Kong   Istanbul   Karachi   Kuala Lumpur
Madrid   Melbourne   Mexico City   Mumbai   Nairobi   Paris
São Paolo   Singapore   Taipei   Tokyo   Toronto   Warsaw

and associated companies in
Berlin   Ibadan

Published in the United States of America by
Oxford University Press, Inc.
198 Madison Avenue, New York, N.Y. 10016–4314
Oxford is a registered trademark of Oxford University Press

Conceived, created, and designed by
Duncan Baird Publishers, London, England

Library of Congress Cataloging-in-Publication Data

Porter, J. R. (Joshua Roy), 1921–
     Jesus Christ : The Jesus of history, the Christ of faith / J. R. Porter.
         p.   cm.
     Includes bibliographical references and index.
     ISBN 0-19-521429-3 (alk. paper)
     1. Jesus Christ—Biography   2. Jesus Christ—Teachings and influence
     3. Jesus Christ—Interpretations   4. Jesus Christ—Art.   I. Title.
     BT198.P675   1999
     232--dc21   98-37404
                                                      CIP

Senior Editor: Peter Bently
Editor: Mike Darton
Designer: Paul Reid
Picture Research: Julia Brown, Julia Ruxton
Index: Lyn Greenwood
Commissioned Photography (see pages 239–40): Eitan Simanor
Maps: Neil Gower
Decorative Borders: Iona McGlashan

Typeset in Sabon 10/15pt
Color reproduction by Colourscan, Singapore
Printed and bound in China by Imago

NOTE
The abbreviations CE and BCE are used throughout this book:
CE Common Era (the equivalent of AD)
BCE Before the Common Era (the equivalent of BC)
Captions to illustrations on pages 1–3 appear on page 240

9 8 7 6 5 4 3 2 1

CONTENTS

Introduction	6
THE SETTING	11
The Geographical Background	
The Land of Palestine	12
Galilee	16
Jerusalem	18
The Political Background	
Hellenism	22
The Herodian Dynasty	24
Palestine under the Romans	26
Jewish Internal Government	28
The Religious Background	
The Law and the Temple	30
The Synagogue and Jewish Festivals	32
Sects and Parties	34
Society and Economy	
Trade and Commerce	38
Farmers and Fishers	40
Marriage and the Family	44
Languages of Palestine	46
THE LIFE	49
Sources	
What is a "Gospel"?	50
The Four Evangelists	52
The Gospel Evidence	56
Jesus in Other Writings	58
Jesus' Life and Times	60
The Birth of Jesus	
The Genealogy of Christ	62

The Nativity 64
The Virgin Birth 68

Infancy and Youth
The First Witnesses 70
The Wrath of Herod 72
The Flight into Egypt 74
Rites of Childhood 76
The Home Life of Jesus 78

The Call to Ministry
John the Baptist 82
The Baptism of Jesus 84
The Temptation 86

The Ministry in Galilee
The Disciples 90
Jesus' Public Career 92
The Healings 94
The Exorcisms 96
The Feeding Miracles 98
Conflicts and
  Confrontations 100

The Approach of the Passion
The Fate of the Baptist 104
Peter's Confession and the
  Transfiguration 106
The Road to Jerusalem 108
The Cleansing of the Temple 110
The Last Supper 112
Betrayal and Arrest 114

Condemnation and Crucifixion
The Trials of Jesus 116
Before the Council 118
Jesus and Pilate 120
Jesus Condemned 122
The Crucifixion 124

The Aftermath
The Risen Lord 128
The Ascension 132

THE TEACHINGS 135

How Jesus Taught
Sayings and Parables 136
Jesus and Scripture 140
Jesus and the Jewish Law 142
Gentiles and Samaritans 144

The Ethics of Jesus
God the Father 146
Sermons and Discourses 148
The Call of the Kingdom 150
The Teachings in John 154

INTERPRETATIONS 157

How Jesus Saw Himself
The Healer of Body and Soul 158
The Prophet 160
Master, Rabbi, Lord 162
Messiah 164
Son of God 166
Son of Man 168

The Man and the Message
The Early Church 170
Jewish and Gentile Christians 172
The Patristic Period 174
Jesus and Gnosticism 176
Founder of the Church? 178
The Apocalyptic Jesus 180
The Revolutionary 182
The Mystic 184
Jesus and Feminism 186

Judaism and the Church 188
Jesus and Islam 190
In Search of the Jesus of
  History 192

JESUS IN ART 197
by Jennifer Speake

Early Christian Art 198
The Nativity 200
Madonna and Child 202
Scenes from Childhood 206
The Ministry 208
The Passion 212
The Resurrection 218
Christ Triumphant 220

Glossary 222
Abbreviations 223
Bibliography 224
Index 227
Picture Credits 239

INTRODUCTION

It need hardly be said that Jesus has always been a figure of great fascination and interest, and by no means only for Christian believers. Over the centuries, a vast amount of literature has been produced about him, and the flow shows no sign of abating. Contemporary research into Jesus is largely conditioned by the developments of the last two centuries, which have tended to detach the historical Jesus—the man who lived and acted in the Palestine of the first century CE—from the Christ of Christian faith. The question "Who really was Jesus?" has produced a bewildering variety of answers. It has been variously claimed that Jesus was essentially, to quote just a few examples, a Pharisaic rabbi; a charismatic Jewish wonder-worker; an apocalyptic prophet; a philosopher similar to one of the ancient Cynics; a social reformer; and a political revolutionary.

   The present volume considers several of the more plausible and suggestive theories concerning the "real" Jesus. Its aim is not primarily to present

The Loaves and Fishes, *a 6th-century mosaic in the church of Sant' Apollinare Nuovo, Ravenna. All the gospels record Jesus' feeding of a large crowd with a tiny amount of food (see pp.98–9). This suggests that the tradition of such a miracle originated very early, perhaps even within the circle of Jesus' first followers.*

another biography of Jesus, but rather to highlight some of the factors that have inspired the continued quest, among present-day New Testament scholars and others, to discover the man Jesus of Nazareth.

One of these factors is our greatly improved—and growing—understanding of the world and society in which Jesus lived. Archaeology in particular, but also sociological studies and the work of historians specializing in the Roman empire, have shown how deeply Jesus' life and teaching were affected by his environment. Thus, the first section of this book (The Setting) deals with the general geographical, political, religious, economic, and social contexts in which Jesus operated. Here and throughout, there is a special emphasis on the Judaism of Jesus' day, which is now much more fully appreciated than was often the case in the past.

The following section (The Life) deals with the career of Jesus from the Nativity to the Ascension, as presented in the four canonical gospels of Matthew, Mark, Luke, and John. Again, the object is not to construct a biography of Jesus in the modern sense but to provide some evaluation of his life and deeds as recorded by the evangelists. How the birth narratives, trials of Jesus, Resurrection, and other episodes are to be assessed remains the subject of intense scholarly debate, as does the value of the gospels as sources. Nevertheless, it does seem possible to provide at least an outline of the course of Jesus' earthly life which would be accepted by a majority of scholars and historians today.

As important as what Jesus did is what he taught and this is the subject of section three (The Teachings). This begins with a survey of Jesus' distinctive teaching methods, as seen in his parables and sayings, which are closely linked to his Palestinian setting, and in the use he made of sources such as the Hebrew Bible and the Jewish law. Here, again, Jesus' background in Judaism is highly significant. The rest of this section is devoted to the main themes of Jesus' message, as these are presented in the four gospels. Overall, the third section raises one of the main areas of contention in New Testament studies: the extent to which it is possible to recover the actual words of Jesus, as opposed to those utterances which—although attributed to Jesus in the gospels—really derive from the early Church. This vital question will also be considered below.

The fourth section (Interpretations) focuses on how the person of Jesus has been understood over the centuries. It begins with an overview of what, according to the available evidence, appear to have been the principal elements of Jesus' own self-consciousness. There follows a series of descriptions—inevitably brief and selective—of some of the many ways in which Jesus' character and mission have been approached and interpreted down to the present time.

The fifth, and final, section (Jesus in Art) is an illustrated survey of the rich and varied traditions of Jesus in the history of Christian art.

It is important to appreciate fully the fact that the gospels constitute

The entrance to the Franciscan Chapel of the Flagellation in Jerusalem, which stands on the spot where, according to Christian tradition, Jesus was flogged by Roman soldiers before the Crucifixion. The Catholic Franciscan order holds the custodianship of numerous Christian sacred sites in Palestine and has been responsible for overseeing many of the archaeological discoveries that illuminate biblical scholarship. The Chapel of the Flagellation was built in the late 1920s on the site of a 12th-century church.

not one but four separate and distinctive accounts of Jesus' life and teaching. Each gospel was written to be of use to a particular early Christian community: it was produced to meet that community's needs and concerns and to give expression to what it believed to be the essential truth of the Christian faith.

The Jesus of the gospels, therefore, is a figure seen through the eyes of the early Church. Full weight must be given to the creative activity of the first Christian communities and to the possibility that they may have invented some sayings and episodes in order to bring out more clearly their own understanding of Jesus.

It has become commonplace in New Testament scholarship to distinguish between the "Jesus of history" and the "Christ of faith," and to stress that all the information about Jesus in the gospels is provided by people who were not his direct disciples and whose view of his significance was, crucially, shaped by their belief in his physical resurrection. Any attempt to discover the historical Jesus depends on whether or not the early Church preserved *any* material that authentically came from Jesus himself and, if so, how this can be sifted from material influenced, or even created, by his first followers. Several scholars would say that such an endeavor is largely unavailing—in fact, that we can only ever meet with the Christ of faith.

Yet it seems likely that the gospel writers worked with a body of existing traditions about Jesus that had many points in common and must, in numerous instances, have derived from the disciples who knew him. Many students of the gospels, therefore, still consider it worthwhile and highly important to look for elements in this material that may be traced back to Jesus himself. They hope thereby to discover a core of authentic sayings of Jesus that encapsulate what he really taught and how he really saw himself.

Once again, this is no easy undertaking. Over the years, scholars have adopted various criteria by means of which they have sought—often, perhaps, with a degree of overconfidence—to prove, or at least suggest, authenticity (see p.194). The most thoroughgoing and widely publicized project to identify the real sayings of Jesus, largely employing the criteria just mentioned, has been that of a group of scholars in the United States known as the "Jesus Seminar" (see sidebar, p.56). The Seminar found that only very few—sixteen percent—of Jesus' recorded words could be considered in any way authentic. It is perhaps unsurprising that, in their own presentations of the historical Jesus, some of the Seminar's individual scholars produce a somewhat minimalist picture. They find little evidence to suggest that Jesus ever thought of himself in the terms suggested by the gospels, such as Son of God, Messiah, performer of miracles or apocalyptic prophet. For them, the Jesus of history must be freed from any theological framework and seen as essentially a radical social reformer.

But many scholars would question how far the Jesus Seminar's findings can be considered definitive and would prefer to conclude simply that it will always be difficult to establish which gospel traditions really go back to Jesus. It may be objected also that the Seminar's researches focus too narrowly on a literary analysis of the gospels, at the expense of other potentially illuminating sources such as the Jewish heritage and the contributions of archaeology and sociology. Also, the contrast between the Jesus of history and the Christ of faith can be exaggerated. A particular saying of Jesus in the gospels may not be formulated in his actual words, but its substance may accurately reflect his teaching—it must not be too easily assumed that the first Christians generally misunderstood their master.

In the end, anyone who attempts a reconstruction, however tentative, of the life and intentions of Jesus cannot avoid a degree of subjectivity. Every idea about Jesus has to be tested by the wide range of criteria and sound historical methods that present-day biblical scholarship has at its disposal.

The Last Judgment, *an anonymous Spanish altarpiece of ca. 1486. Christ, displaying his wounds and seated on a crystal orb representing the world, presides over the resurrection of the dead. Flanking Christ are the Virgin and St. John and two angels, one holding a sword (the symbol of the punishment of the damned) and the other a lily (representing the heavenly bliss that awaits the saved). The complex vision of Christ as cosmic judge derives from the writings of the early Church, but these may well reflect elements of the teaching and self-understanding of the historical Jesus (see box, p.169, and pp.180–81).*

THE SETTING

The Geographical Background	12	**The Religious Background**	30
The Land of Palestine	12	The Law and the Temple	30
Galilee	16	The Synagogue and Jewish Festivals	32
Jerusalem	18	Sects and Parties	34
The Political Background	22	**Society and Economy**	38
Hellenism	22	Trade and Commerce	38
The Herodian Dynasty	24	Farmers and Fishers	40
Palestine under the Romans	26	Marriage and the Family	44
Jewish Internal Government	28	Languages of Palestine	46

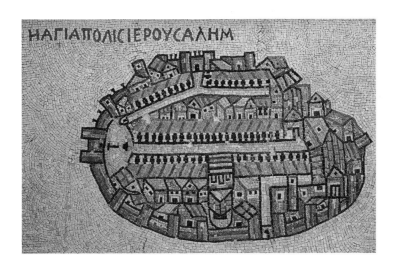

ABOVE: The Holy City of Jerusalem, *part of a famous 6th-century Byzantine mosaic depicting the Christian sacred sites of Palestine.*

OPPOSITE: *The Sea of Galilee near Tiberias. Galilee, especially its lake margins, provided the setting for much of Jesus' ministry.*

THE LAND OF PALESTINE

The main events of Jesus' life took place in Palestine, a region that may conveniently be understood as the land west of the river Jordan, from Dan in the north to Beersheba in the south—the traditional "land of Israel" as defined in the Hebrew Scriptures (for example, Judg. 20.1)—and the territory immediately to the east of the Jordan. Ironically, perhaps, the name "Palestine" comes from the Philistines, Israel's great enemies, who in fact occupied only the southwestern coastal area. The term was first used of the wider region by the Greek historian Herodotus (fifth century BCE). In spite of its small size, Palestine's strategic position as a bridge between two continents gave it a pivotal role in the international politics, commerce and culture of the ancient Near East. However, there is little awareness of this wider context in the gospels as compared with the Hebrew Scriptures.

The region is delimited by the natural boundaries of the Mediterranean to the west, Mount Hermon to the north, and the Syrian and Negeb deserts to the east and south. Within these bounds, Palestine falls into four natural regions, each running roughly from north to south. First, the coastal plain stretches from the Phoenician city of Sidon (just north of Palestine as defined here) down to Gaza, interrupted only by the highlands of Mount Carmel and the Ladder of Tyre. There are brief mentions of a visit by Jesus to the region of Sidon and its southerly neighbour, Tyre (Mark 3.8 and parallels), but generally speaking the Mediterranean seaboard lay outside the sphere of his activities.

To the east of the coastal plain, the central mountain range runs from

The Jordan river in the north of Israel. It forms part of Palestine's natural eastern frontier and features prominently in Israelite history. It was the setting for the ministry of John the Baptist and for the baptism of Jesus.

Galilee to Judea. In ancient times this was the heart of the country. It was the center of its trade and agriculture—although some parts were more fertile than others—and the setting for almost the whole of Jesus' ministry. At the southern end of the range lie the hill country and wilderness of Judea. The hill country encompasses Jerusalem, Bethlehem, and other sites associated with Jesus. The wilderness, to the east of the city, is where John the Baptist began his ministry (see pp.82–3) and Jesus was tempted by Satan (pp.86–7). Adjoining the lower Jordan and Dead Sea region, it is not true desert, but rather uncultivated pastureland, which could provide the Baptist with a sparse diet of locusts and wild honey (Matt. 3.4 and parallels). It

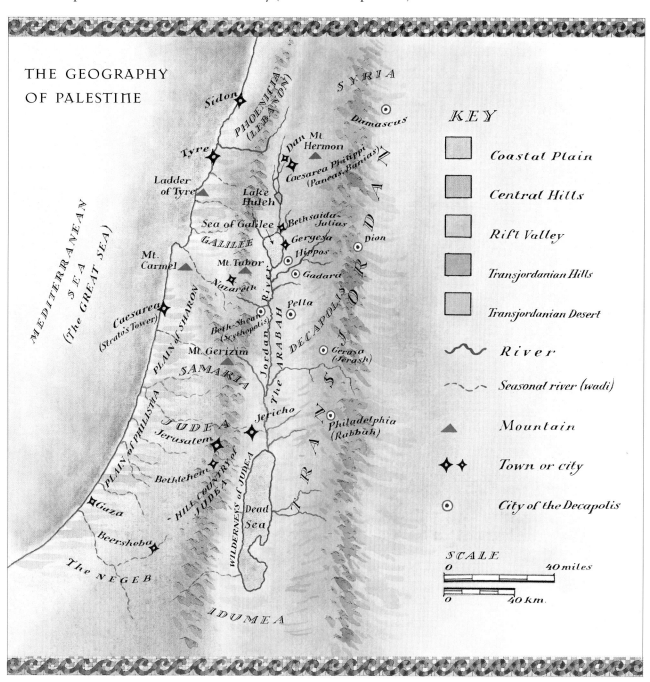

An ornate column capital from Beth-Shean (Scythopolis), the only Decapolis city west of the Jordan. In the 1st century CE these Greco-Roman cities were places of great wealth and splendor.

THE DECAPOLIS

Jesus is recorded as crossing the Sea of Galilee to a region known as the Decapolis. This comprised a league of ten Hellenistic cities, originally independent but assigned by the Romans to the province of Syria. The Decapolis is the setting of the famous episode in which Jesus sent a band of demons into a herd of pigs (see pp.96–7). Early texts of the gospels variously locate this story in the land of "the Gerasenes," "the Gadarenes," and "the Gergesenes." The Decapolis city of Gerasa (Jerash, Jordan) in fact lay a considerable distance from the Sea of Galilee; Gadara, on the other hand, was just six miles (10km) from the lake. Gergesa was also near the lake, but was not in the Decapolis. The confusion suggests that, despite the numerous followers he is said to have had from the region, Jesus' connection with the Decapolis was essentially peripheral.

was well enough watered to allow some basic agriculture.

The third region is the Palestinian section of the Afro-Asiatic great Rift Valley, through which the Jordan pursues a meandering course from north of Lake Huleh via the sea of Galilee down to the Dead Sea. The Jordan valley—which is below sea level for most of its length—is arid terrain except for the verdant margins of the river and freshwater lakes. The Baptist's main activity took place on one or both banks of the lower Jordan, in an area that includes the unlocated sites of "Aenon and Salim" (John 3.23), "Bethany cross the Jordan" (John 1.28), and of Jesus' own baptism (see pp.84–5).

Transjordan is the name given to the fourth broad region of Palestine, the hilly terrain lying east of the Jordan and the Dead Sea. In the north of this region, which is physically quite similar to the central mountain range, the snow-capped heights of Mount Hermon may have been the scene of the Transfiguration (see p.106). It was in Transjordan that Jesus drove an army of demons into a herd of swine, in the region of the Decapolis (Matt. 8.28–33; Mark 5.1–13; Luke 8.26–33; see sidebar, left). The gospel accounts suggest that on his final journey to Jerusalem, Jesus went over the Jordan (Matt. 19.1; Mark 10.1) into the area called Perea ("Land Beyond [the Jordan]"), where he attracted large crowds and performed healings, before crossing the river once more to enter Judea at Jericho (Mark 10.46).

There were two main types of settlement in first-century Palestine: the "town" or "city" (Greek *polis*) and the "village" (*kome*). They were not sharply distinguished in terms of size. A *kome* could have a larger population than a *polis* and perhaps the only real distinction was that "villages" were usually unwalled while "towns" were walled, such as Nain in Galilee, at the gate of which Jesus restored a young man to life (Luke 7.11–17). Archaeological evidence suggests that most settlements were quite small and inhabited mainly by Jews, while the bigger cities were more cosmopolitan, with large non-Jewish populations.

Towns and villages had a simple ground plan. Narrow streets and alleyways lined with modest houses converged on a large open marketplace, the hub of social and commercial life, which lay just inside the town gate if the place was walled. Mark 6.56 records that the sick were regularly brought into the marketplaces for Jesus to heal. The gospels frequently mention the presence of a synagogue in the towns Jesus visited, but otherwise there seem to have been few, if any, public buildings.

Apart from Jerusalem and its environs (see pp.18–21), Jesus is associated with several other towns in Palestine that were very different from those he frequented in Galilee (see pp.16–17). All the gospels relate an important episode that Matthew and Mark locate in the vicinity of Caesarea Philippi (Matt. 16.13; Mark 8.27), in which Jesus is acknowledged as Messiah (see pp.106–7). It was a major city at the foot of Mount Hermon in the far north of Palestine, in the tetrarchy of Philip (4BCE–34CE; see pp.24–5). A typical Greco-Roman settlement, Caesarea Philippi was the site of a sanctuary to the god Pan (hence the city's older name of Paneas, modern Banias) and most of its inhabitants would have been pagans. Jesus may have felt able to move freely in this environment, away from his Jewish detractors. But there is no evidence that he visited the town itself.

The gospels attest to a strong tradition that Jesus went to the non-Jewish region of Tyre and Sidon in Syria-Phoenicia, and even visited the latter city. But he is only said to have gone "by way of Sidon" (Mark 7.31) on his way back to Galilee and it would appear that he made a comparatively brief stay in the region, perhaps in an attempt to extend his influence there—the gospels relate that some of the inhabitants had been attracted to his teaching in Galilee (Matt. 4.24; compare Mark 7.26).

On his final journey from Galilee to Jerusalem (see pp.108–9), Jesus is said to have passed through Jericho, from where a direct road led through the Judean hill country to the capital. New Testament Jericho—situated in a fertile oasis just south of the site of the city of the Hebrew Scriptures—was granted ca. 30BCE by the Roman emperor Augustus to Herod the Great, who adorned it with splendid palaces. Luke records that Jesus spent the night there at the house of Zacchaeus, "a chief tax collector" (Luke 19.2)— a title indicating that Jericho was a regional administrative center.

Orchards in winter in the north of Palestine. In the distance are the heights of Mount Hermon, which may have been the setting for the Transfiguration of Jesus (see p.106).

GALILEE

JESUS' GALILEAN ITINERARY
The gospels record that Jesus taught in the open and mention no visits to the larger Galilean towns, such as Sepphoris, the former capital of Galilee, just four miles from Nazareth, and Tiberias, the new capital founded ca. 18CE. Jesus had good reason to avoid both cities: they were the power centers of Galilee's ruler, Herod Antipas (see p.25), who executed John the Baptist and was reportedly keen to question Jesus (Luke 9.7–9).

However, the evangelists do speak of Jesus regularly visiting other villages and towns, teaching in their synagogues and healing. The mission of his disciples was also directed toward population centers (Matt. 10.23; Luke 9.5–6). As well as Capernaum (see box, opposite) and Bethsaida (see main text), Jesus visited smaller Galilean towns such as Chorazin (Matt. 11.21; Luke 10.13), Gennesaret (Matt. 14.34; Mark 6.53), and Cana (John 2.1–11). Cana, near Nazareth, was also the hometown of the disciple Nathanael.

The Sea of Galilee near Capernaum, focus of Jesus' Galilean ministry. The Church of the Twelve Apostles (Greek Orthodox) commemorates the calling of the disciples.

Galilee, a region in the north of Palestine, was the principal setting for the ministry of Jesus, especially the area around its lake, commonly known as the Sea of Galilee or Lake Galilee. In Jesus' lifetime Galilee was governed by King Herod the Great (37–4BCE) and then his son, the tetrarch Herod Antipas (4BCE–39CE), both clients of Rome (see pp.24–5). It had long had a mixed population of Jews and Gentiles and was described in the Hebrew Bible as "Galilee of the Nations" (Isa. 9.1). According to one theory, this may have been the original name of the region—Galilee simply means "district" (Hebrew *galil*). The non-Jewish population increased around the beginning of the Common Era as Galilee's rulers founded new Hellenistic cities. Galileans were distinguished by their accent (Matt. 26.73), and the Pharisees (see pp.34–6) apparently looked down on them as lax in their observance of the Jewish law and incapable of producing the Messiah (John 7.52). The area was also known as a source of political unrest (see p.103).

Galilee includes the most northerly section of the central Palestinian mountain range (see pp.12–13) and is divided into Lower Galilee, the principal area of settlement and main focus of Jesus' ministry, and the largely mountainous Upper Galilee. In the gospels the most important feature of Galilee is the lake and its environs. The Hebrew Scriptures suggest that its earliest name was Lake Chinnereth ("lyre") which derived either from its shape or the name of a town at its northwest corner. In New Testament times, it was sometimes called Lake Tiberias or Lake Gennesaret after two

NAZARETH AND CAPERNAUM

The Galilean towns most closely associated with Jesus are Capernaum and Nazareth. Jesus' hometown of Nazareth was a small and insignificant village, and virtually nothing of Jesus' time has been preserved. It was a satellite of Herod Antipas's splendid city of Sepphoris, the largest city in Galilee and just an hour's walk away. It has been suggested that the young Jesus and his family may have had contacts with Sepphoris and been influenced by its Hellenistic civilization. As carpenter-builders (see p.75), Jesus and Joseph may conceivably have worked on the reconstruction of the city following its destruction in a rebellion in 4BCE. One early Christian tradition claimed that Mary came from there.

Jesus chose Capernaum (Hebrew, Kefar Nahum, "Village of Nahum") as the headquarters for his ministry in Galilee. He frequently resided there, probably in the house of his disciple Peter. At this time Capernaum was a modest but thriving commercial center, with a toll office and probably a small Roman garrison under a centurion. The town was close to the border of Philip's tetrarchy and on the Via Maris ("Sea Road"), an important highway linking Damascus in Syria with the coast.

When the site of Capernaum was excavated in the early twentieth century, the ruins were discovered of a fourth-century CE synagogue that had replaced one of the first century,

Ruins of 1st-century Capernaum. In spite of the miracles he performed there, Jesus eventually felt rejected by its inhabitants.

in which Jesus may have preached. Close by, under the ruins of an octagonal fifth-century CE church, lay the remains of a first-century CE house owned, according to objects discovered there, by fisherfolk. The early Christians revered this house as that of Peter—hence the church built on the site—and many modern scholars support this identification. It is certainly the kind of dwelling in which Peter and Jesus would have lived.

other towns. It is below sea level and surrounded by high hills, a combination that could produce the sudden squalls mentioned several times in the gospels. The lake was rich in fish and its shores formed a fertile agricultural area that attracted a large population.

Apart from Capernaum (see box, above), the place most frequently mentioned as the scene of Jesus' activity in the region bordering Lake Galilee is Bethsaida, just over the political frontier in the tetrarchy of Philip (ruled 4BCE–34CE), another son of Herod the Great. In Jesus' time Bethsaida would have been only a small place, and Mark calls it a "village." But the later gospels call it a *polis* ("town" or "city"), which may reflect its elevation by Philip in 30CE, when it was renamed Julias in honor of Livia Julia, the mother of the Roman emperor Tiberius. The name Bethsaida means "House of fishing" and archaeologists have confirmed that it was a fishing settlement. According to John's gospel, three of Jesus' original disciples—at least two of whom, Peter and Andrew, were fishermen—came from there. Jesus ultimately curses Bethsaida (Matt. 11.21; Luke 10.13) for failing to respond to the miracles he had performed there (for example, Mark 8.22–26).

JERUSALEM

The most important city in Palestine, then as now, was Jerusalem. Well away from the main regional trade routes and areas of population, it was not a great economic center but primarily a religious and political capital. The New Testament provides comparatively little information about the city in Jesus' day, and the identification of most of the places traditionally associated with him, such as the sites of the Last Supper and the Crucifixion, derives from later Christian sources. But some of these writings may rely on good tradition, while archaeological discoveries and sources such as the historian Josephus (first century CE) and the Mishnah (second century CE) sometimes shed light on the gospel record of Jesus' activities in the city.

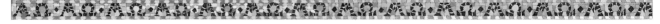

JESUS AND THE TEMPLE MOUNT

At least two episodes that took place in Jerusalem are illuminated by what is known of the topography of the Temple Mount in the first century CE. According to the gospels, Jesus sat down opposite the Temple "treasury," where he observed people making monetary offerings (Mark 12.41; Luke 21.1) and where, according to John, he taught (John 8.20). As a great economic institution (see pp.30–31), the Temple had a treasury chamber, where the bulk of its wealth was stored, but when the gospels speak of the worshipers "putting money into the treasury" they probably mean the thirteen collection chests which, according to the Mishnah, were placed round the walls of the Court of the Women. Each was inscribed with the purpose to which the offerings inside were to be devoted. The specific mention in the gospels of people selling doves or pigeons for sacrifice (as at Matt. 21.12) may imply that these were the main offerings at this time for individual worshipers.

The famous episode of the cleansing of the Temple (see pp.110–11) probably took place in or near the Royal Portico, or Stoa, a magnificent basilica-like covered colonnade which stood at the southern end of the Court of the Gentiles and towered high above the city and the Kidron valley. It was copied by Herod from similar structures that stood adjacent to temples in the Greco-Roman world and served as meeting places for merchants, worshipers and pilgrims. On the occasion of the cleansing, Mark makes a reference (Mark 11.16) to Jesus forbidding the carrying of objects through the Temple precincts—in other words, using it as a short cut. But Jesus' action is supported by Josephus, who says that the practice was officially prohibited.

Jesus is recorded in John as walking in another vast colonnade, known as Solomon's Portico, on the east side of the Temple Mount (John 10.23). The portico, also mentioned in Acts (3.11 and 5.12) and by Josephus (although not by name), was a place where speakers would address the crowds that gathered there. It was therefore a very likely location for Jesus' teaching activities in the Temple.

A reconstruction of the Royal Portico at the southern end of the Temple Mount. The steps (foreground) led down to the Triple Hulda Gate, the Temple's main southern entrance.

The city that Jesus knew was above all the creation of King Herod the Great (see p.24), who constructed a wall around the quarter known as the New City, and built a theater, an amphitheater, a hippodrome, and also a fine palace for himself in the Upper City, the aristocratic quarter. The most impressive of all Herod's achievements was the rebuilding of the Second Temple to create one of the largest and most magnificent religious buildings in the Roman world. The central sanctuary was constructed from massive blocks of masonry and many parts of it were overlaid with gold and silver—the gospels record the wonder of onlookers who beheld its fine large stones and rich ornaments (Mark 13.1; Luke 21.5).

Relating the episode of the Cleansing of the Temple (see pp.110–11), John's gospel says that the building had been under construction for forty-six years (John 2.20). Josephus states that it was begun in 20–19BCE, which would date the cleansing incident to the late 20s CE, a very feasible date for the ministry of Jesus. The sanctuary itself was completed in only eighteen months but work continued on other parts of the Temple Mount, the great platform on which the Temple stood (see box, opposite) almost up to the outbreak of the First Jewish War (66–73CE)—during which the entire Temple complex was destroyed by the Romans.

Situated high in the Judean mountains, Jerusalem is surrounded by hills, of which the Mount of Olives is the most significant for the gospel story. On his final visit to Jerusalem, and perhaps before, Jesus is recorded as spending the night either in Bethany, a village two miles (3.2 km) from

A view westward across Jerusalem. The golden Dome of the Rock marks the site of the Temple sanctuary. The nearest walls follow the eastern and southern sides of the ancient Temple Mount.

THE *PRAETORIUM*

In Jesus' day, the Roman prefect (governor) of Judea was based at Caesarea on the coast, but came to Jerusalem on the occasion of the major Jewish festivals. While in the city he resided at the *praetorium*, mentioned in the gospels (Matt. 27.27; Mark 15.16; John 19.9) as the place where Jesus was tried by Pilate. It is generally accepted that the *praetorium* was either the former palace of Herod the Great or the Antonia, a fortress built by Herod on the site of an earlier citadel at the northwest corner of the Temple Mount and named after his early Roman patron, Mark Antony (died 31BCE). According to Josephus, Pilate stayed at Herod's palace, but it is possible that he moved to the Antonia, the city's main Roman garrison, for at least some of this time, since it was closer to the Temple, where any civil unrest was most likely to erupt.

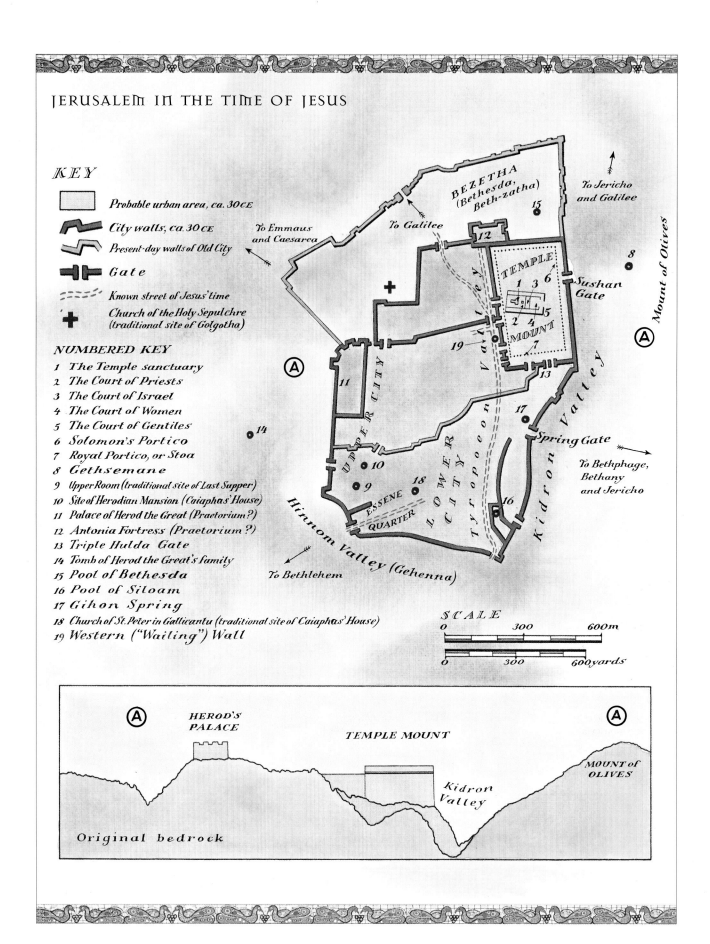

JERUSALEM IN THE TIME OF JESUS

KEY

Probable urban area, ca. 30 CE

City walls, ca. 30 CE

Present-day walls of Old City

Gate

Known street of Jesus' time

✝ Church of the Holy Sepulchre
(traditional site of Golgotha)

NUMBERED KEY

1 The Temple sanctuary
2 The Court of Priests
3 The Court of Israel
4 The Court of Women
5 The Court of Gentiles
6 Solomon's Portico
7 Royal Portico, or Stoa
8 Gethsemane
9 Upper Room (traditional site of Last Supper)
10 Site of Herodian Mansion (Caiaphas' House)
11 Palace of Herod the Great (Praetorium?)
12 Antonia Fortress (Praetorium?)
13 Triple Hulda Gate
14 Tomb of Herod the Great's family
15 Pool of Bethesda
16 Pool of Siloam
17 Gihon Spring
18 Church of St. Peter in Gallicantu (traditional site of Caiaphas' House)
19 Western ("Wailing") Wall

BEZETHA
(Bethesda,
Beth-zatha)

To Emmaus
and Caesarea

To Galilee

To Jericho
and Galilee

Mount of Olives

TEMPLE
MOUNT

Sushan
Gate

UPPER CITY

Kidron Valley

Spring Gate

To Bethphage,
Bethany
and Jericho

ESSENE
QUARTER

LOWER
CITY

Tyropoeon Valley

Hinnom Valley (Gehenna)

To Bethlehem

SCALE

0 ___ 300 ___ 600m

0 ___ 300 ___ 600 yards

Ⓐ HEROD'S
PALACE

TEMPLE MOUNT

Kidron
Valley

Ⓐ MOUNT of
OLIVES

Original bedrock

the city on the eastern slopes of the Mount of Olives, where apparently he had a group of friends (Mary, Martha, and their brother Lazarus); or on the mount itself, probably in the estate of Gethsemane (Hebrew *gath sehnamim*, "Olive Presses") on its lower slopes, where he was arrested. As the name implies, the Mount of Olives was covered by extensive olive groves. On the occasion of his triumphal entry into the city (see sidebar, p.110), Jesus appears to have journeyed from Bethany over the mount, via the village of Bethphage, where he acquired the donkey on which he rode.

Whatever the date and authorship of the gospel of John (see pp.50–51), it is now widely accepted that it contains good historical and topographical information about first-century Jerusalem, which is supported by archaeological and other evidence. The evangelist appears to have known the city well, and he refers to a number of features not mentioned in the other gospels, such as the Sheep Gate and the adjoining pool of Beth-zatha (or Bethesda), where Jesus cured the paralytic (John 5.2–9). There is archaeological and other evidence that the water in the pool—which was located in 1866 and discovered to have five porticoes, as John describes—were believed to possess healing properties. Similarly, only John mentions the pool of Siloam, where Jesus sent the blind man to be cured (John 9.7).

The evangelist also knew that the route from the city to the Mount of Olives crossed the valley of the Kidron brook, which he accurately describes by a word denoting a seasonal river, or wadi (John 18.1). This valley was much deeper in Jesus' day than now (see opposite).

John alone refers to the stone pavement (paved area) outside the *praetorium*, the Roman military headquarters (see sidebar, p.19). It was on this paved area that Pilate sat in judgment over Jesus, and John gives its Aramaic name, Gabbatha ("Raised Place") (John 19.13).

THE POPULATION OF JERUSALEM

It is difficult to assess how many people lived in Jerusalem at the time of Jesus. One estimate has put the number of permanent residents at no more than thirty thousand. But some four times this figure may have flocked to Jerusalem on the occasion of the major Jewish festivals, accounting for the crowds of which the gospels speak (for example, John 12.12) and for the regular presence of the Roman prefect in the city at Passover and possibly other times.

This view across Jerusalem, taken ca. 1950, captures much of the atmosphere of the Old City in the premodern era. In the distance, left, is the tower of the Lutheran Church of the Redeemer; the tower in the foreground is that of a mosque of the Turkish period.

HELLENISM

THE MACCABEAN REVOLT

The impact of Hellenism varied in different regions. For the Jews, the decisive moment was the reign of Antiochus Epiphanes (175–164BCE), ruler of the Seleucid empire founded in 312BCE by Seleucus, one of Alexander the Great's generals. Under Antiochus the empire included Palestine, where he adopted a radical Hellenizing policy. He desecrated the Temple of Jerusalem by erecting an altar of Zeus (whom he equated with the Jewish God) and banned circumcision, the Sabbath, and other Jewish customs.

These actions provoked a revolt led by Judas Maccabeus, who in 142BCE established an independent Jewish state ruled by his successors, the Hasmonean dynasty of high priests. It lasted for around a century until the arrival of the Romans.

Hellenism may be defined as the essentially Greek pattern of civilization that came to dominate the Near East in the wake of the conquests of Alexander the Great (ruled 332–323BCE). It embraced language, lifestyle, education, economy, philosophy, and religion. Its general effect was to bring diverse existing societies within a common culture. For example, it encouraged "syncretism"—the equation of one god with another as forms of the same deity.

Hellenism in Palestine was largely confined to the urban upper classes, while the Maccabean revolt (see sidebar, left) ensured that Jewish religious culture always remained fiercely independent. Under Hasmonean rule, the propagators of Hellenism were regularly forced to reiterate their loyalty to their ancestral Judaism. The later Hasmonean rulers acted as typical Hellenistic monarchs but remained strong Jewish nationalists. Herod the Great, who succeeded them, was a client of Rome and an ardent Hellenizer, who built Greek-style cities that even incorporated pagan tem-

JESUS AND THE CYNICS

Jesus would have had few, if any, links with the sophisticated Hellenism of the Palestinian upper classes. But it has recently been argued that he may have been directly influenced by the Cynics, who followed the principles of the Greek thinker Diogenes (ca. 410–320BCE). The Cynics—their name is the origin of the term "cynical" and literally means "canine" (Greek *kunikos*) because of their snappish attacks on conventional society—were itinerant preachers who, in the late first century CE, were found all over the Roman empire. In vivid and challenging language they proclaimed a lifestyle of austerity and radical self-sufficiency, calling on men and women to renounce all claims of the state, the social order, the family, and the accepted practices of religion in favor of a simple, free life in accordance with nature. The Cynics were often seen as a threat to order and morality, and were frequently expelled from Rome. Like them, Jesus and his disciples were itinerant

A bust of the ancient Greek philosopher Diogenes of Sinope, founder of the Cynic movement in the 4th century BCE.

preachers to ordinary folk, and asked their followers to renounce family ties and material possessions; and Jesus was often at odds with the authorities.

However, the Cynic movement largely died out between ca. 100BCE and the mid-first century CE. It then underwent a great revival, but it is uncertain how far this had begun in Jesus' lifetime. Apparent Cynic resonances in the New Testament (notably Matt. 6.25–29ff. and Luke 12.22–27ff.) are more likely to derive from Cynic influence on the early Church. Unlike Jesus, the Cynics were not exorcists or healers, and nothing in their teaching corresponds to his central message of God's kingdom (see pp.150–53). Jesus remained an observant Jew and an heir of Israel's ancestral faith. The world-renunciation of the Cynics also characterized first-century CE Jewish ascetics, such as the Essenes and John the Baptist (see pp.37, 82–3) and it is with these that Jesus can more fruitfully be compared.

ples. Herod built an amphitheater and a hippodrome in Jerusalem (see p.19) and fostered Greek intellectual culture at his court. However, he also rebuilt the Temple of Jerusalem, the center of Jewish religious life, and maintained its distinctive religious practices. He was careful, too, to observe the Jewish law and to conciliate the most powerful religious faction, the Pharisees (see pp.34–5). The Roman prefects who ruled Judea in the first century CE likewise avoided offending Jewish religious sensibilities, with occasional exceptions—notably under Pontius Pilate (see p.26).

Many Jews were never reconciled to Hasmonean, Herodian, or Roman rule and repeatedly caused trouble for the authorities. They continued to view Hellenism as an alien culture and resented the wealth of its supporters. Such opposition encompassed various groups that responded to Hellenism in diverse ways. Jesus' own outlook is to be placed within this general climate. It has recently been suggested that he may have been affected by the Greco-Roman culture of the city of Sepphoris, which was close to Nazareth. While there is no solid evidence for this, Jesus did regularly criticize the rich and powerful, as in the famous story of the rich man and the poor man (Luke 16.19–31). His opinion of the typical Hellenistic lifestyle of a Herodian ruler is shown in his contrast between John the Baptist and those in royal palaces who "put on fine clothing and live in luxury" (Luke 7.25; compare Matt. 11.8).

A Greco-Roman mosaic from the Hellenistic city of Sepphoris (Hebrew Zippori), four miles from Nazareth. Destroyed in a revolt that followed the death of Herod the Great in 4BCE, Sepphoris was magnificently rebuilt in the early years of the first century.

THE HERODIAN DYNASTY

HEROD ANTIPAS

The most prominent Herodian ruler in the gospels is Herod Antipas (ruled 4BCE–39CE), tetrarch of Galilee and Perea and commonly called simply Antipas to avoid confusion with his father. He was a typical Hellenistic princeling, building the splendid Galilean cities of Sepphoris, four miles from Nazareth, and Tiberias, his capital.

Antipas first appears in the gospels in connection with his execution of John the Baptist (see pp.104–5). According to Luke, some Pharisees warned Jesus that Antipas would kill him, too, if he remained in Galilee (Luke 13.31). In response to the warning, Jesus called Antipas "that fox," a term which in Jewish rabbinic writings denotes a fool—that is, one who cannot prevent Jesus from completing his mission.

Some passages in the gospels are not wholly unfavorable to Antipas. Prime responsibility for the Baptist's death is attributed to Antipas' wife, Herodias. The tetrarch is said to have recognized John as a holy man and to have imprisoned him only for his own safety (Mark 6.17–20 and parallels). Similarly, Antipas regards Jesus, with a kind of superstitious awe, as a reincarnation of John (Mark 6.14); and wants to meet and hear him (Luke 9.9).

Luke alone records that Pilate sent Jesus to Antipas (Luke 23.7) and that Antipas was involved in Jesus' condemnation (Acts 4.27). Luke notes that, as a result of their dealings over Jesus, the prefect and tetrarch became friends, having previously been enemies (Luke 23.12). This enmity probably dates from the occasion when Antipas joined in a complaint to the emperor Tiberius over Pilate's disregard for Jewish religious sensibilities (see p.26).

Some of Antipas' courtiers were among Jesus' followers (Luke 8.3, Acts 13.1).

In 39CE, Antipas was deposed by the emperor Caligula on what were probably trumped-up charges and exiled to Gaul.

Palestine came under Roman control in 63BCE, when the general Pompey captured Jerusalem and ended Hasmonean rule (see p.22). During Jesus' lifetime, imperial authority was exercised either directly, through Roman prefects, or indirectly, through client rulers of the dynasty founded by King Herod the Great (ruled 37–4BCE). According to Matthew and Luke, Jesus was born in Herod's reign—at least four years before the traditional start of the Christian era. Whether historical or not, Matthew's dramatic story of Herod's massacre of the infants of Bethlehem (Matt. 2.16; see pp.72–3) faithfully reflects the king's notorious ruthlessness in preserving his throne. Toward the end of his life—when the massacre story is set—Herod's paranoia led him to execute several members of his own family.

After Herod's death, his territory was divided among three of his surviving sons, Archelaus, Herod Philip, and, most significantly for the story of Jesus, Herod Antipas (see sidebar, left). The Roman emperor, Augustus, granted them not the coveted title of "king" but the lesser status of "ethnarch" ("ruler of the people") or "tetrarch" ("ruler of one-fourth")—although the fact that Matthew and Mark call Antipas "king" (Matt. 14.9; Mark 6.14) suggests that the Roman titles were popularly ignored.

Judea fell to Archelaus (ruled 4BCE–6CE), who shared most of his father's vices but few of his talents. When King Herod died, Archelaus went to Rome to claim his inheritance and encountered a delegation of Jews opposed to his appointment; on his return to Judea as ethnarch he had many of these opponents executed. These events appear to be reflected in

This monumental aqueduct was built by King Herod the Great to supply the coastal city of Caesarea with water. It was one of many remarkable large-scale building projects undertaken during his reign.

PALESTINE UNDER HEROD THE GREAT AND HIS SUCCESSORS

KEY

~~ *Frontier of Herod the Great's Kingdom, 4BCE*

DIVISION of the KINGDOM AFTER HEROD'S DEATH

▨ *Ethnarchy of Archelaus, 4BCE~6CE; under Roman prefects, 6~41CE*

▨ *Tetrarchy of Antipas, 4BCE~39CE*

▨ *Tetrarchy of Philip, 6BCE~34CE*

▨ *Domains of Salome, Herod's sister*

▨ *Under direct rule of Province of Syria*

OTHER POLITICAL AREAS

▨ *Nabatean Kingdom*

▨ *Self-governing cities*

✦ *Town or city mentioned in the New Testament*

◉ *City of the Decapolis*

◉ *Other town or city*

▣ *Fortresses*

Cana¹   *Khirbet Qana, probable site of Cana (John 2.1)*

Cana²   *Kafr Kanna, traditional site of Cana*

SCALE
0   40 miles
0   40 km.

Luke 19.14, and 19.27. Archelaus was hated for his despotic rule and his unsavory reputation probably explains why Matthew says of Joseph that he was afraid to settle in Judea after his sojourn in Egypt (Matt. 2.22). In the end, Augustus deposed Archelaus and exiled him to Gaul.

By contrast, Herod Philip, or Philip (ruled 4BCE–34CE), was renowned for his justice and benevolence. His tetrarchy bordered the eastern shore of the Sea of Galilee and he built the cities of Bethsaida-Julias and Caesarea Philippi (see p.14), which are associated with Jesus. Philip was a Jew, but his subjects were mainly Gentiles, and it was probably because of Philip's tolerance that Jesus felt able to move and preach freely in his territory.

THE "HERODIANS"

The gospels provide the only known reference to a group called the Herodians (Matt. 22.16; Mark 3.6, 12.13). They may have been supporters of the Herodian dynasty, perhaps specifically of Antipas (see opposite); they probably shared his view of Jesus as a danger to public order. The gospels associate the Herodians with the Pharisees, but perhaps only because both factions, for different reasons, were remembered as being hostile to Jesus.

PALESTINE UNDER THE ROMANS

Roman Palestine was linked to the rest of the empire by a network of fine roads. This Roman milestone still stands in the Ela valley, Israel.

A replica in situ of the "Pilate Stone" discovered at Caesarea in 1963. It bears a dedicatory inscription in Latin from a "Tiberieum" (building in honor of the emperor Tiberius) that includes the words [Pon]tius Pilatus ... [Praef]ectus Iudaeae ("Pontius Pilate, Prefect of Judea"). The original stone is in a museum.

In Jesus' day the whole of Palestine was under direct or indirect Roman control. Following the deposition of Archelaus (see p.24), Judea became a subprovince of the Roman province of Syria, under an official called a prefect (*praefectus*). The prefect was in command of auxiliary military units, had full powers of criminal and civil jurisdiction, and was responsible for the collection of imperial taxes. He resided at Caesarea on the coast, but came to Jerusalem on the occasion of the major Jewish festivals.

Little is known of the first four prefects but there is considerable information about the fifth, Pontius Pilate (in office 26–36CE), and not only from the gospels. Pilate's rule was marked by repeated confrontations with his Jewish subjects and this troubled situation forms an important part of the background of the career of Jesus, and especially his trial (see pp.120–21). Pilate showed contempt for Jewish religious feelings by bringing into the holy city of Jerusalem military insignia bearing the emperor's portrait and golden shields bearing his name. Because the Romans revered the emperor as a god, such images were idolatrous to Jews. He also attempted to use the Temple's funds to build an aqueduct. Each of these actions provoked serious riots in Jerusalem. Around the time of Jesus' condemnation, Pilate evidently faced a bloody disturbance in Jerusalem (Mark 15.7), for which Barabbas and other rebels were imprisoned. Jesus was crucified alongside two "bandits," the term that John's gospel uses of Barabbas, and this suggests that they were probably revolutionaries. Pilate's ruthlessness is shown by the reference in Luke to a bloody incident involving Galileans (Luke 13.1). Nothing is known of this event from other sources, but the involvement of the notoriously restive Galileans is probably significant (see p.103).

As Jesus himself pointed out, conquerors inevitably imposed taxes on their subjects. When Judea came under direct Roman rule, the imperial tax system was introduced (see box, opposite), and it appears that the client rulers Antipas and Philip (see pp.24–5) also adopted the Roman system.

Understandably, Roman military might made a great impression on the Jewish world and this is reflected in the New Testament. Matthew 8 and Luke 7 record how Jesus healed the slave of a centurion at Capernaum in Galilee. Such an officer, in command of a comparatively small detachment of troops, would be stationed in an important center to keep order. Centurions were well paid and however much Luke's account may be colored, as is generally thought, by a desire to present Roman authority in a favorable light, there is nothing improbable in his picture of the centurion at Capernaum as a notable citizen of the town and a generous benefactor.

The military was able to requisition individuals for public duty, as when the gospels relate how Simon of Cyrene was ordered to carry Jesus' cross (Matt. 27.32 and parallels; see p.123).

Mark alone uses the proper word "centurion" for the officer who supervises the Crucifixion. The demons who possess a man and are exorcised by Jesus (Mark 5; Luke 8) call themselves "Legion" (Latin *legio*, a large military unit) owing to their great number. According to Matthew, Jesus in Gethsemane declared that he could, if he chose, call on the assistance of "more than twelve legions of angels" (Matt. 26.53). John uses the technical term "cohort" (Latin *cohors*, "tenth of a legion") for the troops who arrest Jesus, although the author may be using the word loosely (NRSV: "detachment").

ROMAN TAXATION

The Roman tax system was quite extensive, involving taxes on crops, a poll tax, and a levy on the transportation of goods. However, during the lifetime of Jesus these taxes do not seem to have constituted an unduly heavy burden.

The job of collecting the taxes was farmed out to tax gatherers (publicans), who were organized under a head official stationed in a commercial center, such as Zacchaeus in Jericho (Luke 19.2). Tax collectors were highly unpopular, not least because they were suspected of exacting more than the tax actually due. The gospels and the Mishnah (see glossary) lump tax collectors with robbers, sinners, and pagans. A Jew who engaged in this occupation was regarded as a traitor, so many tax collectors would probably have been Gentiles. Nevertheless, the gospels speak of Jesus' regular association with tax collectors and one of them, Matthew or Levi, was a disciple. Such links caused offense to pious groups such as the Pharisees.

When Jesus was interrogated about the legitimacy of paying taxes to Rome, his response—"Give to the emperor the things that are the emperor's, to God the things that are God's" (Mark 12.17 and parallels)—is perhaps best understood in the light of a similar episode when he was asked about the payment of the Jewish Temple tax (Matt. 17.24–5). Here, Jesus teaches that his followers, who belong to the spiritual kingdom of God, are free from the obligation but should meet it to avoid giving unnecessary offense.

Zacchaeus the tax collector climbs a tree to catch a glimpse of Jesus in this Russian painting of Jesus' entry into Jerusalem. As was common in the Middle Ages, the artist has conflated this scene with that of Jesus' arrival at Jericho.

THE SANHEDRIN
Central Jewish judicial authority was exercized in Jesus' day by the Sanhedrin, from the Greek *sunedrion* ("council"). There has been much discussion about the nature of this body and its powers, but its basic function was to administer Jewish law for those subject to it.

According to the gospels, the Jerusalem Sanhedrin tried and condemned Jesus, and the evangelists detail its composition. With the high priest (see main text) as president, it comprised three groups: members of the high-priestly family; lay elders, who were the city's other leading Jewish citizens; and "scribes," legal and religious experts (see p.30). It appears that by the time of Jesus many of the scribes would have been Pharisees (see pp.34–5).

The gospels also indicate that there were local Sanhedrins in different parts of the country, made up of elders and presided over by a judge. Jesus predicts several times that his disciples will be hauled before such bodies (for example, Mark 13.9).

JEWISH INTERNAL GOVERNMENT

Under the Hasmoneans (142–63BCE), the last independent Jewish heads of state in Palestine before modern times, the ruler was the supreme civil and religious authority in the land. He could describe himself as "king" to the outside world, which viewed him as a typical Hellenistic monarch (see pp.22–3), but for his Jewish subjects he was also the high priest.

This arrangement came to an end with the Roman occupation and the accession of Herod the Great (see pp.23–4), who appointed high priests from different families and deprived them of many of their political powers. This practice continued under the Roman prefects (see box, below). There was only one high priest at any one time, so when the gospels speak of "high priests" or "chief priests"—the Greek term is the same—they are referring collectively to the members of such notable families, including those who had held the office of high priest.

The high priests, who presided over the Jerusalem Sanhedrin (see sidebar, left), derived much of their wealth and influence from their control of the Temple treasury. The Temple accumulated enormous wealth that made it the most significant single element in the economic life of Palestine. Alongside the Roman revenue system there were specifically Jewish taxes levied by the Temple, in particular a tithe on agricultural produce and a half-shekel tax collected annually from every male Jew in Palestine and the

THE HIGH PRIESTS AND ROMAN RULE

The Romans chose high priests from a small number of wealthy aristocratic families, apparently five in all. Acts 4.6 lists several members of the family of Annas (or Ananos as the historian Josephus calls him), the high-priestly family of the period. Just how influential this dynasty was is shown by the fact that Annas, five of his sons, and his son-in-law Caiaphas all held the high priesthood.

Rome looked to the high-priestly group to keep the populace quiet under their authority, especially in Jerusalem. Thus the prefect Florus (governed 64–66CE) demanded that the high priest and the leading citizens should arrest eighteen agitators and hand them over to him—this probably explains the procedure for the arrest of Jesus.

The high-priestly families are generally considered to have been members of the Sadducean party (see p.35), whose policy was essentially one of collaboration with Rome for the sake of preserving Jewish religious institutions and as much autonomy as possible. The attitude of these priestly groups is well expressed by the statement attributed to them in the Fourth Gospel: if they did not take steps to restrain Jesus, the Romans would sweep away both the Temple and the nation (John 11.48)—this is precisely what happened as a consequence of the Jewish revolt of 66–73CE.

The collaborationist position of the high priests and their supporters made them unpopular with many Jews, especially those who advocated resistance to the Romans. They were also accused of corruption, in that they were known to offer large bribes to the prefects to secure their appointment.

Diaspora (see sidebar, right). In addition, many people made voluntary offerings, as seen in the gospel accounts of the widow and the rich man (Mark 12.41–44; Luke 21.1–4). The Treasury also acted as a kind of bank, where the wealthy deposited valuables for safekeeping.

The high priest's power rested on his position as head of the Temple, its personnel, and religious functioning. He performed a number of religious rituals that were believed to ensure the welfare and prosperity of his people, especially through his unique role in the ceremonies of the great Day of Atonement. The gospels say virtually nothing of these specifically religious functions. Perhaps the only hint is provided by the statement in the Fourth Gospel that Caiaphas was able to prophesy the death of Jesus (John 11.51)—the writings of Philo and Josephus suggest that the high priest was believed to possess prophetic abilities.

Unlike much of the Temple priesthood, the high priest did not live in the Temple precincts but had his own residence, which figures prominently in the accounts of Jesus' final ordeal. According to Josephus, the high priests lived in the Upper City, a wealthy quarter inhabited by the ruling class of Jerusalem (see plan, p.21). Excavations in this area have revealed the remains of a number of grand houses of the Herodian period, the architecture of which corresponds to what the gospels record about the house of the high priest Caiaphas. In particular, they were constructed around a large courtyard, such as Peter would have entered and where Jesus was apparently kept during the night of his arrest.

The houses of the Upper City had space for a considerable number of domestics, both male and female, and boasted one particularly large chamber, sometimes elaborately decorated. Such a room could have accommodated a meeting of the Sanhedrin to interrogate Jesus.

The Tribute Money, by Masaccio (1401–28), a fresco in the Brancacci Chapel in the church of Santa Maria del Carmine, Florence. Jesus (center) instructs Peter to catch a fish (left) containing a coin to pay (right) the Temple tax (Matt. 17.24–27).

THE TEMPLE TAX

In Jesus' day, every male Jew aged twenty and above had to pay half a shekel annually to the Temple. This payment had to be made with the Tyrian *didrachma*, the finely minted silver two-drachma piece from the Phoenician city of Tyre. Like other Tyrian coins, it bore the head of the city's patron god, Melgart (see illustration, p.38), and the presence of this pagan image in the Temple clearly infringed the Jewish law against other gods and idols (Exod. 20.3–4, Deut. 5.7–8). The fact that the Temple authorities evidently turned a blind eye to this fact shows how highly the Tyrian *didrachma* was valued.

Matthew uses the precise term for the coin (Matt. 17.24; NRSV: "Temple tax"). Later in the same passage, when Peter catches a fish with a coin in it to pay the Temple tax for Jesus and himself, Matthew again uses the correct term, *stater* (Matt. 17.27; NRSV "a coin"). This was a Tyrian coin—also called a *tetradrachma*—worth two *didrachmas* .

THE LAW AND THE TEMPLE

THE SCRIBES

Each of the various parties or sects in first-century Judaism (see pp.34–7) had its own approach to interpreting the law. Those who undertook such interpretation were the "scribes," who appear frequently in the New Testament. They are often linked with the Pharisees (see pp.34–6), but not all scribes were Pharisees and the gospels present a somewhat complicated picture of the relationship between them. Scribes were essentially scholars and teachers of the Jewish law, and as such they might belong to one or other of the various religious parties. The gospels and Acts mention specifically Pharisaic scribes (Luke 5.30; Acts 23.9), and it was natural that groups such as the Pharisees should have their own legal experts to expound and defend their special doctrines.

Mark mentions scribes who apparently belonged to the Sanhedrin in Jerusalem (Mark 14.53; see p.28), and he twice speaks of scribes coming from the city to Galilee (Mark 3.22, 7.1). This probably refers to a body that interpreted and applied the law as it was understood by the Temple authorities. But there were scribes in the villages, too, as indicated at Luke 5.17, where the evangelist uses the synonym "teachers of the law." Luke also uses the term "lawyer" (as at Luke 10.25) for "scribe," possibly because it conveyed the sense better to his Gentile readers.

Like the Pharisees, the scribes are generally depicted as opponents of Jesus, but Matthew 8.19 records a scribe's wish to follow Jesus, and Mark 12.28 tells of one impressed by his teaching.

The two fundamental institutions of first-century CE Judaism were the law and the Jerusalem Temple (see box, opposite). In the gospels, the word "law" refers to the written text of the first five books of the Hebrew Scriptures, variously known as the Torah, the Pentateuch, "the law of Moses," and "the Mosaic law." The strict rabbinic teaching on the law is well expressed by Jesus' statement that "until heaven and earth pass away, not one letter, not one stroke of a letter, will pass from the law" (Matt. 5.18; compare Luke 16.17): its words are unalterable and it has perpetual validity.

By the time of Jesus, other writings had also achieved canonical status in mainstream Judaism. The gospels (for example, Matt. 7.12) regularly link the law with "the Prophets," what are now usually called the historical and prophetic books of the Hebrew Bible, such as 1 and 2 Kings and Isaiah. Other works that later came to be included in the Jewish canon of scripture also seem to have been gaining recognition in Jesus' day. When Luke speaks of "the law of Moses, the prophets, and the psalms" (Luke 24.44), the word "psalms" may refer not just to the Book of Psalms but to the other works that make up the "Writings," the third subdivision of the Hebrew canon as we know it. This comprises the following books, given here in the order in which they appear in the Jewish Bible: Psalms, Proverbs, Job, Song of Solomon, Ruth, Lamentations, Ecclesiastes, Esther, Daniel, Ezra-Nehemiah, and Chronicles. Jesus himself is represented several times as quoting from the Psalms.

Thus there was in Jesus' time a large body of sacred scripture, which teachers read and expounded in the synagogues, as Jesus is said to have done at Nazareth (Luke 4.16ff.) By this period the law and the rest of the scriptures were already ancient and needed to be taught and explained in a contemporary context. The Pharisees (see pp.34–6) emerged as the most important interpreters and teachers of the law, and their work—later enshrined in the collections called the Mishnah and the Talmud—was predominant in forming the character of later rabbinic Judaism.

This scholarly activity aimed to clarify, safeguard, and protect the written law, and could be seen as part of the law itself in the literal sense of Torah ("instruction" or "direction"). Jesus is represented as dealing with both the written scripture and its interpretation, and also with the "oral Torah"—customs not found in the law but considered important by teachers. He was recognized as a teacher (see pp.162–3) and there is nothing unlikely in his being challenged by other teaching groups, even if the gospel accounts are colored by later relations between the Church and Judaism. The question of Jesus' attitude to the law is crucial for assessing the nature of his teaching and his place in the Judaism of his day (see pp.142–3).

THE TEMPLE

Jesus was accused at his trial of predicting the destruction of the Temple and, as with the Jewish law, his attitude toward it as a central institution of contemporary Judaism is of great importance for an understanding of his teaching.

The gospels frequently refer to the Temple and its precincts, which were rebuilt by Herod the Great and must have been a magnificent sight. The evangelists also show knowledge of the Temple's rituals and organization. Its primary significance was its claim to be the only place where Jews could offer sacrifices to God. Luke depicts Jesus' parents, as observant Jews, going to Jerusalem to sacrifice on the occasion of Mary's purification (Luke 2.22), and the gospels refer to an individual bringing his sacrificial offering to the altar in the Temple.

Worship in the Temple was carried out by a large body of priests, organized into twenty-four divisions, each of which served for a week in rotation. The father of John the Baptist, Zechariah, belonged to one such division, the order of Abijah, and Luke 1.9 records that he had been chosen by lot from the members of his group to officiate, in accordance with regular Temple practice. Zechariah's particular task was to burn incense on the golden altar in the central sanctuary, just outside the Holy of Holies, a ritual carried out every morning and evening. Luke notes how ordinary worshipers, who were not allowed to enter the shrine proper, had to wait outside (Luke 1.10).

Most priests lived outside Jerusalem and only came to the Temple when they were required for duty. Thus Zechariah returned home to his house in the Judean hills after his tour of duty (Luke 1.23). When Jesus ordered a leper to show himself

The central sanctuary of the Temple, from the scale model of the city in Jesus' day at the Holyland Hotel, Jerusalem. The reconstruction is based partly on written descriptions and depictions of the Temple on, for example, coins and mosaics.

to the priest in confirmation of his cleansing (Matt. 8.4; Mark 1.44), he was not instructing him to go to Jerusalem but referring to a priest who lived locally.

The Levites constituted the other main element in the Temple personnel. They served as singers, doorkeepers, and also as a kind of police force that kept order in the Temple precincts and could also operate in the city at large. It was this force that the Sanhedrin (see p.28) despatched to arrest Jesus in Gethsemane (see pp.114–15) and which, according to John 7.32, had also sought to apprehend him before.

The Temple was not only a place of sacrifice. Jesus quotes Isaiah in calling it "a house of prayer": there were three daily set times for prayer in the Temple, one of which probably provided the occasion for Jesus' parable of the Pharisee and the tax collector (Luke 18.9–14).

Teachers also went to the Temple, where they would find a large audience for their messages, in and around the great colonnades and porticos that surrounded the Temple Mount (see p.18). Jesus is reported to have taught regularly in the Temple during his time in Jerusalem.

The Pharisee and the Tax Collector Praying in the Temple, *a mosaic in the church of Sant' Apollinare Nuovo in Ravenna, Italy (ca. 520CE), illustrating Jesus' parable about righteousness and humility (Luke 18.9–14).*

THE SYNAGOGUE AND JEWISH FESTIVALS

The synagogue at Bar'am in Galilee is later than Jesus' time, but may have replaced one that stood in his day (see Matt. 4.23).

THE SYNAGOGUE AND SOCIETY
The synagogue fulfilled an important social function. Josephus speaks of communal meals there and an inscription of the second or third century CE records a donor building an inn, guest rooms, and ritual baths for a synagogue in Jerusalem. It also functioned as the seat of the local law court—Jesus warned his followers that they would be handed over to local Sanhedrins, or councils (see p.28), which met in the synagogues, and condemned to be flogged. According to the Mishnah, this penalty was administered by a synagogue official, the *hazan*.

Jesus' main contact with his ancestral religion was through the institution of the synagogue (Greek *sunagogos*, "place of meeting"). Its origins are extremely obscure, but by the time of Jesus there were synagogues in Jewish communities throughout the Roman empire. The remains of over a hundred ancient synagogues have been discovered in Palestine, especially in and around Galilee. It has been suggested that the synagogue was the main means through which Judaism was revived in Galilee, which had been largely heathen at the time of the early Maccabean rulers in the late second century BCE (see p.22).

The great majority of the excavated synagogues of Palestine date from much later than the time of Jesus but many of them will have replaced earlier buildings on the same site, as was certainly the case at Capernaum. However, at least three synagogues can confidently be dated to the first century CE: one at Gamala in Galilee and two within Herod the Great's fortresses of Masada and Herodium. All these buildings have much the same plan and so indicate the kind of synagogue that Jesus would have known. They are rectangular, with stepped stone benches around the walls, facing into a central space where the scriptures would have been read and expounded. It was most likely in this area, too, that Jesus sometimes performed healings and exorcisms. In the gospels, the scribes and Pharisees are condemned for monopolizing the best seats in the synagogues (Matt. 23.6; Mark 12.39; Luke 11.43), perhaps those of the uppermost tier. Matthew 23.2 speaks of the scribes and the Pharisees sitting on "Moses' seat," probably a place of honor occupied by experts while expounding the Mosaic law; a basalt chair found in the synagogue of the third or fourth century CE at Chorazin may represent such a seat.

Unlike the Temple, the synagogue was primarily a place of instruction in the Jewish law. The main activity was a weekly assembly on the Sabbath for readings of the Torah and homilies based upon it, although other scriptures were also read. Jesus is recorded as attending the synagogue on the Sabbath and being involved in controversy about the observance of the day of rest. The gospels associate the synagogue with the Pharisees in particular, and this, along with other evidence, indicates that the institution had become very much a Pharisaic preserve—the chief means for propagating and popularizing the Pharisees' distinctive doctrines (see pp.34–5).

A synagogue was headed by an official called "the leader of the synagogue," a prominent citizen like Jairus in the gospels (Mark 5.22; Luke 8.41). He was responsible for the upkeep of the building and the regulation of its meetings. Luke tells of a synagogue leader who angrily rebuked Jesus for healing on the Sabbath (Luke 13.14). There was also an assistant, the *hazan*, who, as seen in the synagogue at Nazareth, had charge of the scrolls of the sacred scriptures and delivered them to the chosen reader for the day.

The reading of scripture always remained the principal purpose of the synagogue. Later Judaism developed annual or triennial reading cycles, whereby certain passages of scripture were assigned to a particular Sabbath or festival day. Some scholars have claimed that such a system was in operation in the first century CE and have even proposed that the structure of one or more gospels follows the pattern of the cycle of synagogue readings. But these suggestions have not gained wide acceptance.

THE JEWISH FESTIVALS IN THE GOSPELS

If Sabbath worship was mainly centered on the synagogue, this was not the case for the major festivals. These were all occasions of pilgrimage, when the law required all male Jews to visit Jerusalem for the ceremonies in the Temple. The most popular festival was Passover, or Pesah, when huge crowds converged on the holy city. Its observance had two parts: the ritual slaughter of paschal (Passover) lambs in the Temple; and their consumption in a domestic meal that had to be held in Jerusalem. The gospels are only concerned with the second part (the meal) and their accounts generally correspond to what is known of the custom at the time. For example, those at the Passover meal lay on cushions to eat, and in their description of the Last Supper, Matthew and Mark use a verb meaning "to recline."

As well as Passover, the Fourth Gospel lists three other festivals for which Jesus is said to have visited Jerusalem. One, simply described as "a festival of the Jews," may have been Pentecost or possibly the Jewish New Year. The second is Tabernacles or Booths, which was marked by the ritual drawing of water and the illumination of one of the Temple courts. On this occasion, according to John, Jesus

appropriately speaks of himself as the water of life and the light of the world. The third is the feast of the Dedication or Hanukkah, held in December to commemorate the rededication of the Temple in 164BCE after its profanation by Antiochus (see p.22). Here, Jesus describes himself as the one whom God had sanctified, which may be intended to indicate that he, as the Messiah, replaces the Temple that is soon to be destroyed.

The Last Supper, *by the Master of Perea (15th century). The paschal (Passover) lamb is on the table in front of Jesus.*

SECTS AПD PARTIES

Judaism in the first century CE was by no means homogenous. It was made up of various groupings with their own views and outlooks, and they were often very hostile to each other. The gospels mention a number of such sects, most notably the Pharisees, but also the Sadducees (see box, opposite), the Samaritans (see box, p.36), scribes (see sidebar, p. 30), Herodians (see sidebar, p.25), and Essenes (see sidebar, p.37).

The attitude of the gospels toward the Pharisees (Greek *pharisaioi*, from Hebrew *perushim*, "separated ones") is mainly hostile and polemical, most notably in the blistering attack in Matthew 23 that includes the catalogue of seven "woes" against them. But allowing for this hostility—which scholars have often regarded as biased and unfair—the New Testament's characterization of Pharisaism broadly corresponds with that found in Josephus and other sources. According to Josephus, the Pharisees were the dominant religious group within Judaism, and this is how

Jesus in the House of Simon the Pharisee. A fresco of 1072 in the basilica of Sant' Angelo in Formis, Capua, Italy, depicting the episode of Jesus and the woman who had sinned (Luke 7.36–50). Although the gospels project a generally critical view of the Pharisees, Jesus is depicted on amicable terms with some of them and he was invited to dine by Pharisees on more than one occasion (see also Luke 11.37).

THE SADDUCEES

One group with whom Jesus came into contact, the Sadducees, are known only from Pharisaic texts, Josephus, and the New Testament—all of which display a somewhat negative attitude toward them. It is generally considered that they were members of the priestly aristocracy, with the Temple as their base, and perhaps the likeliest derivation of their name is that it comes from Zadok, whom Solomon installed as chief priest (1 Kings 2.35). Zadok's successors, the Zadokites, controlled the priesthood until the second century BCE.

However, it would be wrong to overemphasize the specifically priestly aspects of the Sadducees. Not all priests, and certainly not all members of the Jerusalem Sanhedrin (see p.28), were Sadducees. In the New Testament, as in Josephus, they appear alongside Pharisees as a clearly religious party with its own particular interpretation of the Mosaic law, on which they challenge the teaching of Jesus. They were conservatives, who accepted only the written Pentateuch as scripture (as did the Samaritans), and hence opposed those novel Pharisaic doctrines which they did not find there, in particular belief in the resurrection of the dead or an elaborate hierarchy of angels and spirits. Although they rejected the oral law, they were, like the Pharisees, a learned group with their own interpretative tradition. The Mishnah and later writings record disputes between them and the Pharisees over such issues as the religious calendar and sacrificial regulations.

With the destruction of the Temple in 70CE, the Sadducees largely vanish from history. This is consistent with Josephus' description of them as those who held the highest offices but had little following among the general population.

This superbly crafted column capital from Herod's Temple testifies to the wealth of the Temple and the priestly hierarchy that ran it.

JESUS AND THE PHARISEES

Although many things tended to divide Jesus and the Pharisees, they shared a number of important views, especially in contrast to those of the Sadducees (see box, left). The Pharisees actively propagated developments that had arisen in Judaism in the last centuries BCE. They accepted as scripture the Prophets and the Writings (see p.30) as well as the Pentateuch; they had expectations about the end of the present world age (including belief in a future Messiah, who would be preceded by the coming of the prophet Elijah and the general resurrection of the dead); and they possessed a highly developed belief in angels and demons.

The Sadducees rejected all these doctrines, but Jesus shared them, although he might differ in his interpretation of specific issues, such as whether the Messiah had to be descended from King David, and the significance of John the Baptist.

The gospels provide evidence of friendly relations between Jesus and at least some Pharisees (see illustration, opposite). Matthew's statement about the Pharisees sitting on "Moses' seat" (Matt.23.2; see p.32) recognizes them as the authoritative spokesmen for the law, and they are represented as recognizing Jesus as a true teacher of the way of God (John 3.2). It is Pharisees who warn Jesus about Herod Antipas (Luke 13.31).

they appear in their contacts with Jesus. Again, Josephus states that the Pharisees were distinguished on the one hand by their accurate exposition of the written Mosaic law, and on the other by their teaching of the "oral Torah," certain regulations handed down from earlier generations but not in the law as recorded in the Pentateuch. The gospels illustrate the observance of both types of law (see p.30).

Some of the confrontations between Jesus and the Pharisees turn on the correct understanding of the Mosaic law, such as what was meant by the prohibition of work on the Sabbath and the legality of divorce. The Pharisaic position on these and other issues was determined by the unwritten law, "the tradition of the elders" as the gospels call it (Matt. 15.2). According to the Mishnah, a compilation of these oral regulations made ca. 200CE, Moses received the written commandments at Sinai, but also the oral law, which he committed to his successor Joshua, who in turn passed it on to a body of elders, from whom it was handed down by a succession of teachers. The Mishnah sums up the basic message of the unwritten law in three obligations that are a good description of how the Pharisees envisaged their task: "Be deliberate in judgment" (carry out the law's provisions faithfully and accurately); "Raise up many disciples" (bring as many people as possible to the proper observance of the law); and "Make a fence around the law" (employ the oral regulations to preserve and safeguard the written law).

The Pharisees sought to ensure the proper keeping of the law by clarifying various aspects of it. The gospels mention some of the issues that the Pharisees dealt with, for example the degree of cleansing required to avoid ritual impurity; precisely which products of the soil were liable to tithing; and what exactly was involved in vowing property to the Temple.

Josephus states that the Pharisees had the support of the masses and

THE SAMARITANS

The Samaritans, who feature in several important episodes in the gospels, had much in common with other groups. They accepted only the Mosaic law (the Pentateuch) as scripture, like the Sadducees (see p.35), and rejected the Temple, as the Qumran community may also have done.

The Samaritans were marked by three features in particular, all of which are attested in the gospels. As their name indicates, they lived in villages in Samaria, a region that Jesus, like other devout Jews, apparently avoided on his last journey to Jerusalem. They were a distinct ethnic group, all descendants of old northern Israelite tribes, and thus Luke can describe a Samaritan as a "foreigner" (Luke 17.18). Thirdly, they recognized Mount Gerizim, not the Jerusalem Temple, as the sole legitimate place for sacrificial worship, as the Samaritan woman says in the Fourth Gospel (John 4.20).

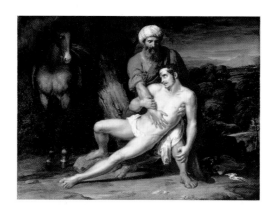

The Good Samaritan *by the Spanish artist Rafael Tejeo (1798–1856). Jesus' famous parable of the Samaritan who, alone of three passers-by, goes to the aid of a man who has been robbed and beaten, is recounted in Luke 10.30–35.*

The gospels' attitude toward the Samaritans varies. For example, in Matthew 10.5, Jesus forbids his disciples to evangelize among them, but elsewhere—especially in Luke—he is more welcoming. In Luke 17.18–19, Jesus commends a Samaritan leper for his piety and likewise praises the Good Samaritan of the famous parable (Luke 10.30–37) for his charity.

This ambivalence was probably reflected more widely in contemporary Judaism. In the Mishnah lawcode, Samaritans are classed among the Jews and are able to enjoy table-fellowship with them. However, Pharisaic Judaism came to harden its attitude towards the Samaritans. John's gospel appears to echo this later situation in its statement that Jews do not share things with Samaritans (John 4.9), and the denunciation of Jesus as a Samaritan possessed by a demon (John 8.48).

The caves at Qumran, 9 miles (14km) south of Jericho, where the Dead Sea Scrolls were discovered by local Arab shepherds in 1947.

that, unlike the Qumran community (see sidebar, right), they were not an exclusive sect but engaged with the population at large. In contrast to the scribes, the Pharisees in general were concerned to move from the passive study of the law toward greater activity in bringing people to its proper observance, as they saw it. Their missionary zeal is highlighted by Matthew's statement that they "cross sea and land to make a single convert" (Matt. 23.15).

The devout Pharisee contrasted himself with "the people of the land," ('am ha'aretz), described by the Pharisees in the Fourth Gospel as those who did not know the law (John 7.49). This expression was particularly applied to the Galileans (see p.103) and so would have characterized Jesus and his disciples, who did not follow the prescriptions of the oral law in such respects as fasting (as at Luke 5.33) and washing (as at Matt. 15.2). In any event, it would often have been difficult for the ordinary peasant or artisan to fulfill all the detailed Pharisaic regulations. Hence, the gospels accuse the Pharisees and lawyers of loading people with burdens hard to bear and of being "hypocrites," who "do not practice what they teach" (Matt. 23.3) —an accusation also found in some Jewish sources. Paul, originally a Pharisee himself, calls them "the strictest sect of our religion" (Acts 26.5).

In sum, the Pharisees might be described as a bourgeois group, on a social level between the Temple aristocracy and the mass of the populace. They had the support of many ordinary people, and with the synagogues as their base, they were crucial to the survival of Judaism following the loss of the Temple as the center of Jewish worship in 70CE. It is generally agreed that the activities of the Pharisees laid solid foundations for the development of rabbinic Judaism in the early centuries CE.

JESUS AND THE ESSENES

The Essenes existed throughout Palestine and it is likely that Jesus and his followers would have come into contact with them, although there is no unambiguous reference to Essenes in the New Testament. Their own writings were thought lost until the dramatic discovery in 1947 of the remains of a community and its literature—the Dead Sea Scrolls— at Qumran on the shores of the Dead Sea. Most scholars believe that the people of Qumran were Essenes.

According to the scrolls, Qumran was founded by a "Teacher of Righteousness," who revealed the true interpretation of scripture and ushered in the final age of history. It has been asserted not only that the Dead Sea Scrolls represent the Teacher as a slain and resurrected Messiah, but even that he and Jesus were the same person. However, the great majority of the scrolls predate the first century CE and so cannot refer to Jesus and his followers.

A more plausible theory is that Jesus (and John the Baptist) started out as Qumranites before leaving to embark on their own distinctive missions. Qumran was a closed body of initiates, similar to a monastery, whereas Jesus and John preached to the whole population and did not exhort their hearers to withdraw from society. Again, central to Qumran was an exact observance of Mosaic law—in contrast to Jesus' more relaxed attitude.

Nevertheless, many ideas and expressions in the gospels have parallels in the Dead Sea Scrolls that illuminate the teaching of Jesus and highlight more clearly the Jewish roots of his teaching (see pp.189, 192–5). In short, Qumran and Jesus represent two independent and distinctive developments within Judaism that draw on a common intellectual and theological background.

MONEYCHANGERS AND BANKERS

The great range of coins and other monetary units in use in Palestine required the services of moneychangers. They were to be found throughout Palestine, but the gospels mention only those who sat at tables in the Temple precincts in order to convert worshipers' money into the Tyrian silver coins that alone were acceptable as Temple donations (see p.110).

The evangelists also mention bankers, but they were probably little different from the moneychangers: the Greek term used of them, *trapezitai*, derives from *trapeza*, "table." The parable of the Talents or Pounds (Matt. 25.14–30; Luke 19.11–27) indicates that the primary function of bankers was lending money at interest, the profits being partly passed on to the bank's investors (Matt. 25.27; Luke 19.23). Jewish law supposedly forbids usury between Jews (Exod. 22.25; Deut. 23.19), and it was considered an act of charity to make a loan to someone in need expecting no return, as Luke says (Luke 6.35). But, as the gospels also show, the acquisition of debt—both financial and in kind—was a common problem, especially for farmers who required help in planting their crops. This situation seems to provide the background to the parable of the Dishonest Manager (Luke 16.1–8).

Silver tetradrachmas (4-drachma pieces) from the Phoenician city of Tyre. Tyrian coins were renowned for the purity of their silver content and were preferred for many payments and transactions.

TRADE AND COMMERCE

Palestine's geographical position gave it an important role as an intermediary between the Mediterranean and the Middle East, and several major roads used by traders and merchants traversed Palestine and Transjordan (see map, opposite). There is hardly any reference to this international commerce in the gospels, although Matthew's image of a merchant in search of fine pearls (Matt. 13.45) no doubt indicates someone engaged in the importation of precious minerals and gems from a region such as southern Arabia. The gifts brought by the wise men to the infant Jesus (see p.70) also indicate the sort of exotic luxury goods that international traders brought to Palestine.

Jesus appears to have avoided the main highways—paved Roman roads such as that linking Galilee with Jerusalem. Along the minor routes, Jesus and his disciples traveled on foot, as was usual for the poorer classes. Most riding was done on the back of the humble donkey—horses are not mentioned once in the gospels, although Jesus does refer to the camel (Matt. 19.24, 23.24; compare Mark 10.25; Luke 18.25). Along the way, there were inns, as in Luke's accounts of the Nativity (Luke 2.7) and the Good Samaritan (Luke 10.34). These would have been typical Eastern caravanserais, providing accommodation for both travelers and their animals. The parable of the Good Samaritan also shows that crossing sparsely populated areas could often be dangerous for lone travelers.

The gospels make frequent, and knowledgable, reference to the wide variety of gold, silver, and bronze coins in circulation. In addition to the Roman imperial currency used throughout the empire, there were coins minted for local use by the client rulers Antipas (see p.105) and Philip, and by the Roman prefects of Judea, such as Pilate (see p.120). Some important commercial cities, such as Tyre, also minted their own coins.

The small imperial silver *denarius* was apparently the most widely circulated coin, probably because this was the standard day's pay for an agricultural laborer (Matt. 20.2; NRSV: "the usual daily wage"). The Good Samaritan generously gave two *denarii* for the care of the man he had rescued (Luke 10.35). The *denarius* was also the main denomination used to pay Roman taxes. It bore the name and portrait of the emperor (see illustration, p.56), as Jesus noted when challenged about the payment of tax to Caesar (Matt. 22.20; Mark 12.16; Luke 20.24).

Also in circulation were small bronze or copper coins of little value. In Mark, the two coins given by the poor widow to the Temple treasury are said to make up one *denarius* (Mark 12.42; NRSV: "a

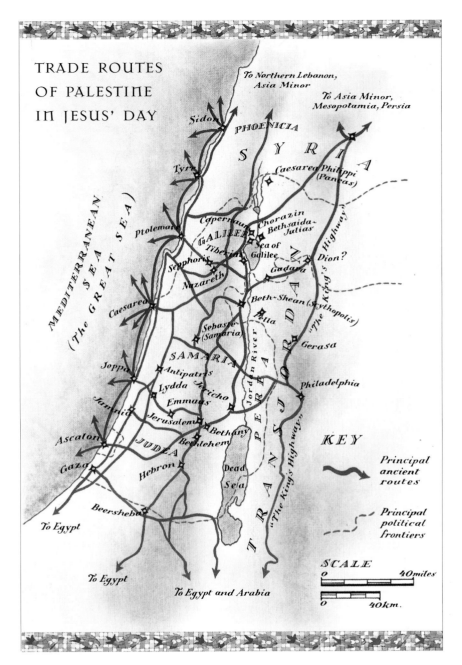

TRADE ROUTES
OF PALESTINE
IN JESUS' DAY

TRADERS AND ARTISANS

The gospels presuppose a mainly agricultural society (see pp.42–3). Otherwise, the Palestinian economy was one of small-scale craftworkers and traders, often operating from the home, who would sell their wares in little shops surrounding the marketplaces of villages and small towns. It was to such people, who tended to be looked down on by the upper classes, that Jesus addressed his preaching and with whom he was chiefly associated.

Tanners produced leather objects such as the sandals, pouches, and wineskins which figure in the gospels, and potters made common objects for domestic use— bowls, cups, dishes, plates, jars, and ovens —as well as more expensive objects, such as the alabaster vase from which oil was poured over Jesus at Bethany (Matt. 26.7; Mark 14.3).

Stonemasons were no doubt engaged in the Greco-Roman cities and on great public works, such as the Temple, which were under construction during Jesus' lifetime. However, many builders worked with mudbrick, which meant that houses were liable to be washed away by a sudden rainstorm, as one of Jesus' parables depicts (Matt. 7.24–27; Luke 6.47–49).

Jesus and Joseph were apparently carpenters, although they may have engaged in more general building work in both wood and stone (see pp.80–81).

penny"). The Temple was the wealthiest institution in Palestine and the focus of a specifically Jewish monetary and taxation system (see pp.28–9).

Coins were a comparatively recent medium of exchange and the gospels show that the older system of using precious metals measured by weight still survived. One such measure was the talent, the equivalent of some seventy-five pounds (thirty-four kilograms) of silver. In Matthew's version of the parable of the Talents (Matt. 25.14–30), the man gives his slaves the extraordinary sum of eight talents. This is probably an exaggeration for dramatic effect: Luke's version of the parable is more realistic in its substitution of the talent with the *mina* (NRSV: "pound"), equal to one pound of silver (Luke 19.12–28).

FARMERS AND FISHERS

Palestine was a primarily agricultural land and this is reflected in the many New Testament metaphors and images drawn from the practices of farming. To quote just two examples, divine judgment is symbolized by the cutting down of unfruitful trees (Matt. 3.10; Luke 3.9), and the growth of a mustard seed parallels the spread of the divine kingdom (Mark 4.30–32 and parallels).

At the time of Jesus, political conditions in Palestine were reasonably stable, allowing agriculture to be a potentially prosperous occupation. In Luke, Jesus depicts a farmer so successful that he has to demolish his barns and build new ones to accommodate all his crops (Luke 12.18). However, the repeated division of landholdings among a family's sons—Luke also

WINE PRODUCTION

The cultivation of vineyards for wine was the third great staple of Palestinian agriculture, and figures prominently in the gospels. Jesus' description of a vineyard in the parable of the Evil Tenants (Matt. 21.33–46; Mark 12.1–12; compare Luke 20.9–18)—however much it may owe to the "Song of the Vineyard" in the book of Isaiah (Isa. 5.1–2)—accurately reflects contemporary practice. There would be a hedge and watchtower for protection and a pit would be dug as a winepress for treading the grapes. The term used for the tenants to whom it was rented probably means "vinedressers." These were skilled agriculturalists, like the gardener in Luke 13.6–9 who knew how to preserve a barren fig tree by digging round it and manuring it. Wine was a common drink—Jesus drank it and was even denounced as a drunkard (Matt. 11.19; Luke 7.34). He quotes what is perhaps a popular saying about the superiority of a mature vintage (John 2.10) and was aware that a worn-out wineskin would burst if filled with newly fermenting wine (as at Matt. 9.17; Mark 2.22; Luke 5.37).

In Judaism, the vine had long been a symbol for the nation of Israel and Jesus continued this idea for the new community of his followers. The kingdom he preaches is a vineyard in which his disciples are laborers. The image is particularly developed in John's gospel: Jesus is "the true vine," his father is the vinegrower, and his disciples are the branches, who, if they prove unworthy, will be pruned and burned (John 15.1–8).

Harvesting the vine and treading grapes. A mosaic from a 5th-century Byzantine church on Mount Nebo in Perea (Transjordan).

tells of Jesus being asked to decide an inheritance dispute between brothers (Luke 12.13)—coupled with the burdens of taxation and bad harvests, meant that many individuals lost possession of their own farms. Sometimes they were forced to sell out to wealthy aristocrats and become tenants, paying rent in kind, often to absentee landlords—a situation presupposed by the parable of the Unjust Steward in Luke 16. Or they were compelled to eke out a precarious existence as day laborers, forced to wait about in the marketplace of a local town each morning for someone to hire them, as in the parable of the Generous Employer (Matt. 20.1–16). Again, many people had to commit themselves to serve as slaves—the Greek term in the gospels usually translated as "servant" often really denotes such an indentured slave.

Farmers in Palestine cultivated three main types of crop: grain, olives, and vines (see box, opposite). Wheat was the staple diet and the principal crop. Barley was also grown, although it was of less importance and in the gospels it is specifically mentioned only once, in John's narrative of the Feeding of the Five Thousand (John 6.9–13).

Plowing and sowing took place in late October or the beginning of November, when the early rains (see sidebar, right) had softened the ground after the hot summer. Lack of water was a major problem, so the farmer would habitually scan the sky carefully to see whether it promised rain or drought, as Jesus said (Matt. 16.2–3). Seed was broadcast by hand, as the parable of the Sower indicates (Mark 4.3–9, 13–20 and parallels), either preceded or followed by plowing. Harvest time was May or June, when sickles were used to reap the crop. After threshing to remove the stalks, the ears of wheat were tossed into the air with a winnowing fork. The wind

The rich agricultural landscape of the shores of Lake Galilee near Bethsaida.

THE CLIMATE OF PALESTINE

Palestine is broadly subtropical, with very hot dry summers and mild damp winters. There are two main rainy seasons, "the early rain and the later rain" (Deut. 11.14). The "early rain," which begins in October and can occur until March, may produce heavy downpours. In this period the ground is plowed and sown. The "later rain," in April, consists of lighter showers, sufficient to ripen late crops. Rain comes on western winds from the Mediterranean, as Jesus remarks (Luke 12.54). The rains were not always dependable and water was often scarce. In Jesus' day it was courteous to offer a guest or stranger a drink or a basin of water to wash dusty feet.

In contrast, hot, dry air is blown in from the desert south of Palestine (Luke 12.55). Palestinian summers are very hot (Matt. 20.12), but at other times the climate can turn chilly, especially at night in hilly areas, where it may even snow. The night of Jesus' arrest, around Passover in the Jewish month of Nisan (March/April), was cold enough to warrant a fire being lit in the high priest's courtyard.

ABOVE: *An ancient olive oil press at Tabgha (ancient Heptapegon) near Capernaum.*

RIGHT: *An olive grove in northern Israel near Mount Hermon.*

blew away the chaff, leaving the heavier grain, which was then cleared from the threshing floor and stored in a granary. The chaff was then burned, as John the Baptist carefully describes (Matt. 3.12; Luke 3.17). Before being stored, the wheat was sieved to remove any remaining impurities, such as small stones—a scene evoked by Jesus when he warns Simon Peter that Satan will sift the disciples "like wheat" (Luke 22.31). Finally, the grain was ground into flour using a large millstone, a process often carried out by women, as the gospels indicate (Matt. 24.41).

After wheat, the most significant staple crop was the olive. Palestinian olive oil, mentioned several times in the gospels, was of renowned quality and one of the region's major exports. It was used for a variety of domestic purposes, including as fuel for lamps, as in the parable of the Ten Bridesmaids (Matt. 25.1–13), and for healing (Mark 6.13; Luke 10.34). The Mount of Olives was, as its name implies, an area of olive groves that included Gethsemane ("[Place of] Oil Presses").

FISHING

Jesus was well acquainted with the fishing trade that was central to the Galilean economy. It was a prosperous activity and those of Jesus' disciples who were engaged in it were men of substance who worked in family partnerships, owning several vessels and employing hired hands. The remains of a first-century CE Galilean fishing boat have been recovered. It has a rounded stern, such as Jesus would have rested on during one of his voyages across the lake (Mark 4.38).

The gospels mention three types of fishing. One method involved throwing a small net from the shore into the water—this was what the brothers Simon and Andrew were doing when they were first recruited by Jesus. A fish could also be taken by angling with hook and line, as in the story of Peter catching a fish containing a coin to pay the Temple tax. Larger nets could be dropped from boats in deeper water and either hauled on board or pulled toward the shore if the catch was too heavy to lift.

Jesus' first disciples were fishermen and the gospels draw vividly upon the symbolism of their profession. In Matthew's gospel (Matt. 13.47–50), the dragnet is the heavenly kingdom that sweeps up all sorts of human beings. The catch is sorted and the "good" fish are kept while "bad" fish are thrown away, prefiguring the last judgment. John 21.11 records a great catch of one hundred fifty-three fish. Ancient Greek zoologists held that there were precisely this number of species of fish in existence, so the catch can be seen as representing the entirety of humankind and the universality of the gospel.

John places the story of the great haul of fish after the Resurrection, but in Luke it occurs at the beginning of Jesus' ministry and prompts Jesus to promise his fishermen disciples that henceforward they will be catching people (Luke 5.10–11). Luke says that the net was so full it began to break, a realistic detail—the gospels describe James and John carrying out the chore of repairing their nets (Matt. 4.21; Mark 1.19). John's account pointedly remarks that the net remained intact, emphasizing the miraculous nature of the catch (John 21.11).

As Christianity developed, fish acquired eucharistic symbolism. This may derive from the gospel accounts of the feedings of the four or five thousand, in which fish feature prominently (see pp.98–9).

The Miraculous Draft of Fishes *by Konrad Witz (1400–1447). It illustrates the episode in John 21 when Jesus, to the disciples' astonishment, tells them to cast their net on the right of the ship and it at once fills with fish. Peter is shown both trying to haul up the net and then jumping into the water to swim toward Jesus on the shore.*

MARRIAGE AND THE FAMILY

Among the Jews of Jesus' day marriage was regarded as virtually an obligation. The Bible records that some of Israel's patriarchs were polygamous, but by the time of Jesus the monogamous family was the social norm. Marriage was essentially a legal contract between two individuals, initiated by their parents. The key stage was the betrothal, when the bridegroom executed a written document, the Ketubbah, in which he undertook to assign his bride a sum of money in the event of his death or if he should divorce her. Betrothal made the woman legally the man's wife, but the marriage could not be consummated until she moved into her husband's house. Unfaithfulness on the part of the woman during the betrothal period was regarded as adultery and grounds for voiding the Ketubbah—this is the situation apparently faced by Joseph when Mary became pregnant while the couple were still betrothed (Matt. 1.18).

After some time, the bride was taken to her husband's house, just as Joseph took Mary as his wife after the angel had allayed his fears. The occasion was marked by a lavish wedding feast, such as the one Jesus attended at Cana (John 2). It is interesting, given the importance of mar-

The Wedding Feast at Cana, by Paolo Veronese (ca. 1528–88). Jesus and his mother are seated at the center among disciples; the chief steward (in white, right foreground) tastes the water that Jesus has miraculously turned into wine (John 2.9).

THE POSITION OF WOMEN

Women in Jewish society were largely confined to the home, but within the household they had a vital and central place, since they were mainly responsible for the whole domestic economy. Jesus sometimes alludes to the activities of women in the family, for example baking (Matt. 13.33; Luke 13.21) and grinding meal (Matt. 24.41; Luke 17.35). Martha, "distracted by her many tasks," represents the typical busy housewife (Luke 10.40).

A wife possessed legal rights that her husband had to respect, including the right to own and control her own property. But it was above all as mothers that women were honored. Normally, the childless woman was an object of scorn and pity, and it is a sign of particular divine favor that the barren Elizabeth becomes pregnant when past the normal age of childbearing (Luke 1).

A coin issued to mark Rome's defeat of the Jewish revolt (70CE). "Captive Judea" (Iudaea Capta) is depicted as a Jewish widow in mourning.

The situation of a widow was an unhappy one but her condition was alleviated by a law, mentioned in the gospels, whereby if a man died without issue his brother had to marry the widow and provide for her (Mark 12.19 and parallels). If a man married his brother's divorced wife during the brother's lifetime it was viewed as incest, hence John the Baptist's opposition to the marriage of Antipas and Herodias, his brother's ex-wife (Mark 6.17–18 and parallels).

Women were exempt from many religious obligations, but they worshiped at the Temple, where they had their own court (see p.21). They were often prominent in the synagogues, at least in the Diaspora, as Acts and Paul's letters indicate.

riage in Judaism, that the gospels do not mention whether Jesus himself was married. It has been suggested that the Cana celebration was his own wedding, but there is no evidence for this. The bridegroom was escorted to the feast at night in a torchlit procession of young women, as described in the parable of the Wise and Foolish Bridesmaids (Matt 25.1–13). Once in their marital home, it was usual for the couple to consummate their union, but Matthew is careful to note that Joseph and Mary had no sexual relations until after the birth of Jesus (Matt. 1.24–25).

Divorce was theoretically easy (see sidebar, right) but it was probably relatively infrequent. The rabbis discouraged it and stressed the blessings of the married state, chief among which were children. Boys and girls were expected to submit to parental authority—Luke mentions that Jesus was obedient to his parents (Luke 2.51) and Jesus reiterates the biblical commandment to honor father and mother (Mark 7.10 and parallels).

The father was definitely the head of the household, but he was bound by the Ketubbah to provide for his family. This obligation underlies Jesus' point when he says how incredible it would be for a father to give a hungry child a stone, a snake, or a scorpion instead of food (Matt. 7.9–10; Luke 11.11). The eldest son had a special status that gave him a double share of the inheritance, and he became head of the family on his father's death. If it is in this capacity that Jesus, on the cross, provided for the welfare of his mother (John 19.26–27), she must have already been a widow.

DIVORCE

Strictly speaking, in Jewish law the initiative for divorce rested with the husband, as suggested by a question that some Pharisees put to Jesus: "Is it lawful for a man to divorce his wife?" (Mark 10.2; Matt. 19.3). A man could give his wife a document stating that he had no further rights over her and that she was free to remarry. He could do this if she had ceased to please him for any reason, as Moses commanded (Deut. 24.1–4).

However, it was also possible for a wife to end her marriage, as Jesus implies (Mark 10.12), by a kind of legal fiction. She could petition the courts to compel her husband to give her a divorce, thus preserving the letter of the biblical law.

The differences between the Pharisees and Jesus on divorce appear to reflect a genuine debate on the issue in first-century Pharisaic circles. The school of the teacher Hillel adhered to Deuteronomy, but the followers of Shammai, another renowned teacher, taught that a wife could be divorced only for unchastity—precisely Jesus' position in Matthew (Matt. 19.9).

LANGUAGES OF PALESTINE

THE SURVIVAL OF HEBREW

While Aramaic was current throughout Palestine and was certainly predominant in Galilee, it would be wrong to think that Hebrew had disappeared as a vernacular language. There are references in rabbinic sources to the use of Hebrew among ordinary people, and it is now known that the Hebrew of the Mishnah, the body of oral Jewish law and tradition that was first written down ca. 200CE, was not devised by scholars as once believed but represents a living form of the language that developed in the last centuries BCE. This variety of spoken Hebrew is also found in some of the Qumran scrolls and in letters and other documents from the time of the Second Jewish War of 132–5CE.

The evidence suggests, therefore, that in Jesus' day Hebrew continued to be spoken in the more southerly areas of Palestine, and it is likely that Jesus would have known some Hebrew, at least, and perhaps spoke it particularly on his visits to Judea. When Jesus addresses God as "Father," "*Abba*"—a word that subsequently passed over into the early Christian communities (Rom. 8.15; Gal. 4.6)—and employs the phrase "*Ephphatha*" (see main text), he could be speaking either Hebrew or Aramaic, because the two were very closely related. Matthew's version of Jesus' utterance from the cross, "*Eli, eli, lema sabachthani*" (Matt. 27.46), is partly in Hebrew and partly in Aramaic (see p.126).

First-century Palestine was a markedly multilingual society. At all social levels, the most common language was Aramaic, a Semitic tongue closely related to Hebrew. It was originally spoken by Aramean tribes of northern "Aram," a term variously used to denote parts of ancient Syria and northern Mesopotamia. These tribes were conquered by the Assyrians, who took Aramean scribes into the imperial bureaucracy. Aramaic subsequently became an official—and the most widely used—language of the Assyrian state and of the Persian empire that supplanted it.

As a consequence, Aramaic was adopted by various peoples at the expense of their native tongues, and it rapidly became an everyday language throughout Syria and in Palestine. Judean exiles returning from Babylon in the sixth century BCE adopted Aramaic in place of Hebrew (see sidebar, left) as the most widely understood tongue in their homeland.

This situation prevailed in the period of the New Testament and it is therefore very likely that Jesus' native tongue was Aramaic. The gospels attribute a number of authentic Aramaic words and phrases to him, such as "*Talitha cum*" ("Little girl, get up!") (Mark 5.41) and probably also "*Ephphatha*" ("Be opened") (Mark 7.34). Both expressions may have been preserved as healing formulae by Jesus' disciples. Mark's version of Jesus' saying from the cross, "*Eloi, eloi, lema sabachthani*" ("My God, my God, why have you forsaken me?") (Mark 15.34), represents the opening of Psalm 22 in Aramaic and not the biblical Hebrew. This may indicate that Jesus acquired his scriptural knowledge from hearing sacred texts read out in the synagogues in Aramaic paraphrases (Targums), which were being made at this time for congregations that no longer understood Hebrew.

The gospels include Aramaic place names, such as Golgotha ("[Place of a] Skull") and Gethsemane ("Oil Presses"), and the Aramaic element *bar* ("son of") rather than the Hebrew *ben* occurs in personal names such as

The name "Jesus" is the Latin form of the Greek Iesous. *This in turn represents the common Jewish name Yeshu or Yeshua, which is inscribed in Hebrew letters on this ossuary of the late 1st century* CE *("YSHWA," reading from right to left).*

GREEK

As a result of the conquests of Alexander the Great in the fourth century BCE, Greek came to be widely spoken in the ancient Near East (see p.22). Herod the Great and his successors fostered the use of the language in Palestine, especially in Jerusalem. The city had a synagogue for Greek-speaking Jews and numerous inscriptions reveal how common the use of Greek was among the inhabitants.

The Greek spoken in this period was not Classical Greek, but a simpler and more colloquial form known as the *koine* ("common [dialect]"). The language of the New Testament is basically *koine*, and it seems probable—if the gospels are to be trusted—that Jesus could speak it. He conversed with foreign officials who would almost certainly have spoken Greek, such as Pilate and the Capernaum centurion, and with a Syro-Phoenician woman whom Mark

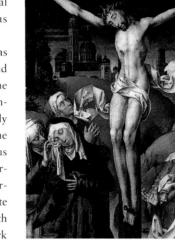

describes as "Greek" (Mark 7.26; NRSV: "Gentile"). As a craftsman, Jesus would also have found Greek useful in his trade among Galilee's mixed population. The names of the disciples Andrew and Philip are Greek, and those of Thaddeus and Bartholomew are Aramaized Greek.

Many Greek words passed into Aramaic and many people would happily have conversed in a *patois* of these two languages. But given the much stronger evidence that Jesus' main language was Aramaic (see main text), it is doubtful whether he was either fully bilingual or —as some scholars have proposed— sometimes even taught in Greek.

The Crucifixion; *French school, ca. 1452. The inscription on the cross (see p.182) is in Greek, Latin, and what the gospels term "Hebrew"—although this probably means Aramaic.*

Bartholomew, Bartimaeus, Barabbas, and Bar-Jonah (Matt. 16.17; NRSV: "son of Jonah"). Jesus would probably have been known in his own tongue as Yeshua bar Y(eh)oseph ("Jesus son of Joseph"). He and his disciples would have spoken the Aramaic dialect of Galilee, which differed from that of Jerusalem, as Matthew's gospel indicates (Matt. 26.73). According to rabbinic texts, Galileans were unable to pronounce guttural consonants properly.

Some scholars have attempted to go behind the Greek of the gospels (see box, above) to recover the original Aramaic words of Jesus. It has even been suggested that there once existed an Aramaic collection of his sayings, which may have been the earliest form of the hypothetical document known as "Q" (see p.57). While such attempts must always be tentative, some passages in the gospels can plausibly be illuminated by reconstructing an Aramaic substratum. It is notable that such instances occur most frequently in the words of Jesus himself. When many of his sayings are turned "back" into Aramaic from Greek, they assume the typical forms of Semitic poetry, with such features as wordplay, parallelism, alliteration, and assonance.

THE LIFE

Sources	50
What is a "Gospel"?	50
The Four Evangelists	52
The Gospel Evidence	56
Jesus in Other Writings	58
Jesus' Life and Times	60
The Birth of Jesus	62
The Genealogy of Christ	62
The Nativity	64
The Virgin Birth	68
Infancy and Youth	70
The First Witnesses	70
The Wrath of Herod	72
The Flight into Egypt	74
Rites of Childhood	76
The Home Life of Jesus	78
The Call to Ministry	82
John the Baptist	82
The Baptism of Jesus	84
The Temptation	86
The Ministry in Galilee	90
The Disciples	90

Jesus' Public Career	92
The Healings	94
The Exorcisms	96
The Feeding Miracles	98
Conflicts and Confrontations	100
The Approach of the Passion	104
The Fate of the Baptist	104
Peter's Confession and the	
Transfiguration	106
The Road to Jerusalem	108
The Cleansing of the	
Temple	110
The Last Supper	112
Betrayal and Arrest	114
Condemnation and Crucifixion	116
The Trials of Jesus	116
Before the Council	118
Jesus and Pilate	120
Jesus Condemned	122
The Crucifixion	124
The Aftermath	128
The Risen Lord	128
The Ascension	132

Christ Pantocrator ("All-Ruling"), *one of a series of 14th-century mosaics in the Byzantine church of St. Savior in Chora (now Kariye Camii mosque), Istanbul, depicting the life of Christ. Surrounded by Israelite patriarchs, prophets, and kings, Jesus is presented as the bringer of the new law, which he holds in his left hand. His right hand is raised in a gesture of blessing.*

WHAT IS A "GOSPEL"?

In recent years, "redaction criticism" has countered the view of the form critics (see main text) that the gospels are basically collections of preexisting fragments of material. Redaction critics, in contrast, see them as unified works by individual authors, each with its own plan and underlying assumptions. According to redaction critics, the gospels can be viewed in the light of an ancient biographical tradition. There are "biographies" in the Hebrew Scriptures (for example, the life of Moses) and such Jewish literature inspired other biographies of prophets and righteous individuals. The rabbinical writings (ca. first–seventh centuries CE) contain nothing corresponding directly to the works of the evangelists, but stories about individual teachers in these texts are often similar in form and content to stories in the gospels.

St. Paul Preaching, *from a Bible produced in France 843–51CE. Before the gospels were written down, the traditions and teachings of Jesus were transmitted orally by the apostles and other early preachers.*

The term "gospel" literally means "good news" and translates the Greek *euangelion*. In this straightforward sense, *euangelion* was in regular secular usage in the Greco-Roman world, but in the New Testament the word takes on a specifically Christian meaning to designate the story of Jesus and his teaching. For Paul, this "good news" is primarily the salvation brought by Jesus' death and resurrection. In the four books known as gospels, it represents the message that the kingdom of God is coming, brought by Jesus.

Until the early twentieth century the four gospels of the Christian canon (see box, opposite) were mainly interpreted as biographies, a view introduced by the writer Justin Martyr (ca. 155CE). It was often thought possible to construct a "life" of Jesus from the gospel evidence, although the pictures produced by different scholars often varied dramatically.

From the 1920s, a school of thought called "form criticism" powerfully challenged the concept of the gospels as biography, portraying them instead as a literary genre with no real parallel. Form critics emphasized that before the appearance of the first written gospels, traditions about Jesus' life and teaching would have circulated orally in small anecdotal units that would have been adapted to meet the needs of individual congregations. Each evangelist assembled these fragments to reflect his own theological interpretation of Jesus' message, and so the gospels cannot be relied on to create a factual, chronologically accurate biography of the historical Jesus.

Much of the work of the form critics remains of permanent value, especially their elucidation of individual episodes and teachings. However,

GOSPELS IN THE CANON OF SCRIPTURE

The Greek term "canon," meaning a "rule" or "standard," is used to denote the collection of writings that the Church accepts as possessing a unique and special status. The first canon that corresponds exactly to the New Testament as we know it was drawn up in 367CE, at the end of some three centuries in which various writings gradually acquired authority among the wider Christian community.

The four gospels began to be perceived as a distinct group in the late second century CE. At this time, there were numerous other gospels in circulation, including the Gospel of Thomas (see box, p.59) and three Jewish-Christian works (see box, p.173). It is not easy to determine exactly why only Matthew, Mark, Luke, and John achieved canonical status, but the Muratorian Fragment (late second century CE), the earliest "draft canon" of the New Testament, indicates two key reasons. Firstly, in spite of their differences, these four gospels present the same basic account of the life of Jesus. Second, they were the earliest gospels written and their authors would have been in contact with Jesus' first followers. There was a sense, too, that these four texts alone were in accord with the emerging consensus about the true nature of the faith.

It has also been suggested that the Christians' remarkably rapid adoption of the newly-invented codex (bound book) played a part in the four gospels being fixed as a group. Unlike a scroll, a codex could contain all of them in a single volume.

Christ in Majesty, *in the church of Sant' Angelo in Formis, Capua, Italy. The winged beasts around Jesus derive from Revelation 4.7–8 and Ezekiel 1.5–14 and symbolize the evangelists: man or angel (Matthew); lion (Mark); calf or ox (Luke); and eagle (John).*

most scholars today would agree that form critics tend to overstress the propensity of early Christian communities to modify a tradition to suit their particular needs. Nor does their skepticism about recovering an authentic picture of the historical Jesus really appear justified.

The gospels can certainly be compared with Jewish writings (see sidebar, opposite), but the most illuminating comparison is with the Greco-Roman genre of popular biography, where the authors related the careers of contemporaries or near-contemporaries with—like the evangelists—a polemical or apologetic purpose. The gospels resemble this type of writing closely enough to be considered a subgenre of it.

Regardless of how they resemble, or differ from, other forms of literature, the works attributed to Matthew, Mark, Luke, and John continue to be identified by the peculiarly Christian word "gospel," instead of the terms "life" and "memoir," which are used of contemporary works. In the end, it is their particular aim—to proclaim the "good news" of Jesus and the salvation he brings—that gives them their unique character.

THE FOUR EVANGELISTS

THE ORIGINS OF MARK'S GOSPEL
There was an early Christian tradition that Mark was written in Rome, a view based on the assumption that the author was connected with Simon Peter (see main text). This claim has been supported by the presence of some Latin terms in the gospel, but these words (such as *quadrans*, the name of a coin) would have been known throughout the Roman empire.

The commonly accepted earliest date for Mark, ca. 65CE, depends on a statement by the late second-century churchman Irenaeus that Mark wrote after the death of Peter, which was assumed to have occurred during the persecution under the emperor Nero in the mid-60s CE. There are somewhat stronger grounds for fixing the latest possible date for Mark. The evangelist's apocalyptic chapter (Mark 13) contains a deliberately mysterious statement (13.14) that is generally taken to be a near-contemporaneous reference to the Roman capture and destruction of Jerusalem in 70CE during the First Jewish War (66–70CE). If so, the gospel would have been written either while the city was already under siege or shortly after its fall.

The gospel of Mark is widely—though not universally—believed to be the earliest of the four (see sidebar, left). Like all the gospels, except perhaps John, the work itself offers no clues as to the identity of its author. The first person to attribute it to someone called "Mark" was the churchman Papias (ca. 130CE), who claimed to have received this information from a figure called "the Elder." The name Mark (Latin Marcus, Greek Markos) was very common in the ancient world, but most scholars believe that Papias means John Mark, who is mentioned several times in the New Testament (as at Acts 12.12, 12.25). John Mark was a minor figure—Papias notes that the evangelist did not know Jesus directly—and this itself argues for the likelihood that he was the author of the gospel. Obscure persons were rarely credited with famous writings unless a very strong tradition demanded it.

For most of Christian history, Mark was seen as basically an abridged version of the gospel of Matthew (see box, opposite). Mark's work came to be assessed as a comparatively simple and reliable account of the life and work of the Jesus of history, based on the reminiscences of the apostle Peter. Papias states that Mark was the interpreter of Peter, but this connection with the chief apostle is now rejected by many critics. It has been pointed out, for example, that John Mark was associated mostly with Paul, not Peter. On the other hand, the first letter of Peter refers to "my son Mark" (1 Pet. 5.13) and in Acts, when Peter is freed from prison, he is said to have gone to the house of John Mark's mother (Acts 12.12).

It was only in the nineteenth century that Mark came to the forefront of New Testament study, with the widespread recognition that it was in fact the first gospel, and that both Matthew and Luke depended on it. "Form

The ruins of the ancient Forum of Rome. According to a very early Christian tradition, the evangelist Mark accompanied the apostle Peter to the imperial capital and composed his gospel in the city.

THE FOUR EVANGELISTS ❖ 53

MATTHEW: THE "JEWISH GOSPEL"

Long considered the earliest of the four gospels, Matthew represents the outlook of Jewish Christianity (see pp.172–3) and is largely concerned with the relationship of Jesus to Judaism. It is written in Greek, but may have drawn on Hebrew and Aramaic sources. If the reference to a burned city in Matt. 22.7 alludes to the Roman sack of Jerusalem, the final form of the gospel must be later than 70CE.

There seems little basis for the traditional attribution of the gospel to the apostle Matthew, although the work does indicate a special interest in him—it alone narrates his calling and records that he was a tax collector. It is also the only gospel to mention how the fame of Jesus spread to Syria (Matt. 4.24): according to another theory the evangelist may have belonged to a Jewish Christian church founded by the apostle at Antioch in Syria (modern Antakya, Turkey).

Although it is basically a story, tracing the career of Jesus from his conception to the Resurrection, teaching is prominent in Matthew, notably in five great discourses of Jesus. Much in the gospel suggests that the author may have trained as a scribe (see p.30). For example, the way he often quotes the Hebrew Bible resembles the Qumran texts, while the Sermon on the Mount (Matt. 5–7) perhaps parallels the rabbinic procedure of modifying a biblical commandment to apply it to fresh circumstances. Matthew's polemic against the scribes and Pharisees is much stronger than in the other gospels, and this should probably be seen as an attack on rival Jewish teachers who did not accept the authority of Jesus.

The evangelist Matthew, from an illuminated gospel book produced ca. 1020 in England. His traditional symbol, the figure of a man or an angel, appears at top right.

criticism" (see pp.50–51) demonstrated that Mark was largely composed of small narrative units handed down in the early Church and not of material derived from a single eyewitness. At the same time, other scholars emphasized that, viewed as a whole, the gospel is clearly the work of a conscientious and sophisticated author with a deliberate theological purpose.

In spite of the undeniable validity of these and other assessments, scholars continue to differ widely in their judgments of Mark's aims and the extent to which he provides authentic historical information about Jesus.

Luke's gospel stands out in many ways, not least because it is the first part of a two-volume work, the second being the Acts of the Apostles. The opening words of the gospel are intended as a preface to both books, in which Luke presents the story of Jesus as part of a broader view of all human history, in successive phases: the epoch of Israel; the epoch of Jesus (from the Baptism to the Ascension); and the epoch of the Church as it

St Luke, *from the 9th-century MacDurnan Gospels produced at Armagh, Ireland. The evangelist holds a book (his gospel) in one hand and a bishop's crozier in the other. He has cloven hooves instead of feet, an allusion to his symbolic creature, the calf or ox (see illustration, p.51).*

awaits the return of its Lord. The gospel is less a biography than a work belonging to the Hellenistic genre of general history. Luke avoids the term "gospel" (*euangelion*) and prefers to describe his work as a narrative in chronological order. His preface, in elegant Classical Greek idiom—he writes the most polished Greek of all the evangelists—conforms to a common type of introduction found in Hellenistic histories, where the author claims to have studied his predecessors in order to produce his own definitive account of events.

For Luke, Jesus' career and its sequel in the growth of the Church were not things that happened in obscurity, or "done in a corner" to use Paul's words in Acts 26.26. To emphasize this, at key points Luke synchronizes the life of Jesus with events in a wider historical perspective. In contrast to Mark and Matthew, he seeks to fix the period of Jesus' Galilean ministry to a definite time by introducing four references to the tetrarch Herod Antipas (see p.25).

The early Church identified the educated and polished historian who wrote the gospel with the Luke who appears in Acts as Paul's traveling companion, and claimed that his work embodied Paul's teaching, just as Mark reflected that of Peter.

Paul's mission was primarily to Gentiles (non-Jews) and the whole tenor of Luke's gospel suggests that it, too, is aimed at Greek-speaking Gentiles. The work was certainly so understood by the anti-Jewish writer Marcion (ca.140CE), who excluded all the gospels except Luke from his canon. But even Marcion only accepted Luke in an expurgated form, since there is a pervasive influence of the Hebrew Bible in many parts of Luke's work. It has also been objected that Luke's portrait of Paul in Acts is very different from that which emerges from Paul's own letters. But biography and autobiography can often differ in the light they cast on the same subject, so this does not necessarily preclude a close link between Luke and Paul.

Luke clearly wrote at a time when the eyewitnesses he mentions had died, and a need had arisen for a reliable account of Jesus. His "predictions" of the destruction of Jerusalem, as in Luke 21, may be after the fact and thus imply a date post-70CE. However, the statement that the city's inhabitants "will be taken away as captives" (Luke 21.24) may be a genuine prophecy, constructed along the lines of the account of the city's destruction in the book of Jeremiah.

Jesus is always the central figure in Luke. Unlike Mark or Matthew, Luke calls him "savior" and pictures him distinctively as a prophet, guided by the Spirit. Above all, Jesus is a being of gracious tenderness and compassion, not least in those parables peculiar to Luke. He shows a forgiving love toward outcasts, sinners, and Samaritans, poignantly expressed in the words from the cross at Luke 23.34 and 23.43. Luke's account possesses a universalism summarized by Jesus' final promise that "repentance and forgiveness of sins is to be proclaimed in his name to all nations."

John's gospel, also referred to as the Fourth Gospel, is an enigmatic work that is in some ways very dissimilar to the other gospels. It received a mixed reception in the early Church, and experts continue to give very different assessments of its theology, composition, and background. There has been much discussion as to whether the author of John (see sidebar, right) used one or more of the other gospels, but it is perhaps more likely that he drew upon similar traditions and developed them in his own way.

Scholars have often attempted to uncover other possible sources for John, such as a "book of signs" or an independent Passion narrative. These remain highly speculative, but if John does largely depend on sources distinct from those used by the other evangelists, much of it could predate the late first century CE, the period usually proposed for its composition.

The content of John may differ, but its differences in form should not be exaggerated. For example, the long discourses of Jesus in John have often been said to constitute the principal feature distinguishing this gospel from Matthew, Mark, and Luke. But—as the five discourses in Matthew demonstrate—lengthy speeches are also ascribed to Jesus in the other gospels.

THE AUTHORSHIP OF JOHN

The issues of the authorship and date of the final form of the Fourth Gospel are highly complex. The gospel itself claims to rest on the testimony of an eyewitness, referred to as the "beloved disciple," and it is not impossible that the first stage of writing did indeed consist of an oral transmission of Jesus' sayings, deeds, death, and resurrection by John, the apostle to whom it is attributed.

The gospel has often been seen as a product of the Greco-Roman world, and the traditional place for its composition is Ephesus in Asia Minor. However, it is now generally agreed that the background of the gospel, or at least of many of the traditions it uses, is Palestine. Archaeology has confirmed that the author gives accurate information about sites and customs of the region. The Qumran texts (see p.37) contain many striking parallels with the language and ideas of John's gospel, and there are other similarities. In fact, the whole book, like Matthew (see p.53), can be seen as rooted in Judaism. Although John refers to "the Jews" as those who should have acknowledged Jesus but rejected him, he also states that "salvation is from the Jews." Jesus is regularly compared with the great figures of Jewish history, such as Abraham and particularly Moses. There are links with Jewish Wisdom theology and considerable concern with the Mosaic law, the Temple, and the Messiah.

However, none of this precludes Hellenistic influence, since it is now known that Palestinian Judaism was deeply affected by Hellenism in the centuries around the birth of Christ (see p.22).

The ruins of the Greco-Roman city of Ephesus in Asia Minor (Efes, Turkey), where the gospel of John is traditionally said to have been written. Paul founded an important Christian community here, and it is to this church that the letter to the Ephesians is addressed.

THE GOSPEL EVIDENCE

A silver denarius of Tiberius (ruled 14–37CE), Roman emperor when Jesus was active (Luke 3.1). As with Jesus, what we know of his life is based on four accounts, each with its own distinct outlook, most notably those of Tacitus (ca. 55–ca. 120CE) and Suetonius (ca. 69–ca. 140CE).

THE JESUS SEMINAR

All the gospels are certainly written "that you may come to believe that Jesus is the Messiah, the Son of God" (John 20.31). But John also claims to be telling the "truth" (21.24)—describing what Jesus really did. This claim must be judged by testing the gospels according to the same criteria applied to similar ancient texts. Notable recent endeavors in this respect include the work of the "Jesus Seminar" of the Westar Institute in the United States, a group of scholars who subjected the words ascribed to Jesus in the four gospels and the Gnostic gospel of Thomas (see p.58) to systematic examination.

Their conclusions (published 1990–93) judged only two percent of the sayings attributed to Jesus to be "most probably genuine" and fourteen percent to be "probably genuine." The Seminar's work is not free of controversy (see Introduction), but on the other hand it is unlikely that any attempt to discover "genuine" evidence about Jesus will ever be the subject of scholarly unanimity.

One of the most assured results of modern New Testament scholarship is that the evangelists provide virtually all that we know about Jesus, and that therefore we can approach him in no other way than through the gospels. Many scholars would assert that these reveal more about the early Church than they do about Jesus himself, since they present Jesus as the object of early Christian belief and preaching—the "Christ of faith" rather than the "Jesus of history."

While few scholars would deny that Jesus ever existed—although this view is still occasionally advanced (see p.193)—the more skeptical would claim that little, if anything, can be known of the man Jesus beyond that he lived, taught, and died in Palestine. However, in assessing the value of the gospels as historical evidence various other factors need to be considered. For example, our knowledge of first-century Palestine has greatly increased in recent years and it can now be seen that much of the gospel picture of Jesus reflects an authentic historical background.

Also, it may be argued that the apparent dichotomy between the Christ of faith and the historical Jesus can be pressed too far, and that what the early Church believed must surely have borne some relation to the actual work and sayings of Jesus. Disciples of a Jewish *rabbi* were expected to memorize their teacher's sayings and transmit them faithfully to future generations. Jesus' followers may have done the same, perhaps even making written notes of his words and deeds in the period before the evangelists composed their accounts.

Much is often made of the discrepancies between the gospels—such as their different versions of the same sayings—and the possibility that much attributed to Jesus may be a creation of the early Church and the gospel writers. While there are obvious legendary elements in the gospels, and no doubt words are attributed to Jesus that he is unlikely to have uttered (see sidebar, left), the same may be said of other biographies of antiquity (not to mention more recent times). It has been pointed out, for instance, that there are also four surviving ancient biographies of Jesus' contemporary, the emperor Tiberius. These disagree very considerably among themselves—two are even biased against him—but scholars find it perfectly possible to produce a generally acceptable historical account of his life.

The extent of the divergences among the gospels can be exaggerated. For example, the wording of the Lord's Prayer varies in Matthew 6.9–13 and Luke 11.2–4, but the prayer is recognizably the same. Similarly, while the present forms of Matthew's Sermon on the Mount and Luke's Sermon on the Plain are no doubt creations of the evangelists, many of the individual sayings of which they are made up could well go back to Jesus himself.

THE "SYNOPTIC PROBLEM"

The question of how each evangelist sourced and shaped his material arises particularly with the gospels of Matthew, Mark, and Luke. These texts have many resemblances that permit them to be set out in parallel and closely compared, and hence they are often referred to as the "synoptic" gospels (Greek *sunoptikos*, "seen together") and their authors as the "synoptists." New Testament scholarship seeks to describe how and why they are so similar to one another.

At present, the most widely accepted explanation of their similarity is the so-called "Two-Document" hypothesis, although this is not an entirely adequate description. According to this theory, Mark was written first and established the distinctive genre of "gospel." Mark was used by the other two synoptists, but some resemblances between Matthew and Luke cannot be explained by their common use of Mark. Scholars have therefore postulated that they employed another source, known as "Q" from the German *Quelle* ("source"). The hypothetical "Q" was not a gospel in the usual sense, but a collection of sayings of Jesus, with some narrative, and could have reached the gospel writers in either written or oral form. It has been compared with the Gospel of Thomas, which also consists of sayings (see box, p.59).

Finally, as well as Mark and "Q," Matthew and Luke also use matter that is peculiar to each of them, referred to as "M" and "L" respectively.

The "Two-Document" theory has attained a wide degree of acceptance but is not without powerful challengers. For most of Christian history, Matthew was considered the earliest and basic gospel, an opinion that still has strong advocates. If this view is adopted, the most plausible account of the relationship between the synoptic gospels is perhaps what is known as the "Two-Gospel" hypothesis. According to this, the three synoptic gospels were written in the order Matthew-Luke-Mark, with Luke dependent on Matthew, and Mark using both Matthew and Luke. Among the evidence used to support this theory is the fact that Mark sometimes seems to abbreviate passages that appear in full in Matthew.

It must be emphasized that there is no surviving independent text of "Q" and many scholars would deny that there ever was such a document. Even if its existence is accepted, there are widely different assessments of its character and purpose. For example, was its original language Aramaic or Greek? Can successive strata, with different characteristics, be discovered within it? Most significantly, does it represent the preaching of a community outside what came to be main-

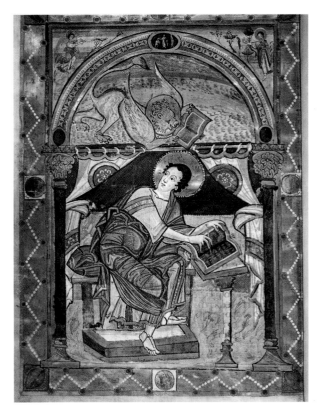

St. Mark, *from the early 9th-century gospel of St. Médard of Soissons, France. Above the figure of the evangelist is his traditional attribute, the winged lion.*

stream Christianity, which had its own particular approach to Jesus? To judge by the sayings that "Q" supposedly included, this group would appear, for example, to have had no interest in Christ's death and resurrection.

These and many other questions mean that the "synoptic problem" remains an issue. It must always be recognized how much is uncertain about the development of early Christianity, such as the fact that there is no hard evidence for the chronological order of the gospels.

Perhaps it is best to conclude that the evangelists employed a wide variety of documents and oral traditions, and were selective in what they used. The author of John acknowledges that he knew of many other acts of Jesus than he records (John 20.30, 21.25). Similarly, Luke's preamble to his "orderly account of the events that have been fulfilled among us" (Luke 1.1) shows that he was aware of many writings already in existence on the life and works of Jesus.

JESUS IN OTHER WRITINGS

EARLY PAGAN AND JEWISH SOURCES
There are a number of early references to Jesus in non-Christian writings. For example, the Roman historian Tacitus (ca. 55–ca. 120CE) relates that the emperor Nero blamed the great fire of Rome in 64CE on the "Christians," who took their name from "Christus." He had been executed by "one of our procurators," Pilate, but his "pernicious superstition" had survived and spread to Rome. Suetonius (ca. 69–ca. 140CE) refers to Jews causing trouble at the prompting of "Chrestus" under Claudius (41–54CE). Jesus is also described in a famous passage in the *Antiquities* of the Jewish historian Josephus (ca. 90CE). Statements such as "He was the Messiah" have led to the dismissal of the entire passage as a Christian interpolation. But stripping out the more obviously Christian words produces a plausible original: Jesus was "a wise man" who "did surprising things"; "a teacher" who "won over" many Jews and Greeks. He was crucified by Pilate at the instigation "of men of the highest standing among us."

Apart from the four canonical gospels, there are numerous references to Jesus and his teaching in other very early sources, the great majority of them Christian, although some are non-Christian (see sidebar, left). The Christian sources include several "apocryphal gospels" of the second to fifth centuries CE, which contain legendary episodes from Jesus' infancy (for example, the second-century Protevangelium of James); narratives of the Passion; or accounts of Jesus' descent into Hell between his death and resurrection. Others reflect the outlook of Jewish Christianity, but survive only as brief extracts in later Christian authors (see p.173).

Among other notable but fragmentary apocryphal gospels are the Gospel of Peter and the Egerton Gospel, which date from the mid-second century. Especially significant in terms of recent discussion are the *agrapha* (literally "things not written"), sayings of Jesus not found in the canonical gospels but occurring elsewhere in the New Testament, in the works of the Church Fathers (see pp.174–5) or in other sources, above all the Gospel of Thomas (see box, opposite).

It would be widely agreed that there is little of historical value in the apocryphal gospels of Christ's infancy and Passion. They are obviously imaginative products, composed in order to supply perceived deficiencies in the information in the New Testament, and to stimulate popular devotion. A number of them were written to present the specific theological viewpoint of Gnosticism (see pp.176–7).

It has been claimed that the Gospel of Peter and the Egerton Gospel predate Matthew, Mark, Luke, and John. But a closer examination reveals that both writings consist of material that represents either a development, or a reproduction from memory, of material in the canonical gospels.

Anna and Joachim at the Golden Gate, by Fra Filippo Lippi (1406–69). It illustrates a scene in the life of the legendary parents of the Virgin, St Anna (Anne) and St Joachim, whose story derives almost entirely from the apocryphal Protevangelium of James.

A stronger case can be mounted for some, at least, of the *agrapha*. Even after the four gospels were written down, traditions about Jesus continued to be transmitted orally and remained highly valued. It is certainly possible that some *agrapha* depend on this oral tradition and preserve Jesus' authentic words. Examples include the saying attributed to Jesus by Paul in Acts 20.35 ("It is more blessed to give than receive") or Paul's poetic quotation of Jesus' words at the Last Supper (1 Cor. 11.24–25).

There is an increasing tendency among New Testament scholars to whittle down to quite a small number any extracanonical sayings that might claim to be genuine words of Jesus, and it is rarely easy to decide in any particular case. In the final analysis, the important conclusion must be that—whatever their interest—the noncanonical sources for Jesus add virtually nothing to the New Testament view of him, and still less require any fundamental revision of it.

THE GNOSTIC GOSPEL OF THOMAS

Among the cache of ancient Gnostic documents discovered in 1945 at Nag Hammadi in Upper Egypt (see pp.176–7) was the so-called "Gospel of Thomas." The manuscript dates from the fourth century CE and is written in Coptic, the Egyptian language of the time, but there is evidence to show that it is actually a translation of a Greek original dating perhaps to the second century CE.

The gospel is unlike the canonical gospels in that it contains no narrative but consists of one hundred and fourteen sayings, or "secret words," that Jesus is supposed to have passed on to the disciple Thomas, the purported author. In this respect it could be compared to the hypothetical "Q" document (see p.57).

The Apostle Thomas, *whom the Gospel of Thomas claims as its author, by Nicolas Frances (ca. 1424–68).*

As it stands, Thomas is clearly a Gnostic text and many of the sayings express Gnostic theology, even when they appear to be drawn from the canonical gospels (seventy of them have New Testament parallels, for example "Let him who seeks not cease seeking until he finds"; compare Matt. 7.7; Luke 11.9). But not all the sayings exhibit this tendency and it has been claimed that the Gnostic coloring was added to the Greek original. Thus the possibility exists that some

sayings with no parallels in the canonical gospels may go back to Jesus. But even scholars who would wish to press this claim believe that the number of plausible cases is very small—perhaps no more than five in all.

Some of the parables in Thomas lack the allegorical interpretations appended to them in the New Testament gospels (see pp.137–8) and so, in the opinion of some, are likely to represent Jesus' own words. Yet even here caution is necessary. For example, the parable of the Great Net (Matt. 13.47–50) occurs in Thomas shorn of Matthew's eschatological interpretation: "And he said, 'The man is like a wise fisherman who cast his net into the sea; he pulled it up from the sea full of small fish; among them he found a large good fish. That wise fisherman threw all the small fish back into the sea, he chose the large fish without regret. Who has ears let him hear'" (Gospel of Thomas 8).

Matthew's parable about the end of the world has become one about human nature, in accordance with Gnostic concerns. It is thus doubtful whether Thomas's version, an apparent example of Gnostic editing, is either original to Jesus or independent of the canonical text.

JESUS' LIFE AND TIMES

The evangelists, with the possible exception of Luke, were not greatly concerned with chronology. Nevertheless, they provide a number of clues that make it possible to place the life of Jesus somewhere within a reasonably certain timespan, from sometime before 4BCE to ca. 30CE or a little later.

Jesus' birth is placed—by Matthew explicitly and Luke implicitly—in the time of King Herod the Great (ruled 37–4BCE). Matthew gives no indication of how long after Jesus' birth Herod died (see pp.72–5), so all that can be said is that Jesus was probably born shortly before 4BCE.

Luke dates Jesus' birth to the time of a census of the Roman empire under the emperor Augustus (ruled 27BCE–14CE) (Luke 2.1). There was never a single, simultaneous census of the whole empire: Augustus intended to carry out a census of all his domains, but on a province-by-province basis. Thus when Luke refers to "the first registration" (Luke 2.2), he means

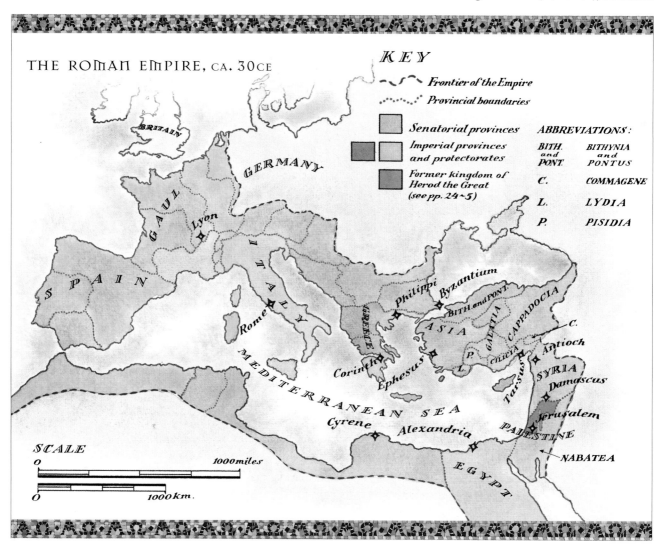

THE ROMAN EMPIRE, CA. 30CE

KEY

〜〜〜 *Frontier of the Empire*

·········· *Provincial boundaries*

▨ *Senatorial provinces*

▨ *Imperial provinces and protectorates*

▨ *Former kingdom of Herod the Great (see pp. 24~5)*

ABBREVIATIONS:

BITH. and PONT.   BITHYNIA and PONTUS

C.   COMMAGENE

L.   LYDIA

P.   PISIDIA

SCALE

0   1000 miles

0   1000 km.

the first census of Judea, for which Quirinius, the legate (governor) of Syria (Luke 2.2), was administratively responsible.

Quirinius was legate of Syria in 6–7CE, but Luke 2.1 says that the census took place "in those days," which in context means around the time of the birth of John the Baptist, which Luke places in the reign of Herod (Luke 1.5). Perhaps Luke believed that Jesus was born ten years after Herod's death, at the time of the census, but also wanted to put the Messiah's birth into the same general time frame as that of his herald, John, who was known to have been born under Herod. At first sight it seems unlikely that Luke, as a careful historian, really believed that the Judean census had taken place under Herod, because it sparked an anti-Roman revolt that was well remembered in Luke's day: he himself mentions it again in Acts 5.37 (see p.182). His contemporary, the historian Josephus, gives the date of the census as 6CE, and there is no evidence that Quirinius held the same post a decade earlier—which in any case would have been highly unusual.

On the other hand, there were also riots after Herod's death, and it has been suggested that Luke erroneously conflated the unrest following the census with these earlier disturbances.

Luke 3.1–2 states that John's ministry began in the fifteenth year of the reign of Tiberius (ruled 14–37CE), probably 28–29CE. This gives an approximate date for the baptism of Jesus and the beginning of his own ministry. Luke 3.23 says that Jesus was "about thirty" when his ministry commenced, which seems very unlikely if Luke is seriously suggesting that Jesus was born in 6CE and began his work ca. 29CE. The age fits better with a birth in ca. 4BCE. But Luke may use the figure of thirty only to indicate that Jesus had arrived at years of maturity (compare Gen. 41.46; Num. 4.47).

All the gospels agree that Jesus was crucified on a Friday, which was either Passover proper (the day that the Passover lambs were sacrificed in the Temple) (John), or the day after Passover (Matthew, Mark, Luke). The sacrifices took place on the fourteenth of the Jewish month of Nisan, and the Passover meal—the synoptists' Last Supper—was eaten at the start of Nisan 15 (in Judaism, days begin and end at sunset). It has been calculated—and the uncertainties of any such calculation must be stressed—that Nisan 14 ended on a Friday evening (April 3) in 33CE, and that Nisan 15 ended on a Friday (April 7) in 30CE. Either year fits Luke's assertion that Jesus died during the prefecture of Pilate (26–36CE), the high-priesthood of Caiaphas (ca. 18–36/37CE), and the reign of Antipas (4BCE–39CE). John's claim that Jesus died on Passover itself, Nisan 14, probably has a theological motive (see p.112–13). So, assuming the synoptists are correct, it may well be that the Crucifixion took place on Friday, April 7, 30CE.

THE LENGTH OF JESUS' MINISTRY
It is often supposed that Matthew, Mark, and Luke assume a one-year ministry, while John presents a ministry covering two or even three years. But the evidence is inconclusive. The three synoptists provide no chronological scheme for the episodes that they select from Jesus' career and these may have occurred over more than a single year. The theory of a longer ministry in John rests on his reference to various Jewish feasts, but the order in which he presents them may be based on theological reasons rather than a concern for strict chronology.

The Baptism of Christ, *by Fra Angelico (ca. 1400–55). This event, which heralded the start of Jesus' ministry (see pp.84–5), is dated by Luke to sometime around the year 29CE.*

THE GENEALOGY OF CHRIST

There are two genealogies of Jesus in the gospels (Matt. 1.1–17; Luke 3.23–38), and there are frequent precedents for both in the Hebrew Scriptures. Recent studies of ancient Near Eastern genealogies have shown that they were compiled for political or religious reasons rather than as straightforward historical records. Genealogies of, for example, a ruler could be adapted to meet changing concerns and different versions might exist side by side without any sense of incompatibility. In postexilic Judaism, such genealogies became particularly important as part of the picture of the expected Messiah.

Similarly, the genealogies in Matthew and Luke are not intended to present a factual family tree and so one should not attempt to harmonize them. Rather, they are artificial constructions with a theological aim, and may have been adapted from earlier Jewish messianic genealogies.

That they are literary creations can be seen most clearly in the case of Matthew. His list is based on a structure of three epochs: from Abraham to David, from David to the Jewish exile in Babylon, and from the exile to Jesus (1.17). Each epoch is of fourteen generations, although the last apparently comprises only thirteen. The evangelist may be reckoning "Jesus … who is called the Messiah" (Matt. 1.16) as two names.

The Tree of Jesse, *an 18th-century icon from the Ionian Isles, Greece. It shows the descent of Jesus from Jesse, the father of King David.*

In any event, the numerical structure stresses God's careful providential plan. Hebrew letters are also used as numbers, and it may be no coincidence that the three letters that spell the name of David add up to fourteen, because David and Abraham are the two most important figures in the genealogy. Abraham is the father of the nation, and thus Jesus is seen as the true Israel, while his descent from King David shows that the divine promise to the Jews of a Messiah from the royal line of Judah has been fulfilled.

A remarkable feature of Matthew's genealogy is his introduction of four women (Tamar, Rahab, Ruth, and Mary). The purpose of this is to demonstrate the precedent in God's plan for the role of Mary, who appears as Jesus' mother at the end of the genealogy. It has often been noted that the first three of these women were morally ambiguous, even scandalous characters. But perhaps too much can be made of this, because by the first century CE Judaism had come to view them in a more positive light. For example, one rabbinic text speaks of Rahab as the ancestor of prophets and righteous men and of Ruth as the ancestor of kings.

THE "PRIESTLY LINEAGE" IN LUKE

In Luke's genealogy, several of the names that appear for the period after the Babylonian exile, such as Levi and Mattathias, imply descent from the Israelite priestly house of Levi (the Levites) rather than the royal house of David. According to Julius Africanus (ca. 220CE), some people saw this feature as highly significant and held that while Matthew's genealogy asserted Jesus' royal descent, Luke emphasized his levitical, priestly, lineage.

It is unlikely, on closer analysis, that the genealogies can really be distinguished in this way. Interestingly, however, Luke presents Elizabeth, the mother of John the Baptist, as a woman of priestly stock, descended from Aaron (Luke 1.5). Mary is Elizabeth's kinswoman, so this could perhaps be taken as indicating that Jesus was of

The shrine under the altar in the 6th-century Church of the Nativity, Bethlehem. Beneath the silver "Star of Bethlehem" is a grotto in which, according to one Christian tradition, Jesus was born.

levitical descent on his mother's side. Curiously, in Luke, Jesus is said to be descended from King David not through the famous King Solomon but through another son, Nathan. Luke may have confused this Nathan with Solomon's contemporary, Nathan the prophet, because the evangelist intended to introduce a prophetic element into Jesus' background. Or Luke may have wanted to avoid referring to Jehoiakim and Jehoiachin, the last two legitimate kings of Judah, because of a prophecy in the book of Jeremiah that they would have no descendants.

Luke's genealogy is less schematic than Matthew's and has more of the character of historical writing. Between David and Jesus he lists forty-two generations, which better suits the time span involved (about one thousand years) than the twenty-eight generations of Matthew. The Lukan genealogy is in the reverse order to that of Matthew, beginning with Jesus. Unlike Matthew, Luke places the genealogy not before Jesus' birth in Bethlehem but at the beginning of his ministry. Here Luke may be following the pattern in Exodus, where the list of Moses' ancestors follows the narrative of his birth and his summoning to God's mission (Exod. 6.16–25).

The other great difference between the two genealogies is that Luke traces Jesus' descent back beyond Abraham to the first man, Adam. This may reflect the universalistic orientation of Luke's gospel (see pp.54–5): Jesus is to be seen as the savior not just of the Jews—unlike Matthew, Luke does not use the term "Messiah" in his genealogy—but for all humanity. Adam is described as "son of God," an expression that may reflect speculation within Judaism about Adam as a heavenly figure. For Luke, though, this description is probably intended to explain why Adam's descendant, Jesus, has been declared the Son of God at his baptism, an event that immediately precedes the presentation of his genealogy (Luke 3.22).

THE NATIVITY

Both Luke and Matthew present the events surrounding Jesus' birth from their own standpoints, but the basic matters on which they agree (see sidebar, opposite) may well point to a reliable early tradition that predates them both. Matthew's version of the birth of Jesus is comparatively brief and colorless: it merely states that Jesus was born, without any accompanying details. Nevertheless, it is not just a factual account but a theological interpretation of events, reflecting ideas present in the Hebrew Scriptures. For example, the heavenly messenger appears in a dream, a regular medium for divine revelations in the Bible.

Also, Matthew draws out the meaning of the name Jesus, in much the same way that the Hebrew Scriptures frequently attach a special significance to personal names. Jesus (Hebrew Yeshu or Yeshua) is a form of "Joshua," which means "Yahweh Saves," and Mary's child is therefore

THE FIGURE OF JOSEPH

In both Matthew and Luke, Jesus' descent from King David is traced through Joseph, which raises the question of whether Joseph was originally regarded as Jesus' actual physical father. In the gospels, Mary and Joseph are referred to as his parents, while Matthew calls Jesus the "son of the carpenter" and Luke refers to him as the "son of Joseph."

However, in their present form, the genealogies of Jesus (see pp.62–3) seem to refute this view. Matthew emphasizes only that Jesus was born of Mary (Matt. 1.16); in one Syrian manuscript this verse makes Joseph the father, but it is very unlikely that this reflects Matthew's original text. Again, when Luke calls Jesus the son of Joseph, he adds "as was thought," and there is no evidence to support the opinion that these words are a later insertion in the gospel.

The early Christians, such as Paul, wished to affirm that Jesus was a descendant of King David and thus the awaited

Bethlehem, the home of Joseph according to the gospels. One theory proposes that Joseph moved to Nazareth to work on the rebuilding of nearby Sepphoris (see p.23).

Messiah. Joseph was known to be of Davidic lineage and it is probably reasonable to suppose that Matthew and Luke present Joseph as Jesus' legal father—as he would have been in Jewish law—in order to give Jesus a claim to Davidic descent.

Joseph's family connections were evidently with Bethlehem, the traditional home of David. Matthew describes Joseph as a "righteous" man and he is depicted as a devout observer of the Jewish law. He was therefore particularly favored to receive angelic messages through the medium of dreams, as Matthew relates (Matt. 1.20–23; 2.13; 2.19). It is possible that the evangelist may be consciously influenced here by the story of the Israelite patriarch Joseph, the great dreamer in the book of Genesis.

Joseph is only really mentioned in the birth narratives. His absence from the rest of the New Testament may indicate that he died before Jesus began his ministry.

The Annunciation, *by Fra Angelico (ca. 1400–55). This illustrates Luke 1.26–38, where the archangel Gabriel announces to Mary that she will conceive by the Holy Spirit (represented here by the white dove).*

THE NATIVITY STORIES IN MATTHEW AND LUKE

The accounts in Matthew and Luke of the birth of Jesus have significant divergences, but nonetheless reveal a number of shared features. These suggest that both evangelists drew upon and adapted much the same basic tradition, which—since each author was writing within a different Christian community—must have been well established for some time. The most notable parallels are as follows:

- The names of Jesus' parents, Mary and Joseph
- The designation of Mary and Joseph as a betrothed couple
- The claim that Joseph is descended from King David
- The annunciation by an angel of the birth of a son (in Matthew to Joseph, in Luke to Mary)
- The angel's message that Mary's conception is by the Holy Spirit, and a command to call the child Jesus
- The representation of Mary as a virgin at the time of conception
- The location of the birth at Bethlehem.

To this list should probably be added the assertion that Jesus was born in the reign of Herod the Great, explicit in Matthew and apparently presupposed in Luke, who synchronizes the births of Jesus and John the Baptist (see pp.60–61).

named because "he will save his people from their sins" (Matt. 1.21).

One characteristic of Matthew's gospel is the evangelist's frequent quotations of biblical prophecies that he sees as being fulfilled in Jesus and his work. These are especially prominent in the opening chapters, where there are no less than five. The purpose of the quotation from Isaiah in the birth story (Matt. 1.23) is not only to confirm Mary's virginal conception but also to attest another significant name for Jesus, "Emmanuel." The author goes on to translate this for his Greek-speaking readers as "God is with us," probably to be understood as indicating a special relationship with God, and Jesus as God's representative.

For Matthew, the main protagonist in the Nativity story, and in the events immediately following Jesus' birth, is Joseph (see box, opposite). He names the child, a very significant event in the Hebrew Bible and Judaism generally, while in Luke it is Mary who does so. The narrative is almost entirely devoted to Joseph's doubts about the proposed marriage and how they are allayed. Perhaps Matthew is developing a tradition of Jewish Christian origin, and is thus concerned to present Joseph as a typically devout Jew, careful to observe the law and customs of his faith. In Matthew he is clearly presented as the patriarchal Jewish head of the family, who could therefore be considered as Jesus' father, whatever his actual physical relationship to his son may have been.

Luke's Nativity account is a moving text of considerable beauty that has always appealed to later writers and artists. Combining poetic imagination and theological interpretation, it is carefully composed with the author's characteristic narrative skill from a series of idyllic scenes pervaded by the ambience of the Hebrew Scriptures. The introduction to the

The town of Ein Karem near Jerusalem, traditionally identified as the "Judean town in the hill country" (Luke 1.39), where Mary went to visit Elizabeth, the mother of John the Baptist.

THE BIRTHS OF JESUS AND JOHN THE BAPTIST

Luke's accounts of the events preceding the births of the Baptist and Jesus are carefully composed and display marked parallels:

- The angel Gabriel appears to Zechariah (Luke 1.11)

  The angel Gabriel appears to Mary (1.26–28)

- Zechariah is troubled at the sight of Gabriel (1.12)

  Mary is troubled by Gabriel's greeting (1.29)

- The angel reassures Zechariah, tells him that God has accepted his prayer, promises him a son, and tells him his name (1.13)

  The angel reassures Mary, tells her that she has found favor with God, promises her a son, and tells her his name (1.30–31)

- The angel foretells John's future in exalted poetic language (1.14–17)

  The angel foretells Jesus' future in a passage of similar quality (1.32–33)

- Zechariah queries the angel: "How will I know that this is so? For I am an old man, and my wife is getting on in years" (1.18)

  Mary queries the angel: "How can this be, since I am a virgin?" (1.34)

- Gabriel gives Zechariah a confirming sign: he is struck dumb (1.20)

  Gabriel gives Mary a confirming sign: her relative Elizabeth is pregnant (1.36).

Further parallels may be discerned in the events that follow the two births:

- John is circumcized and named (1.59–6)

  Jesus is circumcized and named (2.21)

- Events surrounding John's birth cause wonder (1.63, 65–66)

  When the shepherds recount the message of Jesus' birth, "all who heard it were amazed" (2.17–18)

- Zechariah blesses God for John in the form of a prophetic poem (1.67–79)

  Simeon and Anna bless God for Jesus, Simeon with a prophetic poem (2.28–32).

whole gospel is written in good Classical Greek (see p.54), but the author's style then changes dramatically, becoming full of Semitisms and biblical allusions, although Luke does not quote Scripture directly in the way that Matthew does. It has sometimes been supposed that this first section of Luke's gospel has an original Hebrew or Aramaic source, but its linguistic parallels and resonances are with the Septuagint, the Greek version of the Hebrew Bible, rather than the original, and the narrative is best viewed as a literary creation of the evangelist himself.

A distinctive feature of Luke's Nativity story is its close proximity to the story of the birth of John the Baptist. The two accounts come together directly in the meeting of Mary and Elizabeth, who is described as her relative. But the two accounts also have a common form (see sidebar, left), based essentially on various biblical legends in which an angel promises a child to a barren woman (as before the birth of Samson in Judges 13).

That Jesus was in some way closely connected with John, and that Jesus' baptism was of great significance in his own life (see pp.82–5), is one of the most soundly based facts about Jesus. Luke's purpose, perhaps drawing on a tradition current among the Baptist's disciples, seems to be to show that the two men were linked from the very moment of their conceptions, and that they were brought together as part of a great divine plan. However, like all the other evangelists, Luke is also at pains to make clear the superiority of Jesus, which is acknowledged both by Elizabeth and by the child in her womb (Luke 1.41–42). Luke's special contribution is to claim that this was known from the very beginning.

Mary is central to Luke's narrative and his opening chapters have appropriately been described as "the gospel of Mary." It is she to whom Gabriel comes and she who goes to Elizabeth as a kind of messenger of salvation. Her purification after childbirth is mentioned (see p.76), and the righteous Simeon addresses a special prophecy to her (Luke 2.34–35).

Later, Mary takes the lead in speaking to her son when he goes missing and is finally found among the teachers in the Temple (Luke 2.48; see p.76). She is depicted as the perfectly obedient servant of the Lord, suggesting that she is the ideal model of Christian discipleship. Twice the evangelist notes that Mary treasured what she had heard and seen and kept them in her heart (Luke 2.19, 51)—probably an implicit claim that his knowledge of what he records had come from her. It is not impossible that Luke is indeed giving his own version of traditions that go back to Mary herself.

Luke's presentation includes two famous poetic canticles known as the *Magnificat* (Luke 1.46–55) and the *Benedictus* (Luke 1.68–79) from their opening words in Latin translation. They are very probably the evangelist's own composition, based on a string of verses from the Septuagint (the Greek version of the Hebrew Bible). They celebrate the redemption of God's ancient people, Israel, which has now been realized. The *Benedictus* speaks of John as a prophet preparing the way of the Lord. In the *Magnificat* —the position of which is probably suggested by that of the song of Hannah, the mother of the prophet Samuel (1 Sam. 2.1–10)—Mary is the agent whom all future generations will call blessed.

BETHLEHEM AND NAZARETH

The general evidence of the gospels is that Jesus' hometown was Nazareth in Galilee, but both Luke and Matthew record that he was born in the town of Bethlehem, south of Jerusalem. Matthew implies that Bethlehem was also the actual residence of Mary and Joseph (Matt. 2.11)—the couple only move to Nazareth later (Matt. 2.23). In Luke, the couple live in Nazareth (Luke 1.26–27) but go to Bethlehem for a census (Luke 2.4–5). Jesus is born there and the family returns to Nazareth (Luke 2.39).

It is difficult to reconcile these two accounts, and scholars have questioned whether Jesus can really have been born in Bethlehem or whether this assertion rests on theological considerations rather than historical truth. Bethlehem was the birthplace of King David, from whom the Messiah would be descended. Matthew 2.6 quotes a passage of scripture stating that the Messiah would come from Bethlehem.

Luke's account of the census as the reason for the move to Bethlehem also poses problems (see pp.60–61). However, Luke seems to have no ulterior theological motives for the details he gives of Jesus' birth in Bethlehem: the overcrowded inn, the bands of cloth, the manger (Luke 2.7). This may imply—assuming they are not products of Luke's imagination—that they represent an authentic tradition.

Indeed, perhaps the strongest argument in support of Matthew and Luke is the weight of the consistent, and very early, tradition that Jesus was born at Bethlehem. Luke's claim that Joseph's family was from there (Luke 2.4) is hardly implausible, and as a master craftsman he may well have traveled to find employment (see box, p.64). Mary's relative, Elizabeth, also apparently lived not far away (Luke 1.39).

The Adoration of the Magi, *by Jan Gossaert (Mabuse), ca. 1508. The artist depicts the wise men (Matt. 2.11; see pp.70–71) paying homage to Jesus in a picturesque ruin serving as the stable of the inn (Luke 2.7)—note the traditional detail of the ox and ass behind the figure of Mary.*

THE VIRGIN BIRTH

"JESUS, SON OF PANTERA"
It has been argued that the early Christians may have invented Matthew's portrait of a pregnant, unmarried Mary, in order to counter scandalous rumors about Jesus' origins that circulated in non-Christian circles. For example, the early Christian writer Origen (ca. 185–254CE), together with the Talmud and other Jewish sources, record an allegation that Jesus was the offspring of an adulterous liaison between Mary and a Roman soldier, variously called Pantera, Panthera, or Pandera.

Intriguingly, the tombstone of a Roman bowman called Pantera, who served in Tiberius' reign, was found in Germany in 1859. He is described as coming from Sidon, close to Galilee, demonstrating—if nothing else—that the name given to Jesus' alleged "real" father was neither anachronistic nor invented.

Alone in the New Testament, Matthew and Luke relate that Mary was a virgin when she bore Jesus (Matt. 1.18–25; Luke 1.26–35). The historical and literary evidence both for and against the virgin birth—or, more precisely, the virgin conception—is evenly balanced and there are arguments on both sides. Any judgment about the "truth" or otherwise of this event probably has to rest on such considerations as the possibility of the miraculous; the assessment of the gospel texts and what they really mean; and, not least, the religious viewpoint of the individual commentator.

Matthew says that Mary will conceive "from the Holy Spirit" (Matt. 1.18, 20) and Luke that "the power of the Most High will overshadow" her (Luke 1.35). It has sometimes been claimed that neither of these statements necessarily precludes ordinary sexual intercourse, because the evangelists may simply be indicating that God would be present at the moment of conception. Support for this opinion can perhaps be seen in the book of Genesis where Eve, after intercourse with her husband, cries: "I have produced a man with the help of the Lord" (Gen. 4.1).

But the evidence that the evangelists do indeed intend to assert that Mary conceived without human intervention is very strong. Much has been made of the fact that *parthenos*, the Greek word in the gospels usually translated as "virgin," primarily means only a girl who has reached sex-

VIRGIN BIRTH: A PAGAN CONCEPT?

The notion of virgin conception is unknown in Judaism. The possibility of such a phenomenon is in no way implied in the numerous biblical legends of miraculous births to barren mothers—although these accounts certainly influenced the gospel stories of Jesus' birth. Nor can the prophecy of Isaiah (Isa. 7.14) quoted by Matthew (see caption, opposite) be taken as firm evidence of a Jewish belief in the possibility of conception without a human father.

However, the idea of virgin conception was widely current in the Greco-Roman world. Famous royal figures such as Alexander the Great and the emperor Augustus were commonly said to have been born from the union of their mother with a deity, and similar claims were made on behalf of charismatic religious figures. According to later writings, Simon the magician, a figure who appears in Acts 8, claimed

that his mother was a virgin when she conceived him.

The idea of Jesus' virginal conception has therefore often been attributed to the influence of paganism. But it is uncertain how far such ideas would have been acceptable to first-century Christians with a Jewish monotheistic heritage. Also, the pagan parallels with the New Testament stories are not as close as they may seem. Pagan legends tell of intercourse in the usual human manner, between a woman and a god who takes human form.

But the gospels exclude any suggestion of divine anthropomorphism, speaking of the "descent of the Holy Spirit" and the power of God "overshadowing" Mary in language reminiscent of the Hebrew Scriptures. Such terms reflect the Jewish idea of the Shekinah, the divine presence on earth, a concept deliberately designed to exclude anthropomorphism.

THE VIRGIN BIRTH ❖ 69

The Virgin Annunciate (Our Lady of Expectation), *by Naddo Ceccarellli (died ca. 1347). The pregnant Mary reads the verse of Matthew that cites a prophecy in Isaiah 7.14: "Look, the virgin shall conceive and bear a son"(Matt. 1.23). Matthew is quoting from the Greek Septuagint, which translates as "virgin" (Greek* parthenos) *an original Hebrew word that means "young woman." At least as early as the 2nd century, it was claimed that Mary had remained a virgin even after Jesus' birth—an idea that led to the medieval doctrine of her perpetual virginity.*

THE VIRGIN BIRTH IN THE NEW TESTAMENT AND EARLY CHURCH

One of the strongest arguments against the authenticity of the virgin birth is that apart from Matthew and Luke the New Testament never refers to it—in contrast to the central position of the Resurrection. Of course, this is an argument from silence and it may be that the virgin birth began as a private tradition within Jesus' own family, and only became more widely known with the increasing desire to learn more of Jesus' early life (see pp.58–9).

The two evangelists who do not mention the virgin birth may have had very strong reasons for beginning their gospels as they did. Mark opens with the ministry of the Baptist, the new Elijah, perhaps to parallel the way that the prophet Elijah appears suddenly and unannounced in the Hebrew Scriptures. John's prologue could be viewed as an exploration of the implications of Jesus as Emmanuel, "God is with us" (Isa. 7.14; Matt. 1.23).

The absence of the virgin birth in Paul's letters has to be seen in the broader context of his almost complete lack of reference to any part of Jesus' earthly career.

Some Jewish Christian groups, such as the Ebionites (see p.173), rejected the virgin birth, as did the Christian writers Cerinthus (ca. 100CE) and Marcion (ca. 160CE). But Ignatius, bishop of Antioch ca. 112CE, unquestioningly accepted it, suggesting that the belief was early and strongly held. In the succeeding century it became virtually universal among Christians.

ual maturity and not necessarily one who has never had intercourse. But it is clear from the context that the evangelists understand the term to mean "virgin" in the usual sense. For example, when the angel Gabriel announces Mary's pregnancy she expresses surprise: "How can this be, since I am a virgin?" (Luke 1.34).

Luke describes Mary as a "virgin" betrothed to Joseph (Luke 1.26). In Judaism, an engagement could be swiftly broken if a bride was found not to be a virgin, just as Joseph plans to dismiss Mary when he discovers her pregnancy. But the angel reassures Joseph that his bride has not slept with any man (Matt. 1.18–20).

THE FIRST WITNESSES

THE PRECIOUS GIFTS

THE PRECIOUS GIFTS
Christians came to interpret the three gifts brought by the wise men (Matt. 2.11) as each symbolizing an aspect of Jesus' character: gold denoted his royal nature as Son of David and Messiah; frankincense (used in sacred rituals) represented his priesthood (compare Heb. 9.11); and myrrh (used in the anointing of corpses) pointing to his saving death.

However, nothing in the gospel itself justifies this understanding. Matthew is probably reflecting an awareness that such luxury goods were staples of the extensive import trade from southern Arabia.

The second chapter of Matthew recounts the famous story of the "wise men from the East" (Matt. 2.1) who, following a star, come to pay homage to the infant Jesus. This episode underwent considerable development in Christian thought. For example, the evangelist does not say how many wise men there were, and the tradition that there were three of them was deduced from the fact that they brought three types of gift (see sidebar, left).

The visitors are often thought of as kings, an idea that only developed when the Church applied verses in the Hebrew Bible to this episode. For example, there are references in Psalms (as Ps. 72.10–11) to kings bringing tribute to an Israelite ruler interpreted as the Messiah, while Isaiah speaks of kings coming to the brightness of the Messiah and of camels bearing gold and frankincense (Isa. 60.6). It is intriguing that Matthew himself does not cite such passages, in spite of his marked habit of quoting biblical predictions that he sees as referring to Jesus.

THE SHEPHERDS

Luke's story of the shepherds who visit the infant Jesus parallels in some ways Matthew's story of the wise men. Both follow immediately the account of Jesus' birth, and both record a supernatural revelation to a group of people of the true character of the newborn child. In Luke 2, the revelation is to shepherds, the sort of simple folk for whom his gospel generally shows special concern.

The angel tells the shepherds of universal rejoicing at Jesus' birth (Luke 2.10–11) and of the divine gift of peace on earth to those whom God favors—probably meaning the future followers of Jesus (Luke 2.14). Jesus is the Messiah, born in David's city (Luke 2.11). Luke's terms "bringing good news" and "savior"—the sole occurrence of this word in the three synoptic gospels—echo some inscriptions in Asia Minor commemorating the birthday of the emperor Augustus.

The Annunciation to the Shepherds, *a stained glass panel of ca. 1300.*

The shepherds are described as living in the fields to guard their flocks at night (Luke 2.8). This was the usual practice in Palestine, where sheep were turned into the fields after the June wheat harvest to graze on the remains of the crops. If Luke's account has any historical basis, therefore, Jesus is likely to have born in the summer.

Luke's story is a beautiful idyllic tale, perhaps influenced by pagan legends that link shepherds with the birth of famous men such as Romulus and Remus. However, Bethlehem, the city of David, is prominent in the narrative. David began his career as a shepherd. Genesis mentions a place nearby called "tower of flocks," where, according to a Jewish tradition, the king-Messiah would one day be revealed.

+SCS BALTHASSAR +SCS MELCHIOR +SCS GASPAR

The Magi, *a 6th-century mosaic in the church of Sant' Apollinare Nuovo, Ravenna. It gives the "wise men" their traditional names of Balthasar, Melchior, and Caspar (or Gaspar). Each wears a Phrygian cap, a felt hat originally from the land of Phrygia in Asia Minor but widely used in Greco-Roman art to denote a person from the Orient.*

The eastern strangers have sometimes been depicted in art visiting the newborn Jesus in the manger at the same time as the shepherds, whose visit is described in Luke (see box, opposite). But Matthew says that they found Jesus and Mary in a domestic setting (Matt. 2.11), and the fact that Herod felt it necessary to massacre all children under two (see pp.72–3) would suggest that Jesus had been born some considerable time previously.

There have often been attempts to connect the guiding star with astronomical phenomena around the time of Jesus' birth, in particular with the appearance of a comet ca. 5BCE. But it seems more likely that Matthew has developed an imaginative scenario out of a prophecy in the book of Numbers that "a star shall come out of Jacob" (Num. 24.17). Matthew does not quote this passage, but it also occurs in a collection of messianic texts from Qumran (see p.37). Simon bar Kosiba, the leader of the Second Jewish revolt against Rome (132–5CE) was called "bar Kokhba" ("son of a star") by his followers, many of whom proclaimed him as the Messiah.

It has been suggested that the whole episode in which foreign wise men acknowledge Jesus deliberately anticipates the universal Christian mission with which Matthew's gospel ends (Matt. 28.19). If so, the reference is oblique: the *magi* are not depicted as evangelical converts, but simply return to their own country (Matt. 4.12). More likely, the evangelist is expressing the common Jewish expectation that when the Messiah appeared, he and Israel would receive the homage of all nations. Genuine speculation in learned Jewish circles in Jerusalem about the arrival of the awaited Messiah may find echoes in Herod's decision to convene all the chief priests and scribes and seek their advice (Matt. 2.4).

THE *MAGI*

Matthew describes the foreign visitors by the Greek term *magi* (singular *magos*; Latin *magus*), which is probably best rendered as "magicians." Originally of Persian origin, by the first century CE the *magi* had become widespread in the ancient world as a highly influential group of skilled practitioners in esoteric arts, such as astrology and oneiromancy (divination from dreams), both of which figure in the gospel narrative. They possessed secret and arcane wisdom and so may justifiably be called "wise men," the traditional English translation of *magi*.

The Jewish writer Philo commends the *magi* as adepts of "true magic" but elsewhere denounces them as charlatans, concerned only with charms and incantations. The same negative verdict appears in the New Testament in the depiction of other *magi*, such as Simon (Acts 8) and Elymas (Acts 13).

Matthew certainly recognizes the special abilities of the *magi*. Owing to their supernatural wisdom they understand that the guiding star manifests the royal status of Jesus (Matt. 2.2). They also receive a divine message in a dream (Matt. 2.12).

On the other hand, there may be an implied contrast with Jesus. In the gospels Jesus is accused of being a magician and performing miracles in the name and power of Beelzebub, the prince of the demons (Matt. 12.24 and parallels). In introducing the *magi*, Matthew may wish to imply that all practitioners of magic must admit the superiority of Jesus—just as the demons do (as at Matt. 8.29–30; Luke 4.34)—and acknowledge that as the Holy One of God, his power and authority are utterly different in nature from their own.

THE WRATH OF HEROD

This 1st-century tomb in Jerusalem was long thought to be that of King Herod the Great, but more probably belonged to a member of his family. Note the stone rolled to seal the entrance.

HEROD AND ABRAHAM

Jewish embellishments of the story of Abraham in the book of Genesis may have influenced Matthew's narrative centered on Herod the Great. In the Abraham legends, his birth is marked by the appearance over his birthplace of a huge star, which astrologers recognize as presaging the advent of a great future ruler. They relate their prediction to the king, Nimrod, who in consequence slaughters seventy thousand innocent children.

As with the Exodus story of male Israelite babies being slaughtered (see main text), the parallels are not exact, but they may provide some of the elements out of which Matthew constructed his own story.

The figure of Herod the Great (ruled 37–4BCE) features prominently in Matthew's story of the wise men, or *magi* (see pp.70–71), and its sequel. This culminates in the flight of Jesus' family to Egypt (see pp.74–5) and the mass slaughter of the infants of Bethlehem (see box, opposite).

There has been much discussion of how far, if at all, what is recorded of King Herod in Matthew has any genuine historical basis. That the king should have taken such *magi* seriously is by no means improbable, since Jewish interest in astrology is well attested, for example in the so-called *Treatise of Shem* (first century BCE), while horoscopes have been found among the Qumran documents. It has perhaps been too readily assumed that the *magi* were pagans, since by this time there were well-established Jewish communities in the East, notably in Babylonia.

Matthew's general picture of Herod as brutal, hot-tempered, superstitious, and cunning, with a strong instinct for self-preservation, accords well with what is known of his genuine character (see pp.24–5). Herod's expressed wish to pay homage to the newborn king (Matt. 2.8) is, of course, on one level to be understood as a trick. But for Matthew what Herod says, albeit unwittingly, is true: when the king-Messiah comes, the secular ruler must indeed submit to him.

Whatever their historical basis, it can hardly be denied that Matthew's stories involving King Herod are woven from various biblical themes. One of the most important of these is the life of Moses. For example, the Massacre of the Innocents is very likely based on the story in Exodus 1 that Pharaoh ordered the slaughter of all Israelite male children. Thus Matthew is casting Herod in the role of the Egyptian king, the oppressor of Israel.

THE MASSACRE OF THE INNOCENTS

Herod the Great's most notorious act in Matthew's gospel account is to order the massacre of all the children of Bethlehem aged two or under in an attempt to get rid of the infant born there whom the wise men have hailed as Messiah and king of the Jews (Matt. 2.16). Some would assert that this event—known as the Massacre of the Innocents—may be authentic, since the victims would not have been numerous. Bethlehem was a small place and the event could have passed largely unnoticed in the fevered, bloody atmosphere that marked the last years of Herod's reign.

Nor, it is argued, were such acts unheard of in the contemporary world. According to the first-century Roman historian Suetonius, shortly before the future emperor Augustus was born, an omen heralded the birth of a king of Rome, so the republican Senate decreed that all males born that year should die. But this story may be just as legendary as similar Jewish tales. No other source mentions Herod's massacre.

Other scholars hold the view that here, as in all his post-birth narratives, Matthew has manufactured an episode based on a biblical passage, in this case a verse of Jeremiah that refers to a place near Bethlehem (Jer. 31.15), which Matthew quotes (Matt. 2.18). But it is hard to see how he could have drawn what he writes from Jeremiah alone. It is more likely that he relies on a broad range of biblical and other Jewish themes (see sidebar, opposite), introducing particular scriptural passages in order to stress that the events he relates form part of a longstanding divine plan.

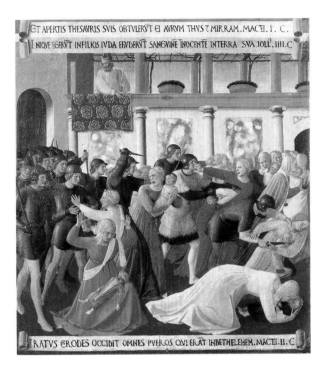

The Massacre of the Innocents, *by Fra Angelico (1387–1455). While Matthew's portrait of a ruthless, paranoid monarch accords well with what is known of Herod's last years, there are various improbabilities in the massacre story. For example, Herod could have found out who the newborn king-Messiah was simply by ordering spies to follow the magi to Bethlehem.*

Similarly, when an angel tells Joseph that Herod is dead and that he can therefore return home from Egypt (Matt. 2.20; see p.75), the angelic words allude directly to God's instruction to Moses to return from exile in Midian (Exod. 4.19).

Matthew may also echo Jewish legends about Moses that were current in the first century CE, although they only occur in later *haggadah*s (accounts of the Exodus read during the Passover meal). According to one of these legends, Pharaoh was warned that the infant Moses would usurp the crown unless he was killed, but Moses was saved by the angel Gabriel. In the gospel, Jesus is preserved from Herod's destruction through the intervention of an angel, who warns Joseph to flee with his family from Bethlehem. Other themes with parallels in Jewish legends of Moses include prophetic dreams and even Joseph's proposal to divorce his bride.

THE FLIGHT INTO EGYPT

After the wise men had paid their homage to the infant Jesus, Matthew relates that an angel warned Joseph in a dream of King Herod's murderous intentions toward the child (Matt. 2.13). At the angel's command, Joseph took his wife and the boy to Egypt, where they remained until after Herod's death. The evangelist gives no details either of the journey or of the family's life in Egypt, and most scholars doubt that the episode has any genuine historical basis. Matthew relates the Egyptian sojourn to biblical prophecy, and cites Hosea 11.1, translating directly from the Hebrew: "Out of Egypt I have called my son" (the Septuagint has "my children").

The "son" represents Moses and, by extension, the Israelite people, whom Moses led from slavery in Egypt. Matthew appears to be alone in taking Hosea's words to refer to the Messiah, but the evangelist may simply wish to stress that Jesus' life echoed and recapitulated key events in the

JESUS THE "NAZOREAN"

Matthew implies that Bethlehem, where Jesus was born, was the original place of residence of Joseph and Mary (see p.67). But he also knew that Jesus was brought up in Nazareth in Galilee and claims that Joseph was directed to go there in fulfillment of a prophecy that "He [the Messiah] will be called a Nazorean" (Matt. 2.22–23). By "Nazorean" (Greek *Nazoraios*) the evangelist appears to mean an inhabitant of Nazareth, and the word has this sense elsewhere in the New Testament; in Acts it is a name for Christians in general.

Matthew's "prophecy" does not correspond closely to anything in the Bible and many scholars think that it is based on Isaiah 11.1, a well-known messianic passage, where the Messiah is described as a "branch" (Hebrew *nezer*) of the tree of Jesse (the father of King David). But Matthew normally cites the Septuagint, the Greek version of the Hebrew Bible, which has nothing like *Nazoraios* at this point. However, he may be translating directly from the original Hebrew, as with his earlier quotation from Hosea (see main text).

There is another explanation. Matthew here claims to cite "the prophets," the term used for one of the three parts of the Jewish Bible (see p.30). In this sense it includes the book of Judges, and in some versions of the Septuagint, Judges 13.7 describes Samson as *naziraios*, a "nazirite" (Hebrew *nazir*), a person dedicated to God by special vows. This seems the most probable source of Matthew's *Nazoraios*. Samson may seem an unlikely model for Jesus, but he is one of the great Israelite heroes and, like Jesus in the gospels, suffered betrayal and agony—only to triumph in death over Israel's enemies. Luke makes a comment on the upbringing of Jesus (Luke 2.40) that may also be influenced by the story of Samson (Judg. 13.24).

The modern town of Nazareth in Galilee. Not mentioned in the Hebrew Scriptures, it was little more than a village in Jesus' day.

story of Israel. The idea that Christ had been present throughout Israel's history was certainly current in early Christianity (for example, 1 Cor. 10.1–4).

Other biblical figures may also be in the background. Most notably, Matthew probably intends to link Joseph of Nazareth with his great namesake, the patriarch Joseph, who was saved from death by being taken into Egypt, enabling God's promise to Israel to be fulfilled. The patriarch Abraham and the prophet Jeremiah—whom Matthew quotes a few verses later—also migrated to Egypt in order to avoid various calamities.

As Christianity developed, a growing interest in the details of Jesus' early life led Christian writers to embellish Matthew's bald account of the Egyptian interlude. These legends are found in the so-called "infancy gospels" (see pp.58–9) and are notable for giving much greater prominence in the story to Mary and the infant Jesus.

The account of the family's return from Egypt (Matt. 2.19–21) is also brief. It, too, is set in motion by an angelic message conveyed in a dream, and once more Joseph is the chief protagonist. Again, the angel's words link Jesus with Moses (see p.73). Matthew says that Joseph feared a return to Bethlehem because "Archelaus was ruling over Judea" (Matt. 2.22). On Herod's death, his son Archelaus became "ethnarch" of Judea and ruled (4BCE–6CE) with such brutality that the Romans deposed him lest he provoke a revolt (see pp.24–5). So Joseph and his family headed not for Bethlehem but for Nazareth in Galilee, outside Archelaus' domains (see box, opposite).

The harsh desert terrain of the Negev desert in southern Israel. If Matthew's account has a historical basis, this is the sort of landscape through which Mary, Joseph, and Jesus would have passed on their journey to Egypt.

RITES OF CHILDHOOD

Following the visit of the shepherds to the infant Jesus (see box, p.70), Luke presents two attractive and moving scenes that display his narrative power and skill. He depicts the parents of Jesus as devout Jews, meticulous in carrying out "everything required by the law of the Lord" (Luke 2.39) with regard to the birth of a male child. The main rituals concerned were those of circumcision, purification, and presentation in the Temple.

Jesus' circumcision took place eight days after the birth, as prescribed by Jewish law (Luke 2.21), and was accompanied by naming the infant in accordance with the angelic command in Luke 1.31.

Childbirth placed a mother in a state of ritual impurity, which lasted for forty days. Luke 2.22 writes of "their" purification, apparently meaning both Mary and Joseph, although Jewish law refers to the mother alone.

JESUS AND THE TEMPLE TEACHERS

The differences between the second chapters of Matthew and Luke suggest that a variety of traditions about Jesus' early years were circulating soon after his death. Luke has selected one episode—the only story about Jesus' boyhood in the canonical gospels—in which the twelve-year-old child goes missing on a visit to Jerusalem at Passover and is found by his parents debating with religious teachers in the Temple (Luke 2.41–49).

This story brings together Jesus and the Temple, a theme in which Luke shows special interest. Other key themes from the story of the Presentation recur (see main text): Jesus' family as devout Jews; the prominence of Mary; and the recognition of Jesus' exceptional nature by figures viewed as representative of Judaism. The setting is to be understood as the precincts of the Temple, where rabbinical teachers congregated to give instruction, as Jesus himself did later in his career and as Luke represents the apostles doing in Acts.

Christ among the Doctors [Teachers] in the Temple, *a fresco by Giotto (ca. 1266–1337) in the Scrovegni Chapel, Padua. According to Luke 2.47, "all who heard him were amazed at his understanding."*

In Judaism, a boy attains the status of religious maturity, *bar mitzvah* ("son of the commandment"), at thirteen, when he takes on the full duties required of males under the Jewish law. Luke may thus intend to present Jesus, while still a minor, as possessing a prodigious understanding of religious matters that amazed his elders (Luke 2.47).

The meaning of the story emerges in the dialogue between Jesus and Mary (Luke 2.48–49), when, for the first time in the gospels, Jesus calls God his Father. Jesus' awareness of a special relationship to God is central to his self-awareness (see pp.166–7). That Jesus' parents do not understand his words at this stage reflects another gospel theme—the incomprehension of his family during his ministry.

Jesus' parents suffer considerable anxiety as a result of his absence (Luke 2.48). Luke is careful to balance this unfilial behavior with the statement that he was otherwise a model Jewish child, whose prime duty was obedience (Luke 2.51).

The Presentation of Jesus in the Temple, *by Giovanni Bellini (ca. 1431–1516). Mary (left) passes the infant into the arms of Simeon (Luke 2.28) as Joseph (center) and others look on.*

The time of purification was completed by a visit to the Temple in Jerusalem for the "presentation" of an animal sacrifice as an act of thanksgiving, which Luke describes as the type permitted for the poorest worshipers (Luke 2.24). This reflects both the "lowliness" of Mary—under Jewish law, the sacrifice would have been offered by the mother—as expressed in the *Magnificat* (Luke 1.46–55; see p.67) and perhaps also Luke's general interest in the poor and the humble.

However, for Luke, the term "presentation" refers primarily to the dedication of Jesus for his future mission. The evangelist quotes the law by which a firstborn child was "designated as holy to the Lord" (Luke 2.23). This passage is probably influenced by the biblical story of the dedication of the infant Samuel at Shiloh (1 Sam. 1). The theme is continued by the prophetic figures of Simeon and Anna, who may have been well-known personalities. Simeon in particular is filled and guided by the Holy Spirit. In the song known (from its opening words in Latin) as the *Nunc Dimittis* (Luke 2.29–32), he foretells the universality of the gospel message—a note that echoes throughout all Luke's work.

Luke's birth narrative is centered very much on Mary and this emphasis continues in his story of the presentation. Simeon has a special message for her (Luke 2.34–35), which strikes a more moving and somber chord than the triumphant note of the *Nunc Dimittis*: the child Jesus is a prophetic sign, which "will be opposed," and his mission will also bring extreme suffering to his mother.

Luke's account concludes with the peaceful return of the family to Nazareth. Jesus grows up blessed by divine favor and "filled with wisdom" (Luke 2.40)—words that prepare the way for the next vivid episode of Luke's gospel (see box, opposite).

THE HOME LIFE OF JESUS

A stone oven dominates the kitchen area of this two-story house in the partly reconstructed village of Qatzrin in the Lower Golan. Although the extant remains at Qatzrin date substantially to the 5th century CE, scholars believe that the form of its domestic buildings and those excavated at other villages in Galilee and the surrounding area, would have changed little since Jesus' day.

Apart from the Nativity and infancy stories in Matthew and Luke, the gospels provide only incidental information about the childhood and youth of Jesus or the circumstances of his home life up until his baptism by John the Baptist and the beginning of his ministry. A number of early texts and "infancy gospels" (see p.58) sought to supply the missing details of Jesus' family background and upbringing, and while their authenticity is at best dubious, they were an important source of several medieval traditions.

Whether or not Jesus was born in Bethlehem (see sidebar, p.67), early nonbiblical sources, such as the second-century Protevangelium of James, claimed that he had family ties with Judea. The Protevangelium says Mary was born in Jerusalem, the home of her legendary parents, Anna and Joachim (see illustration, p.58). In the gospels themselves, Luke calls Mary a relative of John the Baptist's parents, Elizabeth and Zechariah, who lived near Jerusalem in the hill country of Judea (Luke 1.36, 1.39).

The Protevangelium also says that the family of Anna held estates in the region of Mount Carmel, and other early Christian traditions outside the canonical gospels connect Jesus with Galilee and the north of Palestine.

A view of present-day Nazareth. The hill in the background, known as the "Mount of the Precipitation" or "Mount of the Leap," is traditionally said to be the place from which the enraged inhabitants of the town tried to hurl Jesus following his preaching in the synagogue, as described in Luke 4.29–30.

According to one such source, Mary was born in Sepphoris, a city near Nazareth (see illustration, p.23). Some commentators have suggested that for both Jesus and his mother to be invited to a wedding at Cana (John 2.1–2) it must have been a family occasion.

Such legends and speculation aside, it is universally accepted that Jesus was raised at Nazareth in Galilee, and archaeological evidence of life in Palestine in the first century CE means that several aspects of Jesus' early years can now be gleaned with reasonable probability. Recent excavations at a number of nearby sites have given an idea of the sort of house in which he and his family would have lived (see illustration, opposite). Basically, it consisted of a courtyard, around which were a number of rooms of one or two floors, the upper floor resting on wooden beams and reached by an inside ladder or outside stairway. If Jesus' house had accommodated all nine or more members of his family—mother, father, five sons, and at least two daughters—it would probably have required a second story. The gospels indicate that common household items included an oven, a lamp-stand, a meal tub or basket, and mats or mattresses on which to sleep.

Nothing is known directly about any education or intellectual forma-tion which the young Jesus may have received. The fact that his learning later drew comment, and that his followers could address him as *rabbi* ("Teacher"; see pp.162–3) suggests that he was well acquainted with the Hebrew Scriptures as they were taught in contemporary Judaism. By this period, the Pharisees in particular had established schools attached to local synagogues, where children learned to read and write and received instruc-tion in the Jewish law. Jesus might well have attended such a school: he could certainly read and expound a biblical passage during a synagogue service (Mark 1.21, 6.2). The only recorded episode from Jesus' youth, his discussion with the teachers in the Temple (Luke 2.42–51), took place when he was twelve. In later Jewish practice, which may well have applied

This ancient Egyptian bow-drill almost certainly differs little from the sort of carpenter's tool that would have been familiar to Joseph and Jesus. The Greek word tekton, *which is used in the gospels, has a wider sense than "carpenter," by which it is traditionally translated. It can mean someone engaged in construction work in wood, stone, and brick. It is easy to exaggerate the supposed poverty of Jesus' background: a family of general builders could have been quite prosperous.*

JAMES, THE BROTHER OF JESUS

One of Jesus' brothers, James, attained a position of special importance in the early Church. This would appear to have been largely on account of his blood relationship with his elder brother, although Paul also records that James was marked out because he experienced a personal vision of the resurrected Christ. He appears very early as a prominent leader in the Jerusalem Church, perhaps even its chief spokesman, as Acts and Galatians indicate.

In the New Testament, James is portrayed as the representative of the Jewish Christianity that characterized the Jerusalem Church, in contrast to the Gentile Christianity whose chief missionary was Paul (see pp.172–3). Later writings, reflecting the outlook of Jewish Christianity, claim that James had even greater authority, and state that he was the most important apostle, responsible for commissioning all the others. He is traditionally said to be the author of the letter of James and, while this is now disputed, it may well reflect his teachings.

A reliable tradition recorded by the first-century Jewish writer Josephus indicates that James and others were stoned to death in 62CE on the orders of the high priest Ananus, during a power vacuum between the death of one Roman prefect and the arrival of his successor. The second-century Christian historian Hegesippus also has an account of James's death, but its vivid details are seen as largely legendary.

Hegesippus relates that after James's death, another relative, Simeon, assumed a leading position at Jerusalem. This suggests that a dynastic pattern of leadership developed for a time among the followers of Jesus in the city.

in the time of Jesus, a boy became a full adult at thirteen and assumed all the legal and religious responsibilities required of a Jewish male. Luke may intend the episode in the Temple either to demonstrate Jesus' precocity or to be seen as a preparation for his assumption of maturity (see box, p.76).

Mark 6.3 and Matthew 13.55 mention four brothers of Jesus: James (see box, above), Joseph (or Joses), Simon (or Simeon) and Judas (or Jude, possibly the author of the Letter of Jude). The two evangelists also refer to "his sisters," but provide no information about them. Gospel tradition is clear that during his lifetime Jesus was at odds with his family. They are said to have tried to apprehend him as a lunatic (Mark 3.21); the Fourth Gospel states that his brothers did not believe in him (John 7.5); and Jesus himself commented that a prophet had no honor among his own kin and his own house (Mark 6.4; Matt. 13.57). However, his family's attitude seems to have changed, especially after the risen Christ appeared to the eldest brother, James (1 Cor. 15.7). In Acts, Mary and her surviving sons emerge as a distinct unit in the Jerusalem Church (Acts 1.14), alongside the twelve apostles. The sons bear the honorific designation "brothers of the Lord." From at least the mid-second century CE, the Church increasingly emphasized the concept of the perpetual virginity of Mary. This prompted considerable theological debate about the relationship of Jesus to his "brothers," which continues today. For example, it has been proposed that they were either stepbrothers (the children of a former marriage of Joseph), or else Jesus' cousins (the sons of a sister of Mary). The term "brother" in the Bible and elsewhere can signify no more than "kinsman," so neither of these two opinions can be judged wholly implausible.

In Mark 6.3, Jesus is described as "the carpenter" (Greek *tekton*), in Matthew as "the carpenter's son" (Matt. 13.55). It is possible that these descriptions amount to the same thing—in Jesus' time it was common for the eldest son to follow the profession of his father. However, it is clear from the gospels that in later life Jesus did not practice a trade, as Paul and Jewish teachers regularly did. It has also been suggested that the Greek word for "carpenter" in the gospels actually stands for an underlying Aramaic term that is used metaphorically in the Talmud (see glossary) to denote a scholar. But those who call Jesus a carpenter in Matthew and Mark evidently use the word literally, because they are questioning how a mere manual craftsman can display such learning.

The Holy Family with a Sparrow, by Bartolomé Esteban Murillo (1618–82). The sparrow held by the infant Jesus refers to a popular legend from the apocryphal infancy gospels in which Jesus is said to have modeled sparrows in clay and made them come to life (see also p.207).

JOHN THE BAPTIST

Wadi Ze'elim in the Judean desert. John the Baptist is said to have been raised in the desert; it has even been conjectured that the Essenes of Qumran (see main text) adopted him following the deaths of his elderly parents Elizabeth and Zechariah.

THE BAPTIST AND JOSEPHUS
Writing toward the end of the first century, the Jewish historian Josephus calls John by his main title, "the Baptizer" (compare Mark 1.4), and gives details about the form of baptism that was John's primary activity.

According to Josephus, John's baptism was not intended by itself to atone for sin, although it represented a physical purification of those genuinely resolved to change for the better. This parallels John's message in the gospels (see main text).

However, unlike the gospels, Josephus includes nothing of John's prophecy of the coming divine Judgment. This is because Josephus himself was distrustful of the fervent search by contemporary Jews for a Messiah, and desired to portray John as no more than a moral philosopher. Josephus nonetheless finally attests to John's great popularity, and records his execution by Herod Antipas.

One of the most solidly based facts in the New Testament is the close association of Jesus at the beginning of his ministry with John the Baptist (see box, opposite). The Baptist was certainly a historical figure. According to the gospels, John called upon his listeners to mend their sinful ways in advance of the coming Messiah and the advent of the kingdom of God. He performed an act of ritual cleansing called baptism (Greek *baptizein*, "to immerse"), which involved immersion in the waters of the Jordan river. This "baptism of repentance" (Mark 1.1–14 and parallels) was accompanied by the confession of sins. Much of this is confirmed by the description of the Baptist in the writings of the historian Josephus (see sidebar, left).

Most of John's audience were clearly expected simply to return to their ordinary lives and thereafter make a better contribution to society. But there were also those who committed themselves more deeply to the Baptist and became his disciples, thus inaugurating a movement which, according to Acts 19.1–4, spread as far as Asia Minor (and which apparently continued until some time after 200CE). They adopted the ascetic lifestyle of their master, who came "eating no bread and drinking no wine" (Luke 7.33).

Since the discovery of the Dead Sea Scrolls, widely presumed to be the library of an Essene community based at Qumran in the Judean desert (see p.37), it has often been asked whether the Baptist may have been influenced by Essene doctrines, and even whether he and Jesus might have been members of the Qumran community. According to Luke 1.80, John passed his childhood in the desert, and Jesus spent time there (see pp.86–7). Like the Baptist, the Qumranites made much of Isaiah's words about the voice in

JESUS AND JOHN

From the evidence of the gospels, it seems likely that Jesus began as a disciple of John the Baptist. John began his work east of the Jordan and Jesus was with him (John 1.28ff.). John 3.22 states that Jesus began his own work in Judea, baptizing at the same time as John. Following John's arrest, Jesus withdrew to Galilee (Mark 1.14, Luke 4.14). Before this move, Jesus had apparently ceased baptizing in person (John 4.2), and this may well mark the point at which he began his distinct ministry as an exorcist and healer. Two of his followers are said to have begun as disciples of John (John 1.37).

In the gospels, Jesus credits the Baptist with a very special status. He is Elijah (Matt. 11.14), the herald of the Messiah foretold by Malachi 4.5, and the "wilderness voice" of Isaiah (see main text). He is more than a prophet (Luke 7.26). However, each of these utterances is carefully qualified. The Baptist is greater than any ordinary human "yet the least in the kingdom of heaven is greater than he" (Matt. 11.11 and parallels).

The early Christians recognized John's contribution and significance but sought to convince the Baptist movement (see main text) that John himself referred to Jesus as the Messiah in saying that he was not worthy to untie the sandals of the one for whom he prepared the way (Mark 1.7 and parallels). The gospels may increasingly downgrade John—by the Fourth Gospel he is only the wilderness voice and denies being the Messiah, Elijah, or any expected prophet (John 1.19–23)—but he remains a great witness to "the true light" (John 1.6–8). This policy seems to have been successful, because the Church eventually absorbed most of the Baptist's followers.

Madonna and Child with John the Baptist, *by Sandro Botticelli (1445–1510). John, whom Luke presents as the relative of Jesus, wears his desert garb of camelskin (Mark 1.6).*

the wilderness crying: "prepare the way of the Lord" (Isa. 40.3; Mark 1.2–3 and parallels). They too summoned Israel to repentance in the face of imminent divine judgment, and attached importance to ritual washings.

But there is no clear evidence of any direct connection. The Qumran community was only part of the much wider Essene movement, and other contemporary sects in Palestine specialized in baptism. Nor, as an ascetic teacher, was John unique. Moreover, while Isaiah 40.3 had a messianic significance when applied to John, at Qumran the "way of the Lord" meant the study of the Jewish law. The Baptist's ministry was to all the nation of Israel, but the Qumranites were conscious exiles from general society, concerned with their own salvation. At Qumran, washings were a daily ceremony to preserve religious purity, whereas John's baptism was a single, unrepeated rite to prepare for the coming Day of Judgment.

THE BAPTISM OF JESUS

The gospels make it clear that the baptism of Jesus was very different from other baptisms performed by John (see pp.82–3). On this occasion, the Spirit of God descended on Jesus "like a dove" when he emerged from the baptismal waters of the Jordan river. In Mark 1.10 and Matthew 3.16, the descent of the Spirit is a subjective vision, experienced by Jesus alone. For Luke, the dove appears "in bodily form" (Luke 3.22). In the Fourth Gospel (John 1.34), the Baptist himself witnesses the descent. The dove as a symbol of the Spirit would seem to be a distinctively Christian concept: there is nothing clearly comparable to it in the Hebrew Scriptures or other Jewish writings.

For the evangelists, Jesus' baptism marked his formal designation as the Messiah heralded by John, and it was the occasion on which Jesus himself realized the nature of his mission. Later in Luke, Jesus reads a passage from Isaiah that describes a figure anointed for the task of proclaiming God's good news (Luke 4.18). It was with this figure and his work that Jesus identified himself at his baptism, and this was affirmed by a voice from heaven.

In Mark 1.11 and Luke 3.22, the voice addresses Jesus himself, assuring him of his unique relationship with God, as his beloved son. Matthew 3.17 has a public proclamation, while in the Fourth Gospel (John 1.32) it is the Baptist who receives a divine oracle telling him the meaning of the descent of the Spirit on Jesus. The heavenly message combines part of Psalm 2.7 ("you are my Son") with one or more verses from Isaiah (Isa. 42.1, 44.2). Together they form a texture rich in messianic associations.

The Jordan river in evening light near the Dead Sea. The river was the focus of the baptizing ministry of John and was the scene of Jesus' own baptism.

JOHN'S ROLE IN JESUS' BAPTISM

All the gospels record the baptism of Jesus and see it as an event of great significance, dedicating and empowering Jesus for his ministry. However, in some respects it was also a source of embarrassment for the early Christians. The disciples of John the Baptist (see p.82) could claim that Jesus' acceptance of baptism from John, by which he associated himself with John and technically became his follower, proved the superiority of their master.

Mark 1.9–10 gives a straightforward account of the baptism, but the other evangelists introduce elements which in various ways aim to play down John's importance in the event. Matthew 3.14–15, for example, creates a dialogue in which John asserts that it is he who should be baptized by Jesus, not the other way around. Jesus reassures him that their roles must be temporarily reversed, because the baptism is a joint act "to fulfill all righteousness." This seems to mean that it was part of the overall divine plan.

Luke does not explicitly state that it was John who baptized Jesus (Luke 3.21). He may even deliberately exclude the possibility, since he describes John's imprisonment before he mentions Jesus' baptism. However, the evangelist may not intend to provide a precise chronology.

The Fourth Gospel (John 1.32–33) says nothing about Jesus' baptism in the Jordan river but tells only of the descent of the Holy Spirit. The Baptist's declaration at this point that he came baptizing with water in order that the coming one "might be revealed to Israel" may contain the evangelist's own interpretation of Jesus' baptism: it was a revelatory act on the part of the Baptist, which, like the latter's whole ministry, pointed beyond him to his great successor.

The Baptism of Christ, a mosaic (ca. 520CE) in the baptistery of the Arians, Ravenna. As John baptizes Jesus, the Spirit hovers in the form of a dove. The Jordan is personified (left) as a pagan river god with water pouring from a jar.

In some early manuscripts of Luke, the heavenly voice makes no reference to the text of Isaiah but instead quotes the sentence from Psalm 2.7 in full—"You are my son, today I have begotten you." Some groups in the early Church held that Jesus was the human son of Mary and Joseph and only became the Son of God at his baptism. This heretical view might account for text modifications to the Lukan variant, if that represents the evangelist's original words. Yet several early Christian writers knew this variant and saw nothing heretical in it. Moreover, the whole verse of Psalms is cited in Hebrews 1.5 in reference to the preexistent Christ and in Acts (13.33) in reference to the Resurrection. The New Testament evidently sees no contradiction between the supernatural birth of Jesus (as described in Matthew and Luke), his preexistence (as in the Fourth Gospel), and his designation as the divine Son at his baptism.

THE TEMPTATION

The Quarantal monastery (Greek Orthodox) is perched high on the sheer face of the peak near Jericho known as the Mount of the Temptation. It is the traditional site of Jesus' ordeal with Satan in the wilderness.

The three synoptic gospels all bear witness to the tradition that immediately following his baptism (see pp.84–5) Jesus withdrew into the desert, where he was tempted by the devil—that is, he was tested to see if he could be induced to misuse his powers (Mark 1.12–13, Matthew 4.1–11, and Luke 4.1–13). As often in the Bible, such a testing is viewed as part of the divine purpose: Jesus is led, or even driven, to his encounter with Satan by the Spirit that he received at his baptism. Many authorities have tried to suggest what this meant for Jesus, either as a personal experience or as a religious inspiration, but the New Testament provides no real information on the matter. The gospels contain two interpretations of the episode, on the one hand in Mark (see box, below), and on the other in Matthew and Luke.

Matthew and Luke present a dialogue between Jesus and his adversary in three scenes. In each scene Jesus spurns the devil's approach, quoting a verse of scripture in typical rabbinic fashion. Every temptation represents a theme of significance to Jesus' ministry. The first—that Jesus should turn stones into bread to eat—is rejected on the grounds that "one does not live by bread alone, but by every word that comes from the mouth of God" (Matt. 4.4). Later, Jesus was accused of being a magician in league with the ruler of the demons, but in the desert the Son of God demonstrates that he refuses to perform meaningless tricks at the prompting of Satan.

Next, the devil flies Jesus to the "pinnacle" (highest point) of the Tem-

THE TEMPTATION IN MARK

Mark's account of the Temptation (1.12–13) is brief and enigmatic. The Spirit "drove" Jesus for forty days into the wilderness, where he was "tempted by Satan" and lived "with the wild beasts" while "the angels waited on him."

The two possible interpretations depend on the dual symbolism of the wilderness in the Bible. On the one hand, the desert is often a barren and hostile place, the haunt of demonic powers. Wild beasts frequently represent evil forces and the wicked people who assail the righteous. Thus Jesus' entry into the wilderness at once exposes him to the onslaught of satanic powers, and the angels may be understood as aiding him in this conflict (in Matthew 4.11 the angels seem to provide Jesus with sustenance only after his ordeal—perhaps an echo of the provision of food to Elijah in 1 Kings 19.4).

However, the wilderness may appear in a positive light. Israel's forty years in the desert can be seen as a time when the nation enjoyed an ideal relationship with God, which afterward decayed. It was in the desert that the relationship would one day be restored. Mark may intend to say that Jesus lived harmoniously with the wild animals, in allusion to Isaiah's beautiful depiction of the Messianic age (Isa. 11.6–9).

Or the gospel may be hinting at the restoration of Eden, where Adam lived in peaceful coexistence with the animals and where, according to some Jewish texts, he and Eve were waited on by angels. By Jesus' time the serpent of Genesis 3 was frequently identified with Satan. Mark may, therefore, view Jesus as the Second Adam, who reverses Adam's fall and regains paradise (see also pp.170–71).

ple and suggests that if Jesus jumps off, God will surely send angels to prevent him from plummeting to the ground. On his arrest in the garden of Gethsemane, Jesus will say that his heavenly Father, if asked, would at once send legions of angels to thwart his captors (Matt. 26.53). The point is that Jesus will not ask: God is not to be tested in this way (Matt. 4.7).

Finally, Satan offers Jesus dominion over "the kingdoms of the world," that is, secular overlordship like that of a Roman emperor. But in the gospels Jesus teaches that he is not to govern in the manner of Gentile rulers: "my kingdom is not from this world" (John 18.36). Jesus is in the world as the servant of God, and his followers must be the same (Matt. 4.10).

The order of temptations in Matthew is generally held to be the original, with the offer of world domination as an obvious climax. Luke's reversal of the last two temptations allows him to end with the hint at Jesus' passion and death, the climax of his earthly life. At the end, Satan departs "until an opportune time." He reappears again only when he enters into Judas Iscariot (Luke 22.3) and so prompts Jesus' arrest and Crucifixion.

OVERLEAF: *The Wilderness of Judea near the Dead Sea. The biblical quotations in the Temptation story in Matthew and Luke are all taken from chapters 6 and 8 of Deuteronomy, where the setting is the Israelites' 40 years in the wilderness, which is perceived above all as a period of testing for the nation. For the two evangelists, the 40-day temptation of Jesus, who embodies the "New Israel," both recapitulates and transcends the experience of the old.*

Satan Tempting Christ with the Kingdoms of the World, *by William Blake (1757– 1827), an illustration to Book 3 of Milton's* Paradise Regained.

SATAN AND THE DEVIL

In the period following the Babylonian exile, Jewish religious thinkers became intensely preoccupied with the nature and origin of evil. The idea developed of a vast realm of evil ruled by a terrifying figure who was the arch-enemy of the good God and the source of all human woes. This evil principle was itself one of God's own creations. One widespread concept was that of the two ages: a present age controlled by the powers of evil, in which all the kingdoms of the world are given over to the devil (which is why he can offer them to Jesus; see main text); and a future age when evil will be banished forever.

The gospels give various names to the head of the evil forces, such as the devil, Satan, Beelzebul (KJV: "Beelzebub"), and tempter. His minions are the demons, such as those which Jesus exorcises on several occasions (see pp.96–7). Such exorcisms are not simply humanitarian cures, but also signs that a new age has arrived and the grip of evil on the world has been broken.

THE DISCIPLES

THE DUTIES OF DISCIPLESHIP
Jesus instilled in his disciples devotion to one task above all: to proclaim the coming kingdom of God. This was to supersede all human ties and concern for worldly possessions. The ideal disciple abandoned everything—home, wife, parents, children—for the sake of the kingdom, and no one who looked back wistfully to their old life was fit to enter the kingdom. Discipleship also involved sharing the nomadic way of life of Jesus and living in poverty, carrying no money and wearing a minimum of clothing. These restrictions were aimed more at aiding an unhindered dedication to the task than at imposing an ascetic lifestyle, because disciples might accept any hospitality offered, and eat and drink whatever their hosts provided.

Jesus and the Apostles, *a Spanish painting of ca. 1250. The title "apostle" (Greek* apostolos, *"messenger," "ambassador") is given to the twelve leading disciples and Paul, who also appears in the picture.*

The word "disciple" literally means a "pupil" and translates the Greek *mathetes*, a "pupil" or "learner" of the doctrine of a specific teacher or movement. Hence the Fourth Gospel describes the first five of Jesus' followers as committing themselves to the one they call *rabbi*, "teacher" (John 1.37–50). Many who were strongly influenced by Jesus' teaching might also be termed his "disciples," although they never joined him in his itinerant ministry. For example, Joseph of Arimathea is called a disciple (Matt. 27.57) and Nicodemus acknowledges Jesus as *rabbi* (John 3.2).

However, the primary meaning of "disciple" in the gospels is one who follows Jesus—literally accompanies him on his mission—and has made a radical break with a previous lifestyle in order to do so (see sidebar, left). In this sense Jesus appears not so much as a teacher as a charismatic prophet, who issues a direct summons to each disciple. A close parallel in the Hebrew Scriptures is the sudden call of Elisha by the prophet Elijah (1 Kings 19.19–21). Only when Elisha abandons his livelihood as a farmer does he become Elijah's disciple: this story is clearly the model for scenes in the gospels where Jesus rebukes individuals who ask for dispensation to meet

THE NAMES OF THE TWELVE

Lists of the men who comprised the Twelve appear in all three synoptic gospels (Matt. 10.2–4; Mark 3.16–19; Luke 6.13–16). The lists are basically identical: Simon (called Peter, or Cephas) and his brother Andrew; James and John, the sons of Zebedee; Philip; Bartholomew; Matthew (or Levi) the tax collector; Thomas Didymus ("the Twin"); James, the son of Alphaeus; Simon the Zealot; and Judas Iscariot.

The twelfth disciple is variously called Thaddaeus, Lebbaeus, or Judas son of James (Matt. 10.3; Mark 3.18; Luke 6.16). These may be names for the same person, since some early Christians may have wished to distinguish him from Judas Iscariot. He is commonly referred to as Judas Thaddaeus, or Jude, and the letter of Jude has been ascribed to him, although modern scholars tend to ascribe it to Judas the brother of Jesus.

Peter is always listed first, corresponding to his central role in the whole synoptic tradition. His calling by Jesus is immediately followed by that of his brother Andrew and of his friends James and John, the "Sons of Thunder." Andrew plays little part in the synoptic gospels, but Peter, James, and John are a distinct trio, accompanying Jesus at particularly significant and intimate moments, notably at the Transfiguration (see p.106) and in Gethsemane (see pp.114–15).

Khirbet Qana in Galilee, now considered to be the probable site of Cana, where the disciples witnessed Jesus' first miracle (John 2.1–11). The disciple Nathanael came from here. (See also p.93.)

John's gospel has its own traditions about the call of the disciples. Andrew is much more prominent: he brings Peter to Jesus and is named as one of two former disciples of the Baptist (the other is never named, but this may be another veiled reference to the "beloved disciple"—see sidebar, p.55). John also mentions the call of Philip, who in turn introduces a certain Nathanael to Jesus. Nathanael may be the same as the disciple Bartholomew of the synoptic gospels.

family obligations before joining him (Matt. 8.21–22, Luke 9.59–60).

The gospels state that Jesus had many disciples, from whom he chose a select group of a dozen men. To this body, referred to as "the Twelve," Jesus assigned the authority to exorcize, to perform cures, and to preach the kingdom of God (see pp.150–51). Their number corresponds to that of the tribes of ancient Israel. This is deliberate: Jesus promised the Twelve that their supreme reward, at the renewal of all things, would be to sit on twelve thrones and to judge the twelve tribes (Matt.19.28, Luke 22.30).

The Twelve were a fixed and unchanging body that was especially close to Jesus. After the death of Judas Iscariot the number had to be made up to twelve again by the appointment of someone who had accompanied Jesus throughout his ministry (Acts 1.16–26). The new Twelve continued the work of exorcizing, healing, and preaching.

JESUS' PUBLIC CAREER

According to the synoptic gospels, Jesus' public career fell into three distinct stages: the Galilean ministry; a journey to Jerusalem; and the final events of his life. During the ministry in Galilee, Jesus' activity was confined to a small area along the western shore of the lake and the surrounding hills; he also made occasional visits outside Galilee.

It is unlikely that the evangelists intended to present a precise chronological sequence in their accounts of the sayings and deeds of Jesus. The earliest witness to the gospel of Mark states that the evangelist did not set events out in order and, assuming that Matthew and Luke had Mark's work in front of them (see p.57), they evidently felt free to change the order and setting of the individual sections that make up Mark's narrative. However, all three synoptists agree that the Galilean ministry came to an end with Jesus' decision to go to Jerusalem, a journey that took him southward along the Jordan river (Mark 10.1; Matt. 19.1), probably in order to avoid

THE CHARACTER OF JESUS' MINISTRY

The accounts of Jesus' ministry given in Matthew, Mark, and Luke on the one hand and in John on the other differ considerably. While the differences should not be overemphasized (see p.55), it is true that certain features found in the three synoptic gospels—parables, exorcisms, the Sermon on the Mount, the Lord's Prayer, and Jesus' words over the bread and cup at the Last Supper—are absent, or almost absent, from the Fourth Gospel.

Jesus' teaching in the synoptists is largely concerned with moral and religious guidance and is characterized by pithy sayings. In John, Jesus speaks in lengthy discourses and has extensive debates with opponents. These speeches aim to demonstrate the true nature of Jesus and to reinforce his claim to divine sonship.

Jesus does perform miracles in the Fourth Gospel, but mostly different ones from those that appear in the other three.

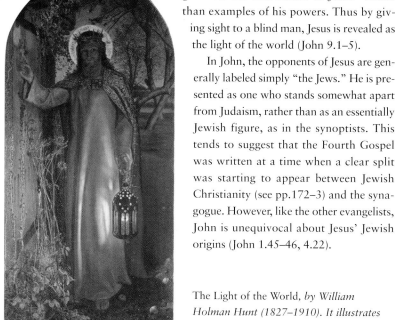

They are "signs"—each with its own special message about the true nature of Jesus—rather than examples of his powers. Thus by giving sight to a blind man, Jesus is revealed as the light of the world (John 9.1–5).

In John, the opponents of Jesus are generally labeled simply "the Jews." He is presented as one who stands somewhat apart from Judaism, rather than as an essentially Jewish figure, as in the synoptists. This tends to suggest that the Fourth Gospel was written at a time when a clear split was starting to appear between Jewish Christianity (see pp.172–3) and the synagogue. However, like the other evangelists, John is unequivocal about Jesus' Jewish origins (John 1.45–46, 4.22).

The Light of the World, *by William Holman Hunt (1827–1910). It illustrates the words of Jesus in John 9.5.*

The Roman Catholic (left) and Greek Orthodox churches at Kfar Kanna, the traditional site of Cana in Galilee, both claim to mark the place where Jesus performed his first "sign" by turning water into wine at a wedding, according to John 2.1–11. John's gospel gives greater prominence to the south of Palestine, especially Jerusalem (see sidebar, below), but it is aware of Jesus' origins in Galilee and that he performed healings and other miracles there. Scholars now consider Khirbet Qana (see p.91) to be a more likely location for the Cana of the gospels.

the direct route through hostile Samaria (Luke 9.51–56, 17.11). Luke develops this journey into an extended travel narrative (Luke 9.51–19.27; see p.109).

Taken as a whole, Matthew, Mark, and Luke present a markedly different picture of Jesus' ministry from that in John (see box, opposite). The Fourth Gospel implies a ministry of two years or longer (see sidebar, right), and this has often been contrasted with the synoptists, who mention only one visit to Jerusalem, at Passover, and seem to imply a ministry of a year or less. The differences may not be entirely irreconcilable, because each of the evangelists is more concerned with theology than precise chronology.

For John, each Jewish festival reveals something of the significance of Jesus. For example, Jesus represents the sacrificial Passover lamb (John 1.29, 36). In the synoptic gospels, Jesus' final journey to Jerusalem is significant not because he was keeping the Passover but because it was the occasion on which he was to meet his death (Mark 10.33 and parallels). The unique significance attached to this particular visit to Jerusalem does not necessarily exclude the possibility that Jesus, as a pious Jew, would have gone to the city on other occasions to observe certain Jewish feasts. The Jewish law (Deut. 16.16–17) called upon all males to visit the Temple at Passover, Pentecost, and Tabernacles, the so-called "pilgrimage festivals." While it seems unlikely, for practical reasons, that every single Jewish male really was obliged to leave home three times a year, it was doubtless considered an act of merit to fulfill the biblical commandment whenever circumstances permitted. This would have been easier for those, like Jesus and his disciples, who were not tied to home or workplace.

THE MINISTRY IN JOHN

In John, Jesus begins his ministry in Judea and the adjacent Transjordanian region of Perea (John 3.22, 26), and moves regularly between there and Galilee. But the greater part of Jesus' ministry, according to the Fourth Gospel, takes place in Jerusalem and its environs. Jesus visited the city on the occasion of Passover and other important Jewish festivals and on most of these occasions visited the Temple.

The evangelist mentions three Passovers and three other intervening festivals. If they are intended to be seen as occurring in strict succession, it is possible to reconstruct a fairly precise chronology of Jesus' life over two or more years.

The first year included a Passover visit to Jerusalem in the spring (John 2.13) and another visit on the occasion of an unspecified festival (John 5.1), either the feast of Weeks (or Pentecost, seven weeks after Passover) or, perhaps more likely, the New Year festival (early autumn).

In the following year, Jesus fed the crowd in Galilee near the time of Passover (John 6.4) and is said to have been in Jerusalem for the feast of the Dedication in December (John 10.22), perhaps having remained in the city since the autumn festival of Tabernacles.

In the third year, after visiting Perea (John 10.40), Bethany (John 11.1–43), and a town near the Judean desert (John 11.54), Jesus returned to Jerusalem for his final Passover (John 12.1, 13.1).

THE HEALINGS

PHYSICIANS AT THE TIME OF JESUS
The professional medical practitioners of Jesus' time are often given a bad name in both pagan and Jewish sources. The Mishnah lawcode quotes one rabbi: "the best among physicians is destined for Gehenna [hell]"; and Jesus cites an uncomplimentary proverb widely known in the ancient Mediterranean world: "Doctor, cure yourself!" (Luke 4.23). The poor reputation of doctors is also reflected in the account of a woman cured by Jesus of chronic hemorrhaging (Mark 5.25–34 and parallels). For years she "had endured much under many physicians and had spent all that she had and was no better, but rather grew worse" (Mark 5.26).

The Blind of Jericho, *by Nicolas Poussin (1594–1665). According to Matthew 20.30–43, Jesus restored the sight of two blind men of Jericho by touching their eyes (compare Mark 10.46–52).*

In Jesus' day, illness and disease were regularly blamed on evil spirits or demons, and for this reason it is hard to distinguish absolutely in the gospels between healing and exorcism (the casting out of spirits that have possessed an individual; see pp.96–7). For example, Peter's mother-in-law suffers a fever that "left her" after Jesus "rebuked" it (Luke 4.39). However, several passages do seem to acknowledge a distinction between curings and exorcisms, especially in Matthew, who displays considerable diagnostic knowledge in his categorization of illness (Matt. 4.24, 10.8).

There were two main types of healer in the time of Jesus: professional physicians, who were held in low regard (see sidebar, left), and "wonder-workers," who enjoyed great popularity. The latter performed healings using age-old magical methods and media, such as spells, incantations, animal parts, potions, and blood. There is no indication that Jesus employed such practices, although on three occasions he is said to have healed a person by applying saliva (Mark 7.33, 8.23; John 9.6). No doubt this was a common folk remedy, but the essential point is that it created a physical bond between Jesus and the sufferer. Most accounts of Jesus' cures involve

RAISING THE DEAD

The gospels record three occasions on which Jesus brought a dead person back to life. In the New Testament, this miraculous ability is part of Jesus' role of prophet, linking him particularly with the biblical figures of Elijah and Elisha. Both of these great prophets restored to life the son of a widow (1 Kings 17.17–23; 2 Kings 4.18–36), and the accounts of these miracles parallel the gospel stories of the raising of the daughter of Jairus, a synagogue leader (Mark 5.22–24, 35–42 and parallels).

All three gospels quote Jesus as saying that Jairus' daughter "is not dead but sleeping." This could be understood literally, but each gospel is at pains to stress that the girl's death was real, as does John in his account of the raising of Lazarus, where Jesus utters similar words (John 11.11–14).

There may be an echo here of the book of Daniel, which says that "Many of those who sleep in the dust of the earth shall awake" (Dan. 12.2): the dead sleep peacefully, awaiting the general resurrection at the Day of Judgment. Paul's letter to the Ephesians has the summons: "Sleeper, awake! Rise from the dead" (Eph. 5.14).

The raising of Jairus' daughter, therefore, is a foretaste of the resurrection assured to all who believe in Jesus. This is also John's clear understanding of the revival of Lazarus, a

The village of Nain in Lower Galilee, the setting for Jesus' miraculous raising of a widow's son, recounted in Luke's gospel.

story only found in this gospel (John 11.1–44): Jesus himself is "the resurrection and the life" (John 11.25).

The raising of the son of a widow at Nain, a miracle unique to Luke (7.11–15), is even more closely modeled on the Elijah and Elisha stories. The miracle prepares the way for Jesus' reply to John the Baptist's messengers (Luke 7.20–23) and marks out Jesus as a prophet as great as his two biblical predecessors. His presence brings God's favor on his people (Luke 7.16).

some sort of bodily contact, touching or laying on of hands. Similarly, the gospels record that people were cured by touching Jesus or even just his clothing, as with the woman with the hemorrhage (see sidebar, opposite). When Jesus healed, power came out from him (Luke 6.19); this is how he himself knew when someone in a large crowd had touched him (Luke 8.46). At such moments, Jesus appears as a holy man similar to several Israelite prophets, possessing a mysterious quasiphysical force that can be directed to the benefit of others.

For Jesus, an equally important means of healing is his authoritative word. Sometimes a simple utterance is enough: "Be made clean" (Mark 1.41 and parallels); "Stretch out your hand"(Mark 3.5 and parallels); "Stand up and take your mat and walk" (Mark 2.9, 11 and parallels). Jesus' word operates even at a distance (Matt. 8.5–13; Luke 7.2–10).

More usually, however, touching and utterance go together, which seems to correspond to the practice of popular healers. An example is the account of the healing of the blind man at Bethsaida, where Jesus both applies saliva to the man's eyes and lays hands on him (Mark 8.22–25).

THE EXORCISMS

The ruins of the splendid synagogue at Capernaum, constructed ca. 400CE to replace the building where Jesus taught and cured a man possessed by an evil spirit (Mark 1.23–26).

A belief in the ubiquitous presence and malevolent activity of evil spirits—also called demons, devils, or unclean spirits—was virtually universal in the ancient world, and there are plentiful references to them in the gospels. Many natural and human calamities (including illness and injury) were attributed to demonic possession. In the synoptic gospels, evil spirits are associated primarily with a specific type of affliction that is accompanied by violent physical symptoms, described in three vivid narratives.

In the synagogue at Capernaum, an evil spirit throws a man into convulsions (Mark 1.26). On another occasion (Mark 9.17–27 and parallels) a boy is similarly hurled to the ground, where he foams, grinds his teeth, and becomes rigid—a combination of symptoms that is currently understood to describe an epileptic seizure. The boy is said to have been frequently impelled by the spirit to attempt suicide. Most dramatic of all are the accounts of the Gerasene, or Gadarene, demoniac, who lived naked in a graveyard and wandered the hills, howling and bruising himself. He possessed such supernatural strength that no chains or fetters could restrain him (Mark 5.1–13; Luke 8.27–33; compare Matt. 8.28–33).

EXORCISTS IN JESUS' DAY

The limited medical knowledge at the time of Jesus allowed little understanding of severe mental illness: "demonic possession" was the standard diagnosis. Over a long period there had developed a class of exorcists, to whom people turned in order to expel evil spirits and restore a sufferer's peace of mind. The techniques they used were essentially magical. Exorcists depended for their success (or at least their reputation) on the correct performance of elaborate rituals involving incantations and spells and the use of various substances believed to possess supernatural properties.

To people who did not know of him, Jesus may well have seemed like other Palestinian wonder–workers and exorcists. At one stage he was certainly accused by his opponents of being no more than a magician, and moreover one whose power derived from the prince of demons, Beelzebul (KJV: Beelzebub). But the purpose of such accusations was not to deny the success of his exorcisms but to attribute them to sorcery. Different as Jesus undoubtedly was, it is possible to discern parallels between his exorcisms and those of Jewish and

pagan exorcists. Mark (9.38) and Luke (9.49) record that a man went around casting out demons in Jesus' name—that is, at least one exorcist had come to realize that Jesus' name could be used effectively in magical conjuration.

Jesus himself acknowledges the existence of other successful exorcists including, according to Matthew (12.27), some of the Pharisees, who, like many other Jewish religious teachers, may well have had a great interest in exorcism. The process of exorcism demanded that the exorcist wield self-evident authority over the evil spirits to be cast out, and a teacher might well be assumed to possess such authority.

For the synoptic gospels, Jesus' authority over demons is closely associated with his authority as a teacher, in that his healings and exorcisms confirmed the truth and power of his preaching. To the jealousy of his opponents, Jesus possessed authority over the demons because he was recognized by the people at large as a charismatic prophet who—like the prophets in the Hebrew Scriptures—was directly inspired by the spirit of God.

In contrast to other healers (see box, opposite page), Jesus made no use of magical techniques, but cast out demons simply with words of power: "Come out!" There did not have to be physical contact with the demoniac—indeed, in the case of the daughter of the Syro-Phoenician woman (Mark 7.25–30), Jesus never even saw the sufferer. The reason that his methods were different, according to the gospels, was that Jesus had a special understanding of his activity as an exorcist: he saw the demons as not just random and individual spirits but as the agents of the mighty power of evil in the world. They worked under the direction of their leader, who is known by several names and titles, including the devil and Satan (see sidebar, p.87). Casting out the demons was in itself a prophetic sign, to those that could comprehend it, that the power of evil was losing its grip on the world—that the new kingdom of God was beginning, heralded and inaugurated by the mission of Jesus.

If most Jews, apart from Jesus' own followers, did not recognize this sign, some of the demons cast out by Jesus certainly did. They verbally acknowledged him as the Holy One or the Son of God, and were terrified at his power over them. In the case of the legion of spirits who possessed the Gerasene demoniac, they implored Jesus not to make them go back into the "abyss"—suggesting that the gospel writer equates the demons with the fallen angels who were placed in such a confinement. Jesus' response portrays the demons as in reality powerless and contemptible figures. He sends them not into the cosmic abyss but instead—and the narrative is not without a touch of humor—into a herd of pigs who, maddened by this invasion, rush headlong to destruction.

The Gadarene Swine, *depicted in the 6th-century mosaics of Sant' Apollinare Nuovo, Ravenna. Jesus (center) casts evil spirits out of a demoniac—ancient manuscripts of the gospels disagree on whether he was from the region of Gerasa or Gadara—into a herd of pigs (right), which hurtle down a bank into the Sea of Galilee.*

DEEDS OF POWER

Scholars today distinguish between Jesus'
miraculous cures, which may seem more
credible to modern people, and the so-
called "nature miracles" such as the
feedings of great multitudes. It is doubtful
whether Jesus' contemporaries would ever
have made such a distinction. Charismatic
Jewish teachers of the time were often
thought able to control the forces of
nature, and the same was true of biblical
prophets such as Elijah, with whom Jesus
was identified by some contemporaries. It
is therefore quite understandable that Jesus
should have been credited with various
miraculous feats, even if some—such as the
fish with a coin in its mouth (Matt. 17.27)
—must be regarded as legendary.

How the gospels interpret the nature of
miracles is significant. The accounts of Jesus
stilling a great storm (Matt. 8.26 and
parallels) and walking on water (Matt.
14.25 and parallels) recall God's power
over the waters of the Red Sea (Exod.
14–23) and the crossing of the Jordan by
the Israelites (Josh. 3.14–17) and the
prophet Elisha (2 Kings 3.13–14). In Luke,
the story of Peter and the miraculous draft
of fishes (Luke 5.3–11) symbolizes both
Jesus' divine authority and the mission of
his followers to make converts.

Jesus sometimes warned against anyone
being unduly preoccupied with his "deeds
of power": his audience were to take note
of his person and message rather than his
miracles. Thus when the Pharisees asked
Jesus for a miraculous prophetic sign, he
simply refused (Mark 8.11–12). When he
effected cures, he told those he had healed
not to publicize what he had done.

THE FEEDING MIRACLES

All four gospels relate how Jesus employed a tiny amount of food to feed a crowd of five thousand or more, and Matthew and Mark also describe a broadly similar feeding of four thousand people. If there is a relationship between the two episodes, as is commonly supposed, it is not easy to determine. The feeding of the five thousand seems to be aimed at a Jewish audience, especially in Mark's account (Mark 6.34–44). The setting is Galilee and the crowd is described as "like sheep without a shepherd"—an image for Israel in the Hebrew Scriptures. They are divided into groups of hundreds and fifties, which recalls the way Moses divided up the Israelites (Exod. 18.25), and the leftover food is collected in twelve baskets, recalling the twelve tribes of Israel.

Mark's account of the feeding of the four thousand (Mark 8.1–9) is preceded by a healing in the Decapolis (see p.22), a largely Gentile area. So it is possible that the two feedings originally symbolized the call, first to Jews and then to Gentiles, to share in the new life that Jesus bestowed.

The feeding narratives in the gospels are accompanied by passages that seek to bring out their deeper meaning. In Matthew and Mark, this takes the form of a discussion between Jesus and his disciples on the subject of food (Matt. 16.5–12; Mark 8.14–21). On a crossing of the Sea of Galilee, the disciples realize that they have brought no bread or, at most, a single loaf. Jesus warns them against "the yeast of the Pharisees," and the disciples take this as a reference to their forgetfulness. But Jesus upbraids them for their lack of perception and reminds them how, in each of the miraculous feedings, a small number of loaves had fed great multitudes and produced a vast quantity of leftover pieces.

In Mark, Jesus does not go on to explain what he actually means by "yeast"—the evangelist's primary concern is simply to show how the disciples repeatedly fail to understand their master's words and actions. In Jewish rabbinic writings, yeast is commonly used as a metaphor for human evil. One teacher of the third century CE concluded that what hindered people from doing God's will were oppressive pagan empires and "the yeast in the dough"—the evil impulse in all human beings. In the gospels, the term is broadly to be understood as the hostility of Jesus' opponents, of whom his followers are to beware. To the "yeast of the Pharisees" Mark adds "the yeast of Herod," while Matthew includes the Sadducees. In Matthew, "the yeast of the Pharisees and Sadducees" refers specifically to the teaching of these groups (Matt. 16.12). Luke, who has the "yeast" reference in a different context (Luke 12.1ff.), equates it with the Pharisees' hypocrisy.

Two other motifs emerge from the accounts of the feeding of the five thousand. Firstly, the setting is a desert place, and there is a clear analogy

The Sea of Galilee at Tabgha. The modern Church of the Multiplication of Loaves and Fishes (foreground) marks the spot where Jesus is said to have miraculously fed some 5,000 people with a mere 5 loaves and 2 fishes (Mark 6.38 and parallels). Dedicated in 1982, the church incorporates remains from a 3rd-century CE Byzantine basilica that originally stood on the site.

between Jesus' action and Moses' provision of food for the Israelites in the wilderness (Exod. 16). Second, Jesus' taking, blessing, breaking, and distribution of the bread and fishes foreshadow the events of the Last Supper (and probably the Christian Eucharist).

Both motifs are explicitly developed in the Fourth Gospel, especially in the accompanying discourse of Jesus (John 6.25–59). The miracle takes place at the time of Passover, when Jews eat a meal to commemorate the Israelite deliverance from Egypt. The food Jesus provides is contrasted with the manna of Moses: those who ate the manna eventually died, but Jesus himself represents the true bread from heaven, the gift of his Father who alone confers eternal life and the assurance of resurrection (John 6.48–50). The discourse moves on from the image of consuming bread to the eating of Jesus' flesh and drinking his blood (John 6.51–57), whereby a believer is united with him, the true source of life. The Fourth Gospel contains no account of the Last Supper, and John's narrative of the feeding is to be understood as its equivalent.

CONFLICTS AND CONFRONTATIONS

The gospels contain many accounts of opposition to Jesus and his teaching, and there is a distinct class of "conflict stories," such as the five grouped together at the beginning of Mark's gospel (Mark 2.1–3.6). These were preserved because they contained words of Jesus that were considered important to his message.

It has often been said that the stories of Jesus' confrontations with various Jewish groups, especially the Pharisees, really reflect later disputes between Christians and Jews that developed after Jesus' death. It is not impossible that the gospels may have been influenced by later circumstances, but many aspects of Jesus' message and actions would certainly have provoked hostile reactions during his lifetime.

To begin with, Jesus came into conflict with his own relatives, who even attempted to restrain him as a dangerous lunatic (Mark 3.21). This is something that the early Church would have been unlikely to invent, and that it caused embarrassment is shown by the fact that some New Testament manuscripts alter Mark's original to make the participants "the scribes and the others" rather than "his family." Jesus and his followers were dedicated to a peripatetic life of poverty, and he could be seen as challenging the ties of home and kinship, when he taught that his disciples were

Christ and the Woman Taken in Adultery, by Lucas Cranach the Younger (1515–86). John 7.53–8.11 records that "the scribes and Pharisees" wanted Jesus to endorse the penalty—death by stoning—against a woman guilty of adultery. Jesus replied: "Let anyone among you who is without sin be the first to throw a stone." The crowd dispersed and Jesus dismissed the woman with a warning not to sin again.

Ruins of the Roman-period synagogue at Chorazin in Galilee, one of the towns that Jesus cursed—together with Capernaum and Bethsaida—for rejecting the message of his "deeds of power."

his only true family (Matt. 12.49–50) and that discipleship meant the renunciation of family and possessions (Mark 10.28–30 and parallels; Matt. 10 37–39; Luke 14.26–27).

The gospels record the success of Jesus' Galilean ministry but they also show that this was by no means unmixed: Jesus was ejected from the synagogue at Nazareth, his own hometown (Luke 4.16–30), and could perform no miracles there because the inhabitants would not recognize his prophetic authority (Mark 6.1–6 and parallels). Jesus cursed several Galilean towns for their failure to respond to his message (Matt. 11.20–24; Luke 10.13–15).

The gospels record a number of confrontations on specific issues between Jesus and the Pharisees, the "scribes" (see p.30–31), and other experts in Jewish law closely associated with them. For example, they accused Jesus of being possessed by Beelzebul, the ruler of the demons, and performing exorcisms by his power (Mark 3.22 and parallels). This accusation—that Jesus was a false magician—was a way of isolating him as a threat to the established religious and social order.

However, the Pharisees represented a fairly wide range of religious opinion and the evangelists do show that they were not invariably hostile to Jesus. There was much in Jesus' teaching that corresponded with the Pharisaic outlook, such as his refutation of the arguments of the Sadducees (see p.35) against the resurrection of the dead (Luke 20.27–39). Jesus' words on this occasion gained scribal approval, and his definition of the supreme commandment of the Jewish law is also represented as being in harmony with that of the scribes (Mark 12.28–34; Luke 10.25–28).

The "woes" that Jesus pronounces against the Pharisees, especially in Matthew (Matt. 23.13–29), probably echo later tensions and largely represent the evangelist's version of similar lists of denunciations and prophesied woes in the Hebrew Bible (such as Isaiah 5.8–24 and Habakkuk

Jesus in the House of Simon the Pharisee, *by Jean Fouquet (ca. 1420–ca. 1481), from* The Hours of Etienne Chevalier. *According to Luke 7.36–50, Jesus was invited to dine by a Pharisee, but criticized his host for giving him a poor welcome compared with that of a woman—described as "a sinner"—who washed and anointed Jesus' feet and dried them with her hair. The woman is traditionally identified with Mary Magdalene, the first person to see the resurrected Christ, as depicted in the inset scenes below (see John 20.11–17). (See also pp.34 and 186–7.)*

2.6–19). Jesus, like very many Jews of his day, apparently recognized the Pharisees as authoritative teachers (Matt. 23.2–3), and he is recorded as enjoying the hospitality of individual Pharisees. It is worth noting that the three synoptists make no mention of Pharisaic involvement in the moves leading to Jesus' arrest and condemnation.

All the same, there remain important differences in outlook between Jesus and the Pharisees. The fundamental issue is summed up in Jesus' complaint that the Pharisees have neglected "the weightier matters of the law: justice and mercy and faith" (Matt. 23.23). According to Jesus, Pharisaic rules about such matters as tithing, fasting, and priestly purity, which were intended to protect and strengthen the Mosaic law, went so far beyond it that they were in danger of obscuring its real priorities. The observance of such meticulous rules could become a burden and lead to an attitude of contempt toward the social and religious outcasts with whom Jesus so closely identified, as seen in the parable of the Pharisee and the tax collector (Luke 18.9–14). It is Jesus' priority of humanitarian concern, as in the healing of disease or relief of hunger, that is at stake in the controversies about the proper observation of the Sabbath (Mark 2.23–28 and parallels).

The Pharisees no doubt saw Jesus as a threat to their religious authority and teaching. In their eyes, he was a provincial (see box, below) with no background of religious training, and they inevitably questioned whether his teaching, so different from scribal learning (Mark 1.22; Matt. 7.29), could possess the authority of their own (Mark 11.27–33 and parallels).

GALILEE: A LAND OF REBELS

Jesus and his immediate followers were natives of Galilee, particularly of the Galilean countryside, and as such they were a ready object of suspicion to both the religious and civil authorities. In the gospels, the Pharisees and scribes seem to have a background in Jerusalem (Mark 3.22, 7.1), where Galileans seem to have been widely regarded as boorish provincials, with a marked regional accent (Matt. 26.73), ill-educated in the Mosaic law, and lax in its observance. This attitude is reflected in John, where some of the Jerusalem crowd question whether the Messiah could come from Galilee (John 7.41) and the Pharisees describe Jesus' followers as "this crowd, which does not know the law" (John 7.49).

When a sympathetic Pharisee, Nicodemus, intervenes with the "chief priests and Pharisees" in Jesus' support, he is taunted with being a Galilean (John 7.51–52). From the Pharisaic point of view, Jesus could appear to be guilty of the religious impropriety that was seen to characterize Galileans in general: he accepted hospitality from the hated tax collectors; consorted with "sinners" and prostitutes; and his disciples did not observe the strict Pharisaic rules (see main text).

Galilee had long been a center of resistance to the Roman power and its client Jewish rulers. For example, the New Testament mentions a revolt led by "Judas the Galilean" (Acts 5.36–37) in 4BCE, following the death of King Herod the Great (see pp.24–5). During the uprising the capital of Galilee, Sepphoris (see p.23), was looted and destroyed.

A blocked-up triple arch has been identified as the Triple Hulda gate, the main south entrance of the Temple Mount and used by worshipers coming from the southern end of the Mount of Olives, Bethany, or Jericho. It was probably where Jesus made his entry for the Cleansing of the Temple (see pp.110–1).

According to the Jewish historian Josephus, John the Baptist was executed by Herod Antipas, the ruler of Galilee (see pp.24–5), because he was afraid that the success of John's preaching would provoke another rebellion. The gospels suggest that Antipas saw Jesus as a similar figure (Mark 6.14–16 and parallels) and likewise sought to remove him (Luke 13.31–33). The gospels describe a group called the "Herodians" conspiring to destroy Jesus (Mark 3.6) or trying to catch him out on the issue of Roman taxation (Mark 12.13–17). It is possible that the Herodians were the partisans of the Galilean ruler, although Mark associates them with the Pharisees, who were generally hostile to the Herodian dynasty.

In the Fourth Gospel, the Temple authorities in Jerusalem are also afraid that Jesus' activities will earn him a large following and provoke a drastic intervention from the Romans (John 11.47–50). All four gospels record the "Cleansing" incident, a disturbance caused by Jesus in the Temple (see pp.110–11) near Passover—a time when the Roman military was on special alert in case of trouble in the crowded city.

THE FATE OF THE BAPTIST

The Beheading of John the Baptist, *by Massimo Stanzione (1585–1656), as recorded in Matthew 14.10 and Mark 6.27. According to Josephus, Antipas imprisoned and executed John at the fortress of Machaerus in southern Perea, near the Dead Sea (see map on p.25).*

The arrest and execution of John the Baptist made a profound impression on the early Christian community. It is mentioned several times in the gospels, and the fact that the Jewish writer Josephus, writing in the last quarter of the first century CE, also records it shows that the events remained well known.

The three synoptists claim that Herod Antipas, the tetrarch (ruler) of Galilee and Perea, arrested John mainly because the Baptist had condemned his marriage to his former sister-in-law while her ex-husband was still alive—an act that Jewish law regarded as incest (see sidebar, p.45). However, according to Josephus, Antipas imprisoned and executed the Baptist because he feared that his popularity would provoke an insurrection. Both stories are plausible, because Josephus wrote in Rome for a Gentile audience that would not have been concerned with the niceties of Jewish marriage law. Matthew, though, implies that John's popularity was why Antipas did *not* want to execute him—he feared the reaction of "the crowd," who regarded the Baptist as a prophet (Matt. 14.5).

Mark presents a vivid narrative of the death of the Baptist (Mark 6.17–29) and there is a more summary account in Matthew (Matt. 14.3–12). Both evangelists probably rely on a common tradition, preserved among the Baptist's disciples and perhaps told to people visiting his tomb (Mark 6.29; Matt. 14.12).

Mark's version has the character of a Jewish folktale, with echoes of the Hebrew Bible. The daughter of Herodias, Salome—it is from Josephus that we have her name—dances for Antipas, who makes her a rash promise: "Whatever you ask me, I will give you, even half of my kingdom." This promise occurs twice, in almost identical form, in the book of Esther (Esth. 5.6, 7.2), where the setting is also a great royal banquet. Esther's response to the monarch's promise brings about the execution of her enemy, Haman. In Mark, Salome is prompted by her mother Herodias to ask for "the head of John the Baptizer."

Mark's story also reflects the resentment of ordinary people, such as the followers of the Baptist and Jesus, at the splendor and intrigue of the courts of the Herodian dynasty (see pp.24–5). Elsewhere, Jesus contrasts the Baptist with those who put on fine clothing and live in luxury in royal palaces (Luke 7.25; Matt. 11.8). The decadence of the Herodian royal family is emphasized by the performance of a dance (probably understood to be of a lascivious character), by a royal princess (Mark 6.22)—this sort of entertainment was usually provided by professional courtesans.

A coin issued by Herod Antipas (ruled 4BCE–39CE). The obverse (right) bears the Greek legend "Herod the Tetrarch" and the reverse has the name of his capital city, Tiberias in Galilee.

JOHN AND ELIJAH

Mark's account of the Baptist's death has significant echoes of the biblical story of the prophet Elijah. In each case the ruler's wife is the prophet's real and determined enemy, while her husband displays a more ambiguous attitude. Herodias, like Queen Jezebel in 1 Kings, appears as the dominant partner in the marriage, and it is at her instigation that John is jailed (Mark 6.17; Matt.14.3). Again like Jezebel, it is she who plots the prophet's death (Mark 6.19; 1 Kings 19.2).

Some people believed that Jesus was Elijah (Mark 6.15; Luke 9.8), but Jesus himself identified Elijah as the Baptist (Matt. 11.14). In one key passage (Mark 9.9–13; Matt. 17.9–13), the disciples asked Jesus whether Elijah would return to usher in the messianic age, in accordance with scripture (Mal. 4.5–6). Jesus replied that Elijah had already come, but "they did to him whatever they pleased" (Mark 9.13)—a reference to the Baptist's execution that is explicit in Matthew (Matt. 17.12–13).

Matthew states that the "Son of Man"—Jesus—will suffer in the same way (Matt. 17.12) and that his fate and that of the Baptist-Elijah are foretold in scripture (Mark 9.12–13). In this respect, the gospels see the death of John as foreshadowing the inevitable fate of Jesus himself.

Salome with the Head of John the Baptist, by Andrea Solario (ca. 1470–1524), illustrating Matthew 14.11 and Mark 6.28.

PETER'S CONFESSION AND THE TRANSFIGURATION

All four gospels record an episode in which the disciple Peter made a confession (avowal) of faith in the special character of Jesus (Matt. 16.13–23; Mark 8.27–33; Luke 9.18–22; John 6.67–69). Matthew and Mark locate this scene in the vicinity of Caesarea Philippi, in the far north of Palestine. At the heart of Peter's confession is his declaration of the disciples' belief that Jesus is the Messiah. In Matthew, Mark, and Luke, Jesus never uses the term "Messiah" of himself, and in their accounts of the Galilean ministry it occurs only once, in the mouth of the demons (Luke 4.41). It is only after Peter's avowal of faith that the issue assumes significance.

There was a wide variety of messianic concepts in contemporary

THE TRANSFIGURATION

Peter's confession is followed by the episode known as the Transfiguration, when Jesus appears transfigured—illumed in glory—on a mountainside in the company of Moses and Elijah (Matt. 17.1–8; Mark 9.2–8; Luke 9.28–36). The experience provides divine confirmation of Jesus' vocation as Redeemer and of his words (Mark 8.34–9.1 and parallels) on suffering as a condition of discipleship.

A privileged trio of disciples, Peter, James, and John, witness the event and perceive the reality of the divine world to which Jesus belongs. They are overshadowed by a "bright cloud" (Matt. 17.5), a sign of the presence of God, from

which a heavenly voice utters words recalling Jesus' baptism (Mark 9.7 and parallels). Just as the Baptism (see pp.84–5) empowered Jesus for his earthly ministry, so the Transfiguration is a foretaste of the glory of the resurrected Christ.

The Transfiguration episode contains a variety of biblical motifs. Moses is clearly in mind (Exod. 24.15–18; compare also Exod. 34.29 and Matt. 17.2). He and Elijah are usually understood to symbolize the law and the prophets respectively, two of the three subdivisions of the Hebrew Bible (see p.30). They thus represent the old covenant with Israel, which Jesus supersedes. In rabbinic traditions, Moses and Elijah were expected to appear at the end of the world, so their presence may be intended to indicate that a new age—inaugurated by Jesus' death and resurrection—was about to commence.

Nonbiblical Jewish writings tell of individuals who ascend to the divine presence, where they are transfigured into heavenly beings and learn divine secrets. They become clothed in shining white garments, the dress of angels. Such accounts seem to be derived from the personal visions of seers, and the Transfiguration may represent a similar mystical transformation experience on the part of Jesus, which was also shared by the three disciples.

Mount Tabor in Galilee is identified in Christian tradition as the "high mountain apart" (Mark 9.2) of the Transfiguration. Many modern scholars tend to favor Mount Hermon.

The springs of Banias, ancient Paneas, in the Golan. It was an important town in the territory of the tetrarch Philip (ruled 4BCE–34CE), a son of Herod the Great (see pp.24–5) and halfbrother of Antipas, the ruler of neighboring Galilee. Paneas was in a largely Gentile region and was named from its important shrine to the Greco-Roman god Pan, around which Philip constructed the city of Caesarea Philippi ("Caesarea of Philip"). Jesus may have crossed into Philip's lands to escape the attentions of Antipas following the execution of John the Baptist (see Matt. 14.1–2; Mark 6.14–16).

Judaism, but almost all involved a belief in God's intervention in history through an intermediary who would "redeem Israel" (Luke 24.21) from its oppressors. At Caesarea Philippi, the disciples recognized Jesus as this intermediary: he is more than the Redeemer's forerunner, more than a prophet, teacher, or wonder-worker: he is the Redeemer himself.

However, Jesus saw his redeeming work as different from what most Jews expected of the Messiah (see pp.164–5). It was to be accomplished through his death and resurrection, a truth that Jesus drives home in the three predictions of the Passion (see p.108). He told the disciples that the Jewish religious authorities would reject him and, far from overthrowing the heathen oppressors, he would be handed over to them. When Peter cannot accept this Jesus rebukes him (Mark 8.32–33; Matt. 16.22–23).

A crucified Messiah would have seemed a contradiction in terms to most Jews and to announce Jesus as Messiah would have aroused false expectations. So Jesus insisted that this truth must be kept secret among his disciples, to be revealed only when he had been vindicated by actually rising from the dead (Mark 9.9; Matt. 17.9). Until then, not even the disciples would be able to understand the true meaning of Jesus' mission.

The confession marks the virtual end of Jesus' ministry in Galilee—he returns there only briefly—and the beginning of his final journey to Jerusalem. In Matthew and Mark, the content of the narrative also changes strikingly: they recount just two healing miracles and emphasize Jesus' teaching, which is imparted chiefly to his closest disciples. Luke also gives much prominence to Jesus' teaching, but the shift is less marked and his account of the journey to Jerusalem includes a variety of themes (see p.109).

From Caesarea Philippi onward, the gospels strike an increasing note of tragedy. Jesus becomes increasingly isolated and the narratives reach a climax when all his disciples have abandoned him (Mark 14.50; Matt 26.56).

THE ROAD TO JERUSALEM

The Jericho-Jerusalem road passes through the rugged landscape of Wadi Qelt, 8km (5 miles) west of Jericho. High above the valley floor is the Greek Orthodox monastery of St George, originally founded in the 5th century CE.

THE MEANING OF FAITH
Another prominent theme at this point in the gospels' story is how faith is to be understood. Following the Transfiguration (see p.106), there is an account of Jesus curing an epileptic boy (Mark 9.14–29 and parallels). On this occasion, the disciples had tried to effect a cure but failed, and their failure is a sign of a faithless generation. Mark emphasizes the faith of the boy's father, and in Matthew and Luke the disciples are instructed about the supreme power of such faith. In Mark, the disciples are taught that exorcism must rely on prayer, presumably following the example of the boy's father, who prays to Jesus (see also box, opposite).

The synoptic gospels present varied accounts of the period in which Jesus and his disciples journeyed from Caesarea Philippi to Jerusalem, via Galilee and Jericho (Matt. 17.9–21.11; Mark 9.9–11.10; Luke 9.51–19.28). The versions of Mark and Matthew are broadly similar, while that of Luke is quite distinctive and much longer (see box, opposite).

In all three gospels, a growing shadow is cast by Jesus' three predictions of the Passion, before and after the Transfiguration (Mark 8.31, 9.31, 10.33–34 and parallels). The first prediction is followed by a warning that Jesus' disciples must also be prepared for rejection and even death. But such suffering will guarantee them the ultimate reward for true discipleship (Mark 8.34–9.1 and parallels; see pp.90–91).

The gospels relate disputes about leadership of the community of Jesus' followers (Mark 9.33–37 and parallels; Mark 10.35–45; Matt. 20.20–28). These lead to Jesus' teaching that members of the Christian community are to follow their master and seek to serve rather than to rule. To belong to the kingdom of God they must have the unquestioning trust of a child. The child represents the ordinary believer, whose welfare must be paramount to the community (Mark 9.42–48 and parallels).

Concern for the future community of believers is most clearly seen in one of the several discourses that punctuate Matthew's gospel (Matt. 18.1–19.2). It has been described as "a manual of Church discipline" and some of it seems to envisage a situation that must have existed only later than Jesus' lifetime, such as regulations for resolving disputes in the congregation (Matt. 18.15–17). For Jesus, the society of the faithful is to be characterized by unlimited forgiveness (Matt. 18.21–22). The parable of the Unforgiving Servant drives home this great truth (Matt. 18.23–35).

The parable of the Rich Man (Mark 10.17–31 and parallels) again illustrates the absolute demands of God's kingdom and both the hardships and eternal rewards of discipleship. In Matthew, the parable of the Vineyard Laborers is intended to make the same point (Matt. 20.1–16; compare Matt. 19.30 and 20.16).

Just prior to Jesus' arrival at Jerusalem occurs the episode of the healing of one or two blind men at Jericho (Mark 10.46–52 and parallels; see illustration, p.94). Here Jesus is hailed as "Son of David," anticipating the cry that will greet his entry into the Holy City (see sidebar, p.110).

THE JOURNEY IN LUKE

Luke's extensive account of Jesus' journey to Jerusalem (Luke 9.51–19.28) forms the core of his gospel and it has been claimed that it is crucial for understanding his distinctive message. The dominant purpose of Luke is to present Jesus' career as "the way of the Lord" (Luke 3.4). As a travel narrative, it has been linked with Acts, the evangelist's second volume, which records the spread of the faith.

However, Luke's actual references to traveling are brief and generalized, very different from the detailed movements recorded by the same author in Acts. They are no more prominent than those in the accounts of the journey in Matthew and Mark, and Luke seems to have no more precise knowledge of the course of events than they do.

As with the other gospels, Luke's presentation of this part of Jesus' ministry focuses far more on Jesus' teaching than on healing miracles. The evangelist has grouped traditions of Jesus' teaching on such important topics as prayer, wealth, and forgiveness. Many of these teachings occur in the other gospels, but here they are brought together to provide a corpus of teaching for the followers of Jesus on their mission. Like Mark and Matthew, Luke has in mind the situation of the Church after Jesus' death.

Luke has also introduced his own distinctive contribution to his account of this period of Jesus' life, notably several famous, and striking, parables that occur in his gospel alone: the Good Samaritan, the Prodigal Son, the Rich Man and Lazarus, the Pharisee and the Publican (Tax Collector), and many others.

The Good Samaritan, *by Rembrandt (1606–69). Jesus employs this famous parable (Luke 10.30–37) to illustrate the meaning of the term "neighbor" in the commandment "you shall love your neighbor as yourself" (Lev. 19.18).*

THE CLEANSING OF THE TEMPLE

JESUS' ENTRY INTO JERUSALEM
Matthew, Mark, and Luke place the
Cleansing incident immediately after Jesus'
triumphal entry into Jerusalem on a
donkey's colt, accompanied by nationalistic
enthusiasm from the crowds (Matt.
21.1–11; Mark 11.1–11; Luke 19.29–40).

In Matthew, the crowds hail Jesus as a
prophet (Matt. 21.11), and the Cleansing
of the Temple is probably to be seen as
the sort of dramatic symbolic act that
was typical of the prophets in the Hebrew
Bible. They often criticized the Temple
and looked forward to a time when the
institution would be purged of the
corruptions that they believed had invaded
it. Jesus' action may have been influenced
by a prophecy that, in the coming new age,
there would "no longer be traders in the
house of the Lord" (Zech. 14.21).

Almost immediately after his final arrival in Jerusalem, at Passover time,
the synoptic gospels record that Jesus caused a public disturbance in the
precincts of the Temple. John also records the event, but places it at the
beginning of Jesus' ministry (see box, opposite). The incident is usually
called "the Cleansing" but what happened is not altogether easy to interpret. It appears that Jesus carried out an attack on traders on the Temple
Mount who catered to worshipers by changing money for them, because
the Roman coins in common circulation were not acceptable for Temple
donations as they bore images of the emperor—a Roman god—and other
idolatrous symbols. The traders also sold animals for sacrifice (Matt.
21.12; Mark 11.15; Luke 19.45; John 2.14–16).

At one level, Jesus was no doubt making a protest against the com-
mercialism surrounding Temple worship. The Jewish historian Josephus
and rabbinic texts attest to a degree of corruption and intrigue among
Temple personnel that merited Jesus' denunciation: "My house shall be
called a house of prayer, but you are making it a den of robbers" (Matt.
21.13 and parallels, citing Isa. 56.7).

It has been suggested that in calling the Temple "a house of prayer"

*The Cleansing of the Temple, a fresco in
the Scrovegni Chapel, Padua, by Giotto
(1266–1337). Whatever Jesus' precise
motives, there was certainly much popular
resentment against the wealth and splendor
of the Temple, which was lavishly rebuilt
by Herod the Great partly as a monument
to his dynasty. The scale of the undertaking
was such that it was finally completed only
half a dozen years or so before its
destruction in 70CE.*

THE CLEANSING IN JOHN

In its distinctive presentation of the Cleansing of the Temple (John 2.13–22), the Fourth Gospel develops certain themes that are only hinted at in the accounts of Matthew, Mark, and Luke. John places the incident at the beginning of Jesus' ministry, although its position in the other gospels, shortly before Jesus' arrest, is more likely to be historically correct. But the Fourth Gospel is primarily concerned with the theological significance of the event as an example of God's judgment against the Judaism of his day—a judgment that the evangelist sees as present in Jesus' actions from the very beginning. In John, the Cleansing demonstrates that Israel's existing religious practice, centered on blood sacrifice, is to be abolished—a fact emphasized by Jesus' driving out of all the sacrificial animals (John 2.15).

Unlike the other evangelists, John does not deny that Jesus spoke of the destruction and rebuilding in three days of the Temple (see main text), but characteristically provides his own interpretation. Here, as repeatedly in his gospel, "the Jews" fail to understand the true importance of Jesus' words. They take them to refer literally to the Temple building, whereas Jesus actually means "the temple of his body," which will suffer death but then be resurrected (John 2.21–22). Through Jesus' death and resurrection a new Temple—the Church—will arise. Elsewhere in the New Testament (for example, 1 Cor. 12.27) the Church is referred to as "the body of Christ." It represents a wholly new type of worship, "in spirit and in truth"—which supersedes all previous forms (John 4.19–26).

The el-Aqsa mosque stands over the main southern exit of Herod's Temple Mount. Traces of the Herodian gate can be made out (right of center).

Jesus was advocating an end to the institution's sacrificial practices. However, the gospels do not suggest that Jesus was opposed to sacrifices. The Isaiah quotation points to a future age, when (as the Qumran sect and others believed) the Temple would be replaced by a new, purified institution. It may be that Jesus himself shared this outlook.

The gospels certainly suggest that Jesus' negative attitude toward the Temple was a central factor in his subsequent condemnation by the priestly authorities. He was accused before the Sanhedrin (see pp.118–9) of claiming that he, personally, would destroy the Temple and rebuild it in three days (Mark 14.58, 15.29; Matt. 26.61, 27.39; Acts 6.14). But the New Testament regards this accusation as false and it does seem unlikely that Jesus would actually have made such a claim. His earlier prediction of the destruction of the Temple (Mark 13.2 and parallels) mentions no involvement on his part and introduces the so-called "Synoptic Apocalypse" (Mark 13.5–37), foretelling a general catastrophe for Jerusalem.

The best conclusion may be that Jesus did speak against the existing Temple in some way, and that his violent behavior there was understood by the religious authorities as some kind of prediction of its destruction. Certainly, Jesus' actions implied much more than simply ridding the Temple of commercial practices.

THE CLEANSING: A POLITICAL ACT?

Scholars who see Jesus as a political revolutionary (see pp.182–3) have proposed that he actually occupied the Temple at the head of a band of militant followers. However, anything on such a scale would have provoked an immediate intervention by the Temple's own police force or by the Roman troops stationed in the nearby Antonia fortress. The Roman garrison was reinforced at Passover precisely to deter any disturbances among the crowds attending the Temple. Moreover, such a demonstration would certainly have led to a round-up of all Jesus' followers—but the gospels speak only of a plot to arrest Jesus himself.

THE LAST SUPPER

The gospels recount that Jesus and his twelve closest disciples had one final meal together before his arrest. Matthew, Mark, and Luke make it clear that the Last Supper was the Seder, the special meal that is traditionally eaten by Jews in celebration of the feast of Passover, or Unleavened Bread. All three gospels record that the proper preparations were made for this festival supper, including the sacrifice in the Temple of the paschal (Passover) lambs that would form the main part of the meal (Mark 14. 12–16 and parallels).

However, according to the Fourth Gospel, the meal cannot have been the Passover supper because Jesus was crucified at about noon on the day of Passover preparation (John 19.14). There have been many attempts to reconcile the discrepancy between John and the synoptic gospels. One theory is that Jesus and his disciples were following the practice of the Qumran sect, which had its own ritual calendar and sometimes celebrated Passover earlier than other Jews. The Qumranites were very likely Essenes (see p.37), and the traditional site of the disciples' final meal with Jesus is in the ancient Essene Quarter of Jerusalem (see plan, p.20). But all the

THE LAST SUPPER AND THE EUCHARIST

There has been a great deal of discussion about the significance of Jesus' words at the Last Supper (Mark 14.22–25 and parallels). The event is clearly related to the Christian sacrament variously known as Eucharist (Greek *eucharistia*, "thanksgiving"), Holy Communion, and Lord's Supper, and the extent to which Jesus intended to inaugurate such a rite is also the subject of much debate.

Jesus offers the disciples bread to eat with the words: "this is my body" (Mark 14.22 and parallels). He then offers them wine to drink, saying: "this is my blood of the covenant, which is poured out for many" (Mark 14.24; Matt. 26.28). Just as the old Israel was established by the "blood of the covenant" (Exod. 24.8), Jesus establishes a new covenant with the "many"—all humankind—whose sins, as Matthew 26.28 makes explicit, are forgiven through the sacrifice of Jesus' body.

Jesus says that it is only in the coming kingdom of God that he will again eat the Passover meal or drink wine (Mark 14.25; Matthew 26.29; Luke 22.16, 18). This suggests that he saw the Last Supper as prefiguring the great banquet presided over by the Messiah, which it was widely believed would mark the advent of the final age. In Matthew and Mark, Jesus implies that the Last Supper will be repeated only in the messianic age, and hence he does not appear to envisage the meal being commemorated by his followers in a regular rite. But the first Christians may have believed that they had already entered the final age, and celebrated the Eucharist as a foretaste of the imminent messianic banquet.

It is only in Luke that Jesus explicitly founds a new rite: most manuscripts of the gospel record that Jesus broke the bread with the command "do this in remembrance of me" (Luke 22.19). Some early manuscripts of Luke omit these words and many scholars think that they were interpolated from Paul's first letter to the Corinthians (1 Cor. 11.23–25). This is not to say that they are necessarily inauthentic: Paul's letters are the earliest documents in the New Testament and in the passage quoted he claims to describe a rite "received from the Lord"—indicating a very early Christian tradition.

references in the gospels point to a Passover celebrated in accordance with the practices prevalent in Jerusalem.

Christian tradition certainly closely associated the final events of Jesus' life with the Passover, and the anomalous timing of the meal in the Fourth Gospel probably arises from John's interpretation of the symbolic significance of the festival. In the Fourth Gospel, Jesus is presented prominently as the true sacrificial Passover lamb, and as such his destiny is accomplished when he dies at the time of the slaughter of the lambs in the Temple (John 19.36). In John's interpretation of the feeding of the multitude (John 6.4ff)—which in many respects parallels the accounts of the Last Supper in the synoptics—the evangelist also appears to view Jesus as the paschal lamb. The feeding takes place near Passover time (John 6.4) and the discourse that follows centers on Jesus' gift of his body and blood to confer eternal life (John 6.48–58; see also p.99). The synoptists may also see Jesus as the paschal lamb in offering himself as food to his disciples within the context of the Passover meal (Mark 14.22, 24 and parallels).

None of the gospels explicitly mentions the consumption of the lamb at the Last Supper, but they do refer to other rites that were, and remain, a part of the Passover meal: the blessing and sharing of unleavened bread and wine (Mark 14.22–23 and parallels). The gospel writers mention only those elements of Passover ritual to which Jesus' words gave a new and distinctive interpretation (see box, opposite).

The Last Supper (1480), by Domenico Ghirlandaio (1449–94), a fresco in the refectory of the Ognissanti monastery, Florence. Peter, depicted as a man of mature years, is on Jesus' right; reclining on Jesus' left is the "disciple whom Jesus loved" (John 13.23). Judas Iscariot, who will betray Jesus, sits apart, without a halo. The Latin legend around the walls quotes words spoken by Jesus to the disciples during the meal: "I confer on you, just as my Father has conferred on me, a kingdom, so that you may eat and drink at my table in my kingdom" (Luke 22.29–30).

BETRAYAL AND ARREST

THE KISS

In the synoptic gospels, the arrest of Jesus begins with the dramatic and poignant moment when Judas Iscariot (see box, opposite) identifies his former master with a kiss or attempted kiss (Mark 14.44–5 and parallels). The kiss emphasizes that Jesus alone is to be the victim, while his followers escape (Mark 14.56 and parallels).

Judas addresses Jesus as "Rabbi" (see p.162), and a kiss was the regular salutation of a disciple to his rabbinical master. The gesture may also be inspired by biblical passages where an apparently friendly kiss conceals treachery, for example, 2 Samuel 20.9–10 and Proverbs 27.6. It also serves to highlight Judas' responsibility for Jesus' arrest, in which his real role was probably comparatively minor—if obviously momentous.

The four gospels broadly agree in their accounts of the arrest of Jesus. Following the Last Supper (see pp.112–13), Jesus and his disciples set out for the garden of Gethsemane, an olive grove on the Mount of Olives, after singing the final part of the Jewish hymn sung at the end of the Passover celebrations (Mark 14.26; Matt. 26.30). The depiction of the group in Gethsemane suggests that on this occasion they intended to withdraw for a special time of prayer and meditation. During his time in Jerusalem, Jesus apparently spent all his nights outside the city, either on the mount (Luke 21.37) or at nearby Bethany (Mark 11.11; Matt. 21.17).

On the way to Gethsemane, according to Matthew and Mark, Jesus

The Agony in the Garden, *by Corrado Giaquinto (1690–1765), depicts Jesus' solitary vigil and prayer in the Garden of Gethsemane. The angel (Luke 22.43) bears a eucharistic chalice, a literal interpretation of Jesus' words: "Father, for you all things are possible; remove this cup from me" (Mark 14.36 and parallels).*

JUDAS ISCARIOT

The gospels and Acts all record that the disciple Judas Iscariot was instrumental in the arrest of Jesus. According to John, Iscariot was a surname, borne also by Judas' father, Simon (John 6.71, 13.2). It is commonly understood to mean "man of Kerioth," a village in southern Judea, and some manuscripts actually say "Judas from Kerioth" at John 6.71. John is well informed about Judean matters and this appears to be the best explanation of the name. Thus Judas was alone among the disciples in not hailing from Galilee.

As for his motives, the gospels explain only that Judas was possessed by Satan (Luke 22.3; John 6.70, 13.2, 27) and betrayed Jesus for money (Mark 4.10–11 and parallels). John emphasizes Judas' interest in money and his cupidity (John 12.5–6). Recently, however, some scholars have suggested that Judas could not accept

The Roman Catholic Church of All Nations, constructed in 1924, adjoins the site of the Garden of Gethsemane and commemorates the events leading to the arrest of Jesus.

Jesus' coming death and wished to force him to show his power as Messiah. Another "rehabilitating" theory is that Judas wished to help Jesus to achieve his purpose—in Matthew and Mark, the mention of Judas' treachery immediately follows the scene at Bethany where he predicts his death (Mark 14.3–9; Matt. 26.6–13). However, perhaps all that can be said with certainty is that Judas showed the Temple priests how Jesus could be arrested away from the public glare, as they planned (Mark 14.1; Matt. 26.4; Acts 1.16).

Whatever the facts, the gospels tend to depict Judas in the light of the fulfillment of scripture. Thus in Matthew he is paid "thirty pieces of silver," a reference to an obscure biblical prophecy (Zech. 11.12). The details of Judas' repentance and death (Matt. 27.3–10; Acts 1.16–20) are similarly constructed from biblical passages.

---

solemnly predicted that his followers would desert him and that even Peter would deny him (Mark 14.27–31; Matt. 26.31–35; compare Luke 22.33–35, John 16.32, and John 13.36–38). Peter's subsequent denial of Jesus is probably authentic—the early Christians are unlikely to have invented such an unflattering story about one of the Church's leading figures.

On arrival at the garden, Jesus withdrew for a moving prayer in which he accepted the destiny decreed by his heavenly Father (Mark 14.32–42 and parallels). He counseled his disciples to pray that they might escape the coming time of trial. John's gospel has no account of this "agony in the garden"; its equivalent is Jesus' final prayer at the Last Supper (John 17).

At this point a party arrived to arrest Jesus, guided by Judas (see box, above), who knew where Jesus might be found (John 18.2). All the gospels describe some kind of brawl, during which a sword was drawn and the ear of the high priest's slave was cut off (Mark 14.47 and parallels). Mark records the episode simply but the other gospels make clear that Jesus himself repudiated the violence. A somewhat obscure passage in Luke probably means the same thing: when the disciples produce two swords, Jesus says curtly "It is enough" (Luke 22.35–38).

THE ARRESTING PARTY

According to the synoptists, the body that arrested Jesus was an armed troop sent by the Temple authorities. The Fourth Gospel identifies this troop as the regular police force of the Temple and claims that it was accompanied by a Roman cohort under its commanding officer (John 18.3, 12).

There is nothing improbable in such cooperation between the Roman and Temple authorities, because it was in the interest of both to avoid disturbances at Passover time, when Jerusalem was very crowded. But it seems unlikely that so many people—a cohort consisted of two hundred men or more—would have been needed to apprehend a single individual. However, what they had heard about the manner of Jesus' entry into Jerusalem (see p.110) may have led both authorities to overestimate the scale of his following.

THE TRIALS OF JESUS

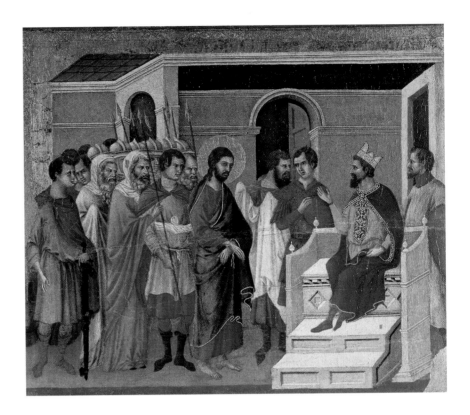

Jesus Before Herod, *by Duccio di Buoninsegna (ca. 1260–1318). Luke alone records that Pilate sent Jesus for a hearing before Herod Antipas, the ruler of Galilee (Luke 23.6–12). The gospel describes the scene: "Herod with his soldiers treated him with contempt and mocked him; then he put an elegant robe on him, and sent him back to Pilate" (Luke 23.11).*

JESUS BEN ANANIAS

Josephus records an interesting parallel to the gospel account of the two trials of Jesus from the time of the Roman prefect Albinus (62–64CE). It concerns one Jesus ben Ananias who, during the feast of Tabernacles, repeatedly prophesied the destruction of Jerusalem in the Temple. As a result, he was arrested by some of the leading citizens and soundly beaten, but he persisted in his prophesying and was brought before the prefect, presumably for execution. When Albinus asked the man who he was, where he came from, and why he acted as he did, Jesus ben Ananias made no reply but continued his ranting. Albinus concluded that he was insane and let him go after a flogging—rather as Pilate is said to have wished to do in the case of Jesus.

Around one-fifth of each gospel is devoted to the Passion (Latin *passio*, "suffering")—the final days of Jesus' earthly existence, from the Last Supper to his burial (Mark 14–15; Matt. 26–27; Luke 22–23; John 18–19). While it is virtually impossible to fix any clear chronology of Jesus' earlier ministry, the Passion narratives present a detailed and remarkably consistent sequence of events. This suggests that the evangelists all relied on a narrative tradition that was well formed by the time they wrote; Luke and John also appear to draw on other, distinct, traditions.

The synoptic gospels—John is less clear on this point—record two consecutive trials and condemnations of Jesus, one before the high priest and Sanhedrin, or council (see p.28), and one before Pontius Pilate, the Roman prefect of Judea. Scholars have examined the accounts of the trials of Jesus in the context of what is known about contemporary Jewish and Roman legal processes (see pp.119–21). But such material has to be assessed with caution: for example, most of the evidence for Jewish legal practice comes from the Mishnah lawcode, which was compiled ca. 200CE. While the Mishnah undoubtedly records numerous longstanding practices, it is not certain how many of these were in force in Jesus' day. Also, the Mishnah represents the outlook of the Pharisees (see pp.34–7), and it cannot necessarily be assumed that the Sadducee-dominated Temple authorities, before

THE DEATH PENALTY IN ROMAN PALESTINE

The Fourth Gospel explains that the Temple authorities had to hand Jesus over to Pilate because the high priest and the Sanhedrin did not have the power to impose capital punishment (John 18.31–32). There has been much argument as to whether this statement is historically accurate or whether it is an invention of the evangelist to confirm Jesus' own predictions that he would meet his end by being "lifted up" on a Roman cross.

It does seem to have been regular policy throughout the provinces of the empire to restrict the ability to pass a death sentence to the Roman authorities. But there may have been exceptions. For example, a famous Greek inscription from the Temple threatens death to Gentiles who trespass in areas restricted to Jews. This has been taken as evidence that, even under Roman rule, the Sanhedrin retained the right to carry

This ossuary dating from the 1st century CE was discovered in 1990 in a family tomb, 2km (1.2 miles) from the Temple Mount. It bears the name Yehoseph bar Qypa— Joseph Caiaphas—the high priest who tried Jesus, according to the gospels.

out executions—a right it could certainly claim under Jewish law. Further support for this theory has been seen in the stoning of the first Christian martyr, Stephen (Acts 6–7), and later, in 62CE, of Jesus' brother James.

But both deaths—and possibly the right to execute trespassers in the Temple—are best explained as special cases. The death of James, recorded by Josephus, seems to have been unauthorized: it took place between the death of one prefect and the arrival from Rome of another. Once in Judea, the new prefect deposed the high priest responsible for the execution.

whom Jesus is said to have been tried, would have accepted Pharisaic rules. Nor are the evangelists the equivalent of today's court reporters. Their primary concern is a theological presentation of the facts of Jesus' suffering and death. Moreover, as history often shows, in a situation of crisis precise legal niceties may not always be observed.

However, while there is no inherent improbability in Jesus being tried twice in fairly rapid succession (see sidebar, opposite), there is considerable uncertainty about the gospels' claim that the priestly hierarchy of Jerusalem was primarily responsible for arresting and trying Jesus and accusing him before the Roman governor. Some scholars have proposed that the religious authorities only acted at the instigation of, and in collusion with, the Romans, or, more radically, that the whole story of the trial by the Sanhedrin is a Christian fiction designed to slander the Jews. While it is lamentably true that anti-Judaism and anti-Semitism have often sought justification from these and other passages in the New Testament (see pp.188–9), it is very hard to reject the unanimous gospel view that the Jewish priestly authorities, headed by the high priest, were involved in the arrest of Jesus and subsequently handed him over to the Romans. That Jesus was arraigned before Pilate is generally accepted, because it is almost certain that he alone could impose the death penalty (see box, above).

BEFORE THE COUNCIL

THE GROUNDS FOR JESUS' ARREST
The gospels note several different reasons why the Temple authorities ordered Jesus' arrest. But these accounts are not necessarily contradictory and all the factors mentioned by the evangelists may have contributed to the final decision to apprehend him.

Mark states that the priestly authorities reacted to Jesus' dramatic expulsion of the traders from the Temple by actively seeking a way to get rid of him (Mark 11.18; see pp.110–111). They may also have been alarmed by the circumstances of his entry into Jerusalem (see p.110), which in Matthew and Luke culminated in his entry into the Temple.

Luke states that "the chief priests, the scribes, and the leaders of the people" sought to eliminate Jesus because of his teaching in the Temple (Luke 19.47–48), and all the synoptics say that an attempt was made to arrest him because of a particular example of his teaching there: the parable of the Wicked Tenants (Mark 12.1–12 and parallels; see p.167).

According to the Fourth Gospel, the Sanhedrin was alarmed by Jesus' popularity—boosted by his raising of Lazarus from the dead at Bethany, just outside the city (see pp.97, 210–11)—which was liable to lead to large gatherings, unrest, and severe Roman intervention as a consequence (John 11.45–53).

The gospels record that Jesus was taken under arrest before the high priest and the Sanhedrin, the Jewish governing council (see p.28), which judged him to be deserving of death. Various grounds are given for Jesus' arrest (see sidebar, left), but taken as a whole they suggest that Jesus was viewed as one who stirred up discontent with the accepted religious and social order, and as such posed a threat to the stability of the whole region. Luke in particular shows that this was the accusation made against Jesus before Pilate (Luke 23.2, 5, 14; see pp.120–21).

To justify a capital charge, the Sanhedrin had to prove that Jesus was guilty of a serious offense against the Jewish law. The priestly authorities may have been provoked by Jesus' alleged prediction of the destruction of the Temple (see p.111). This accusation was made at his trial, although Matthew and Mark relate that Jesus made no answer to this charge and, for whatever reason, it apparently could not be substantiated.

Christ's Entry into Jerusalem, a Russian icon of the Novgorod School (14th century). News of this dramatic episode, recounted in all the gospels (see p.110), may well have been a factor in the decision to have Jesus arrested.

The Roman Catholic Church of St Peter in Gallicantu (St Peter at the Cockcrow) was built in 1931 on the traditional site of the high priest's house, the scene of Jesus' trial in the gospel accounts. The church commemorates Peter's sorrow in the courtyard of the house when he realized that he had denied his master three times, just as Jesus had predicted: "Before the cock crows twice, you will deny me three times" (Mark 14.30, 66–72 and parallels).

According to the gospels, the high priest and council finally condemned Jesus after the high priest asked him whether he claimed to be the Messiah. Jesus' reply is variously given by the synoptists: "I am" (Mark 14.62); "You have said so" (Matt. 26.64); "If I tell you, you will not believe" (Luke 22.67–8). Whatever his actual words, his answer was judged to be affirmative. In Matthew and Mark, the high priest describes Jesus' response as "blasphemy." According to the Mishnah, blasphemy applied only to speaking the sacred and unutterable name of God (YHWH), but there is no evidence that Jesus did so. However, elsewhere in the gospels "blasphemy" seems to mean anything causing serious theological offense (Mark 3.28–29 and parallels).

A claim to be the Messiah was not technically against the Jewish law. However, in Matthew and Mark, the high priest's question couples "Messiah" with "Son of God," and this might be the more crucial term: "Tell us if you are the Messiah, the Son of God" (Matthew 26.63); "Are you the Messiah, son of the Blessed One [God]?" (Mark 14.61). In Luke, the Sanhedrin puts two separate questions to Jesus (Luke 22.67, 70), and it is only following the second ("Are you, then, the Son of God?") and Jesus' reply ("You say that I am") that he is condemned. The Fourth Gospel reports only an allegation that Jesus called himself "Son of God" (John 19.7).

The term "Son of God" had a range of connotations in contemporary Judaism; it was used by some charismatic wonder-workers to describe themselves. Such individuals were at times accused—like Jesus (see pp.96–7)—of performing magic through the agency of demons. If the Sanhedrin considered that "Son of God" denoted Jesus as a magician, they could condemn him as a false prophet, tempting the people of Israel to trust in miracles performed by supernatural beings other than the true God. For this, in the Mosaic law, the penalty was death (Deut. 13.1, 5; 18.20). (See also pp.166–7.)

THE TRIAL AND JEWISH LAW

The accounts of Jesus' trial before the Sanhedrin have often been examined in the light of Jewish process of law and the known powers of the Sanhedrin, especially as set out in the Mishnah. It has been proposed that Jesus' appearance before the high priest was only a preliminary hearing before he was referred to the Roman jurisdiction. But Matthew, Mark, and Luke all speak of Jesus before "the council," indicating a formal assembly.

The Mishnah states that a capital trial could not be held on the eve of a festival or the Sabbath. This conflicts with the gospel accounts, but this provision may not have been in force as early as Jesus' time. Matthew and Mark appear to suggest—it is not entirely explicit—that Jesus was tried at night in the house of the high priest, which would infringe another Mishnaic ruling, that capital cases had to be tried in the daytime in the council chamber in the Temple. Luke indicates a trial by day, before the full council (Luke 22.66).

John has no details of a trial before Caiaphas, the incumbent high priest, and the council, although some charges made against Jesus in the synoptic accounts appear in John in a different context (John 10.24–25, 33–36). He does include an interrogation by the ex-high priest Annas, who handed him over to Caiaphas (John 18.13, 19–24). Annas had been deposed from office, but remained influential (Caiaphas was his son-in-law).

JESUS AND PILATE

A bronze coin issued in Judea by Pontius Pilate. One side (left) gives the date, in Hebrew, as "Year 17"—that is, 30–31CE, the 17th year of the reign of the emperor Tiberius. The Greek legend on the other side (right) reads "[Of] Tiberius Caesar." The coins issued by Pilate have no imperial portrait, to avoid giving offense to Jews.

LEGENDARY EPISODES OF JESUS' ROMAN TRIAL

While the gospel accounts of Jesus' trial before Pilate generally reflect regular Roman judicial procedure, some episodes are of more dubious historical value.

For example, there is no evidence for a Passover amnesty under which the prefect freed a prisoner of the people's choice, in this case a rebel called Jesus Barabbas (Mark 15.6 and parallels). Luke makes no mention of an amnesty and records the release of Barabbas without giving a reason for this concession (Luke 23.18–19).

In Matthew, Pilate washes his hands of responsibility for Jesus' death (Matt. 27.24–25). Again, this was not a Roman custom, but echoes scripture (Deut. 21.6–9) and, like the dream of Pilate's wife (Matt. 27.19), the episode is probably best regarded as the invention of the evangelist.

John has two exchanges between Jesus and Pilate inside the *praetorium* (John 18.33–38, 19.8–11). It is not impossible that Pilate, like Herod Antipas (Luke 23.8), was interested to find out more about Jesus, but John could hardly have known anything that was said between the two men in private. The dialogues contain distinctive themes of this evangelist and must be judged to be his own creation.

Jesus' final condemnation followed his appearance before Pontius Pilate, the Roman prefect of Judea. Scholars agree that the principal reason for Pilate's decision to execute Jesus is reflected in the placard fixed to the cross upon which he was crucified: he had claimed to be "King of the Jews" (see p.184). The wording of the whole inscription differs among the four gospels, but they all agree on this key phrase, and the issue of Jesus' kingship is central to all their accounts of his trial before Pilate (Mark 15.2, 9, 12 and parallels). This would be compatible with a judgment by the Sanhedrin that Jesus had claimed to be the Messiah (see pp.118–19), because it was popularly expected that the Messiah would be of royal blood, a descendant of King David, and would free Israel from Gentile domination. In Matthew and Luke, Jesus' messiahship is an issue in both his Sanhedrin trial and that before Pilate (Matt. 27.17, 22; Luke 23.2).

When Pilate asks Jesus if he is "king of the Jews," Jesus gives an evasive answer (Mark 15.2 and parallels; John 18.37), similar to the response he gives to the high priest when asked if he is the Messiah (see p.119). The Romans would have been well aware of the threat to public peace which a claim to kingship could pose. As the Jewish historian Josephus records, following the death of Herod the Great in 4BCE, Palestine lapsed into a state of anarchy in which several dangerous rebels proclaimed themselves king and enjoyed considerable, if temporary, success.

Each gospel presents the Roman trial in its own way, but together they indicate that it followed regular judicial procedure as followed in the provinces of the empire, with certain exceptions (see sidebar, left). According to the gospels, the court was held in public outside the *praetorium*, or military headquarters, on a paved space—the local name of which, Gabbatha, is preserved in John 19.13—where the final verdict was pronounced. The trial began with formal charges being laid by the prisoner's accusers, after which the defendant was questioned and given the opportunity to respond. In Roman practice, the accused had three opportunities to make a defense before the presiding official gave his verdict. When, after repeated questioning, Jesus remained silent, Pilate had no choice but to find him guilty.

The gospels record that Pilate was reluctant to impose the death penalty, and it may well be true that he thought Jesus should be let off, again in accordance with Roman custom, with a warning flogging, as Luke says (Luke 23.16, 22). (Luke employs the precise Greek term for such a comparatively mild whipping; Mark 15.15 and Matthew 27.26 use a word that means the very severe flogging inflicted before execution.) It is also

reported that the prefect sought to avoid responsibility for Jesus, either by returning him to the Sanhedrin court (John 18.31, 19.6) or by sending him for trial by Herod Antipas, the ruler of Galilee, Jesus' place of origin (Luke 23.6–12), who happened to be in Jerusalem (see illustration, p.116). Whether or not these episodes are historical, they were certainly legitimate options for a Roman governor.

Whatever Pilate's unwillingness to execute Jesus, he changed his mind. All the evangelists represent his final decision as a response to the demands of the crowd, led and incited by the Temple authorities, for Jesus' crucifixion (Mark 15.15 and parallels). The chief concern of a Roman governor was the maintenance of public order, and the gospels record that Pilate's initial resistance to the crowd's demands threatened to provoke a riot (Matt. 27.24). Pilate himself knew the sort of trouble a mob could cause (see p.26), and probably felt that it was not worth risking a serious disturbance for the life of an individual whom he considered to be unimportant. According to John, he finally gave in to the crowd when accused of disloyalty to the emperor (John 19.12). Such accusations were not infrequent in the politics of the Roman empire and often had the gravest consequences for the accused.

Ecce Homo, by Antonio Ciseri (1821–91). The Latin title of this scene is taken from the words of Pilate when he presents Jesus to the crowd, according to the Fourth Gospel: "Here is the man!" (John 19.5).

JESUS CONDEMNED

All the gospels record that Jesus was mocked by Roman soldiers prior to his execution (Mark 15.16–20 and parallels). They also claim that Jesus had already been treated roughly during his appearance before the high priest, apparently by the Temple police, who engaged in a brutal game of blind man's buff designed to show that Jesus was not a genuine prophet (Mark 14.65; Luke 22.64).

Jesus' abuse at the hands of the Roman soldiers centered on his alleged claim to kingship, the charge on which he was evidently finally condemned. Luke locates the mockery of Jesus not in the *praetorium* during the trial by Pilate but during Jesus' interview with the Galilean ruler Herod Antipas. The Fourth Gospel places it not at the end of the Roman trial but in the middle of it. With characteristic irony, John depicts Pilate presenting Jesus as a parody of monarchy and a mere ordinary human being (John 19.4–5); but the gospel wishes it to be understood that Jesus is indeed a king, and one far greater than any earthly sovereign (John 18.36–37).

THE DAUGHTERS OF JERUSALEM

Luke alone mentions an encounter on the journey to Golgotha between Jesus and a group of women who bewail his fate (Luke 23.27–31). There is nothing inherently improbable in this: mourners accompanying a condemned person remain a common sight in the Middle East. Jesus addresses the women as "Daughters of Jerusalem," a term with scriptural precedent, and movingly foretells the tragic end of the city.

Although Jesus is likely to have prophesied the destruction of Jerusalem at some point in his ministry, his words here seem rather to be those of Luke. The lament weaves together biblical reminiscences, influenced perhaps by a strange passage in Zechariah that describes a great mourning ceremony among the inhabitants of Jerusalem for "the one whom they have pierced"—where the sorrow of the wives is specifically mentioned (Zech. 12.10–14). The episode is related to another prediction of Jerusalem's fall, also unique to Luke, when Jesus weeps over the city (Luke 19.41–44).

This sculpture in a chapel on the Via Dolorosa—the traditional route followed by Jesus to Golgotha—marks the spot where Jesus is said to have fallen for the first time under the weight of the cross, shortly before meeting the women of Jerusalem.

The spectacle in which the Roman soldiers dress Jesus up as a mock sovereign has been compared with similar practices that marked the Persian festival of the Sacaea at Babylon and the Roman Saturnalia. But a much closer parallel is found in the account by the Jewish writer Philo of the lampooning of King Herod Agrippa I at Alexandria in 38CE. On that occasion, a wretched lunatic was crowned with a piece of bark, given a scrap of papyrus for a scepter, and dressed in a rug for a royal robe, while the spectators pretended to pay him homage and addressed him as king.

Perhaps this anecdote became widely known in Palestine and the evangelists used it to elaborate a simpler story that Jesus had been derided and spat upon by the soldiers. However, it is not improbable that the soldiers acted on their own initiative, mimicking the imperial insignia by what they had to hand—a soldier's cloak and plants from the *praetorium* gardens—and parodying the regular greeting to the emperor, "Hail Caesar" (Mark 15.18 and parallels).

The punishment of crucifixion was carried out by the military. When the soldiers had ended their sport, they dressed Jesus again in his own clothes and marched him out to the place of execution, Golgotha, which means "Place of a Skull" in Aramaic. The preservation of the name in the gospels suggests that the site was well known, but it can no longer be certainly identified. Its description as a skull points to a small rounded eminence, probably just outside Jerusalem: both Jewish and Roman executions were carried out outside the city walls, and later Christian tradition (for example, Heb. 13.12–13) recalled that this had been the case with Jesus. The Fourth Gospel states that near the place of crucifixion there was a garden containing a tomb (John 19.41), and archaeology has confirmed that burials also took place outside the urban area.

In his narrative of the road to Golgotha, Luke mentions that Jesus was accompanied by two other condemned criminals, which suggests that Jesus' trial was part of a wider process of rounding up troublemakers (Luke 23.32). It is likely that Jesus was accompanied by a crowd, since various texts show that the practice of parading a criminal through the streets served to provide a visual warning lesson to the population.

Jerusalem on the Day of Christ's Death, by Olivier Pichat (died 1912). The artist has imagined the expectant crowds lining the route to Golgotha (foreground, right). The city is his own reconstruction, but the landscape is accurately depicted. The three large towers—still partly extant—belong to the former palace of Herod (see plan, p.20).

SIMON OF CYRENE

A condemned man had to carry his cross to the place of execution and it seems that Jesus began by doing so (John 19.17). But Matthew, Mark, and Luke relate that Jesus could not continue, perhaps owing to the flogging and other privations he had suffered. A bystander, Simon, was thus "pressed into public service" to assist him (Mark 15.21; Matt. 27.32). He is said to have come from Cyrene in North Africa, where there was a Jewish community. Cyrenian Jews had their own synagogue in Jerusalem (Acts 6.9). The mention of Simon's sons, Alexander and Rufus (Mark 15.21), is strong evidence for the historicity of the event, because the casual and unadorned way in which Mark refers to them suggests that they were known to the community for which he wrote.

Mark and Luke state that Simon came "in from the country," which some have taken to imply that he was breaking the prohibition against journeying on the Passover and so could not have been a Jew. But the words are too vague to warrant this conclusion. Nor do his sons' non-Hebrew names prove that the family was Gentile, since Greek names were common among contemporary Jews (see p.47).

THE CRUCIFIXION

The heelbone, pierced by a nail, of a 1st-century CE crucifixion victim called John (Yehohanan), whose remains were discovered near Jerusalem in 1968.

LEGENDARY ELEMENTS OF THE CRUCIFIXION ACCOUNTS

In their narratives of the Crucifixion, Matthew, Mark, and Luke describe supernatural events that can hardly be accorded historical value. They are designed to demonstrate that, contrary to appearances, Jesus' death on the cross was a victorious occurrence that heralded the messianic age, the final period of history.

The three hours of darkness from noon (Mark 15.33 and parallels) cannot have been an eclipse of the sun, as perhaps suggested in Luke 23.45, since this is not astronomically possible at Passover time. Rather, it represents one of the phenomena marking the great "Day of the Lord," the onset of the final age (Amos 8.9; Joel 2.31).

The tearing of the Temple curtain, the veil that shrouded the Holy of Holies (Mark 15.38 and parallels), represented the supreme desecration of the Temple—in effect its destruction, as Jesus had prophesied. In Matthew, the tearing of the veil is followed by an earthquake and the bodily resurrection of the righteous (Matt. 27.51–53), both of which were regularly expected in Judaism to accompany the arrival of the last age of history. For the evangelists, this is when Jesus will arrive in glory as the Son of Man, as they have described earlier in apocalyptic passages with many echoes of the Hebrew Bible (Mark 13.24–27 and parallels).

In the Roman empire, crucifixion was regarded as the most humiliating and painful of all penalties. It was confined to slaves and foreigners, Roman citizens being exempt. Not the least reason for believing that the crucifixion of Jesus was a historical event, therefore, is that the first Christians were unlikely to have invented so degrading a fate for their master. They well knew how unfavorably the world viewed it (1 Cor. 1.23).

In depicting the Crucifixion, the evangelists include legendary features (see sidebar, left) and present their own special interpretation of events at Golgotha. Above all, they are concerned to demonstrate that the manner of Jesus' death had been foretold in scripture and so fulfilled God's purposes. They—Luke especially—seek to present Jesus as the perfect example of how they themselves should respond to suffering and persecution.

Notwithstanding their theological concerns, the gospels can also be shown to contain good historical information. Before being affixed to the cross, Jesus is said to have been given a drink (Mark 15.23; Matt. 27.34). The Talmud indicates that it would have been a narcotic, intended to deaden the pain. This was a Jewish custom, and while the gospels seem to imply that the drink was offered by the Roman soldiers, they do not explicitly say so. Matthew apparently understands the gesture as a fulfillment of Psalm 69.21 ("for my thirst they gave me vinegar to drink") and thus makes it a hostile act rather than a humane one. The gospels say that Jesus refused the drink, perhaps to demonstrate his own power to conquer pain.

In another preliminary act, Jesus was stripped of his clothing, since criminals were hanged naked on the cross. In Roman custom, the clothes and other small possessions of a condemned man were a perquisite of his executioners. The soldiers are said to cast lots for them (Mark 15.24; Matt. 27.35), but this scene may be influenced by Psalm 22.18, which John actually quotes at this point (John 19.23–24). John's reference to a squad of four soldiers may be authentic, since this was a regular Roman unit for guard duty (Acts 12.4), and his mention of Jesus' seamless tunic accurately describes the kind of loose garment commonly worn next to the skin.

There were various ways of crucifying a person, but it seems certain that Jesus was nailed to the cross. In John, the risen Christ explicitly shows the nail marks on his hands (John 20.24–27) and Luke 24.39 implies the same. Luke 24.40 indicates that Jesus' feet were also nailed, like those of a crucified man discovered recently in a tomb near Jerusalem (see illustration, above left). Josephus twice mentions victims being nailed to a cross.

The crucified Jesus is mocked by the crowd, the Temple authorities or (in Luke) the soldiers, and the two criminals (Mark 15.29–32; Matt. 27.39–44; Luke 23.35–39). It is very likely that passers-by would indeed

The Crucifixion, *by Antonello da Messina (ca. 1430–79). At the foot of Jesus' cross are his mother and the "beloved disciple" (a reference to John 19.26–27). In contrast to his two fellow victims, Jesus betrays no sign of his torments. Above his head is the* titulus *(Mark 15.26 and parallels), the placard on which the reason for execution was written. It would have been carried in front of him or hung around his neck as he was led to the execution ground. The letters* INRI *stand for* Iesus Nazarenus Rex Iudaeorum *(Latin, "Jesus of Nazareth, the King of the Jews"), the version of the inscription given in John 19.20 (see also p.182).*

THE TWO CRIMINALS

All the gospels state that Jesus was crucified between two other victims (Mark 15.27 and parallels) and there seems to be no reason to suppose that this is not historically accurate. Mark 15.28 quotes a scriptural precedent: "And he was counted with the lawless" (Isa. 53.12: "and [he] was numbered among the transgressors"). But it is widely accepted that this verse was not part of Mark's original text. It was probably added under the influence of Luke, who quotes the verse in a different context (Luke 22.37).

have insulted a crucified man, and the crowds abused Jesus for his alleged threat to destroy the Temple. But the gospel accounts at this point also include biblical reminiscences (for example, a reference to Psalm 22.7–8), and generally display the careful artistry of the evangelists.

According to the timescale in Mark's gospel (Mark 15.25, 34), which is broadly supported by Matthew and Luke, Jesus was alive on the cross for some six hours, from nine in the morning until three in the afternoon. John suggests an even shorter period, since in his account Jesus is hanged at least three hours later (John 19.14). Crucifixion victims often survived for a considerable time—even days—so when Pilate was asked to release Jesus' body, he is reported as expressing some surprise (Mark 15.44).

The early Christians remembered that Jesus had spoken from the cross,

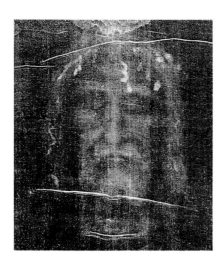

The image on the Turin Shroud is best viewed, as here, in negative. It accurately depicts the type of crucifixion wounds described in the gospels. Interestingly, the figure displays wounds to his wrists—this is widely accepted as a more likely method of crucifixion than nailing through the hands.

THE SHROUD OF TURIN

For centuries, a linen cloth preserved in the cathedral of Turin, Italy, has been venerated by many Christians as the very shroud in which Jesus was buried. The 4.5-meter (14-foot) length of cloth bears the faint but remarkably powerful image of a man who has apparently been crucified and laid out for burial.

In recent years, the cloth has attracted widespread world attention because of the possibility that modern scientific methods might determine its date and provenance. In 1988, a carbon-14 test dated the cloth to ca. 1260–ca. 1390CE, with a margin of a century on either side, thus branding it a pious medieval forgery.

However, this verdict has not quite settled the issue. Other evidence suggests an earlier date, for example a number of early medieval images of Christ that closely resemble the facial features of the shroud image. It is not a painting and it has proved difficult to explain how it could have been created in late medieval times. Whether or not it dates back as far as the first century CE—let alone depicts the actual body of Jesus—the shroud retains, for many, its mysteries.

although it is unlikely that he spoke all seven of the utterances attributed to him in the gospels. The authenticity of one famous saying—"Father, forgive them; for they do not know what they are doing" (Luke 23.34)—is questionable, since it is absent from several early manuscripts. Also in Luke, Jesus' promise to one of the two criminals hanged alongside him ("Truly I tell you, today you will be with me in paradise"; Luke 23.43) may reflect the evangelist's own belief that the righteous enter a realm of bliss immediately upon death (Luke 16.22).

John 19.26–27 records a moving scene between Jesus and his mother and "the disciple whom he loved," who is referred to several times in the gospel (see p.55). Jesus says to Mary, "Woman, here is your son" and, to the disciple, "Here is your mother." The scene does not appear to be dictated by the theology of the Fourth Gospel and may reflect a tradition that, at some stage in his life, Jesus had made special provision for his mother.

The gospels include four utterances at the moment of death, all influenced by the Psalms. Mark and Matthew report only one of these, and it has perhaps the best claim to historicity: "My God, my God, why have you forsaken me?" (Mark 15.34; Matt. 27.46). The early Church may have come to understand this utterance—the opening line of Psalm 22—as God's rejection of Jesus, and hence the other gospels omitted or replaced it. But these words need not be taken as a cry of hopelessness: Psalm 22 goes on to reassure the sufferer of God's help. Mark gives the saying in Aramaic, Jesus' own tongue, which argues for its authenticity. Matthew replaces *eloi* ("my God") with the Hebrew *eli*, perhaps to make it clear why some bystanders thought Jesus was invoking the prophet Elijah (Matt. 15.35).

Mark and Matthew state that Jesus expired with an inarticulate shout, for which Luke substitutes the more edifying "Father, into your hands I commend my spirit" (Luke 23.46), which quotes Psalm 31.5.

The two last sayings of Jesus in John (19.28, 30) display the double meaning so frequent in that gospel. The first, "I am thirsty," is an apparently simple expression of human need but also echoes the spiritual thirst found in the Psalms (Pss. 42.2, 63.1). The second, "It is finished," is an acknowledgment both that Jesus' physical end has arrived and that the Savior has accomplished his mission.

All the gospels relate that Jesus received a drink of "sour wine," in Luke and John from the soldiers, in Mark and Matthew from an unspecified bystander (Mark 15.36 and parallels). This could be understood as a kindly act, since in Jewish sources "sour wine" is generally a refreshment (see, for example, Ruth 2.14). But Luke, at least, regards it as a mockery, and all the gospels probably have Psalm 69.21 in mind (see p.124). The reference to the sponge and reed with which the drink was proffered have no theological significance and may well be authentic. However, John says the branch was of hyssop, a herb used in the Passover ritual (Exod. 12.22), reflecting the evangelist's view of Jesus as the true paschal lamb (see p.113).

THE DEPOSITION AND ENTOMBMENT

Usually, a body was left hanging on the cross until it was devoured by vultures, but sometimes an influential person might secure the right to bury it. In Jewish law, a hanged man had to be buried before nightfall (Deut. 21.31), and John says that "the Jews"—probably meaning a delegation from the religious authorities—asked Pilate to have Jesus and his two companions removed from their crosses, so as not to desecrate the approaching Sabbath (John 19.31).

The delegation assumed that the victims would still be alive and requested that their legs be broken in accordance with the Roman custom (*crurifragium*). This caused the dying victim to collapse, putting unbearable weight on the chest and causing rapid suffocation and death. The soldiers broke the legs of the two criminals, but Jesus appeared to be already dead. Perhaps to make sure, one of them thrust a spear into his side, releasing a flow of blood and water. John claims that a reliable eyewitness vouched for this (John 19.35), and apparently the phenomenon is medically possible. But John invests this whole episode with a profound symbolism, and sees what happened to Jesus as the fulfillment of scripture (Exod. 12.46; Zech. 12.10). In the first letter of John, which was written in the evangelist's circle, water and blood reveal Jesus as the savior who has come (1 John 5.6).

A man executed as a criminal would hardly have received a decent burial, and Jesus' body and those of his companions would very likely have been thrown into a ditch. It was probably from there that Jesus' corpse was retrieved by Joseph of Arimathea who, notwithstanding Luke 23.53, would have found it very difficult to remove it from the cross on his own. This man was of sufficient standing to persuade Pilate to commit Jesus' body to him. Matthew and John make him an actual disciple of Jesus (Mark 15.42–45 and parallels).

John relates that Joseph and his companion Nicodemus embalmed the body in accordance with Jewish custom (John 19.39–40). But the synoptists say only that the corpse was wrapped in a shroud before immediate burial (Mark 15.46 and parallels). This seems more likely: the quantity of spices that John specifies is excessive, and there are hints that the looming Sabbath deadline imposed a degree of haste that precluded full burial rites (Luke 23.54; John 19.42; see also p.129).

All the gospels agree that Joseph interred the corpse in a hitherto empty rock tomb (Mark 15.46 and parallels), no doubt belonging to his own family (Matt. 27.60). The entrance was sealed by a large stone (Mark 15.46; Matt. 27.60; see illustration, p.128).

The Entombment, *Castile school, ca. 1475. Joseph of Arimathea and Nicodemus lay Jesus in the tomb; the other mourners are John (the "beloved disciple") and the "Four Marys," including the Virgin (center) and Mary Magdalene (right).*

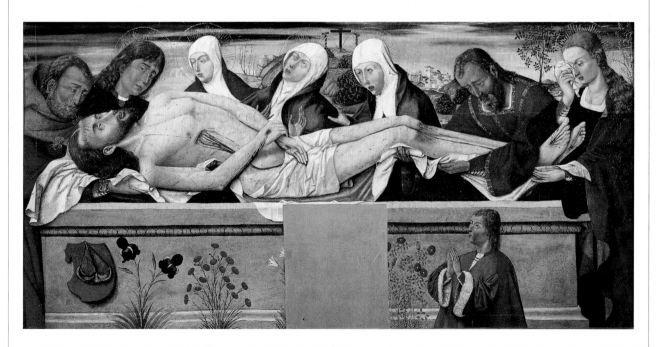

THE RISEN LORD

The interior of a tomb in Jerusalem dating from around the time of Jesus. As in the gospel accounts of Jesus' burial place, the tomb was sealed by rolling a large stone in front of the entrance.

Each evangelist presents his own individual account of the events that followed the entombment of Jesus, and although scholars have often sought to reconcile the four narratives, this is not really possible. However, the four versions share underlying thematic and structural patterns, which indicates that they all rely on a common and well-established tradition.

Most significantly, the gospels all agree that, on the third day after his burial, Jesus' tomb was discovered to be empty. Matthew, Mark, and Luke are at pains to stress that those who made this discovery knew for certain that the tomb they went to was the one in which Jesus' body had been placed (Mark 15.47 and parallels). In Matthew, the Temple authorities bribe the tomb guards to say that the disciples have stolen the corpse (Matt. 28.15). This story is unlikely to be historical, but it strongly suggests that knowledge of the empty tomb was widespread and accepted.

A second shared element is that one or more women found that the heavy stone sealing the tomb had been rolled away, and that Jesus' body had gone (Mark 16.3–4 and parallels). They had visited the tomb because they were anxious that Jesus' body had not received a proper burial (see p.127). Such concern was consistent with the way female disciples had provided for Jesus during his ministry (Mark 15.40–41 and parallels). An element common to the synoptists is that the women were confronted by one or more supernatural beings, who assured them that Jesus had risen from the dead. In Mark and Matthew, the women were then commanded to tell the disciples that Jesus was going ahead of them to Galilee, where his followers would meet him (Mark 16.5–7 and parallels).

For women to be credited with the first testimony to the Resurrection is remarkable for the time, and this alone makes a strong case for accepting that the gospel accounts have some sort of historical basis. Under Jewish law, women were not permitted as witnesses in court, and the male disciples at first rejected what the women told them (Mark 16.11; Luke 24.10–11).

The gospels go on to record various appearances of the risen Jesus, and here they begin to diverge considerably. Very likely, each writer has chosen particular traditions of special theological interest to himself. Paul—whose

THE ENDING OF MARK'S GOSPEL

All the accounts of the appearances of the risen Jesus in Mark's gospel occur in its final verses (Mark 16.9–20). Scholars generally agree that these passages are a later addition and that the work originally concluded with Mark 16.7–8: an angelic being, having announced that Jesus "has been raised," commands the three women who have come to the tomb to tell the disciples that Jesus would be preceding them to Galilee. But the women fled "and said nothing to anyone, for they were afraid."

Did Mark never complete the gospel, perhaps because death intervened, or was the original ending lost? Both theories have been discussed, but many scholars now believe that Mark did indeed intend to conclude at 16.8. In doing so, he ends on a note that demonstrated simply the tremendous and awesome effect of the Resurrection on ordinary believers. It has been pointed out that Mark reports three times Jesus' prediction that he would rise on the third day (Mark 8.31, 9.31, 10.34). The angelic "young man" simply confirms the fulfillment of Jesus'

The Resurrection, *by Fra Angelico (1387– 1455). "A young man, dressed in a white robe" (Mark 16.5) greets the women in the tomb. The risen Christ holds a banner symbolizing his resurrection.*

promise and no further proof is needed. Moreover, accounts of Jesus' appearances would have been well known to his readers.

At an early stage, many readers evidently felt uncomfortable with Mark's apparently abrupt ending and lack of Resurrection stories. Verses were added that read like a digest of post-Resurrection appearances in the other gospels: the appearance to Mary Magdalene (compare Matt. 28.1–10); the meeting on the road to Emmaus (Luke 24.13–32); Jesus' appearance to the disciples and their commissioning (Matt. 28.16–20; Luke 24.36–53; John 20.26–29, 21.1–23). Its only distinctive feature—the promise that believers would possess special powers (16.17–20)—reflects the experience of the early Church (Luke 10.17, 10.19; Acts 2.1–4; 5.16, 28.1–6, 8; 1 Cor. 12.10).

The Miraculous Draft of Fishes, *by Antoniazzo Romano (fl. 1460–1506). The scene depicts the events surrounding the appearance of the resurrected Jesus recounted in John 21.1–8 (compare illustration, p.43).*

THE RESURRECTION IN JOHN

The Fourth Gospel describes appearances of the risen Christ that are not especially different in kind from those in the synoptics, but, as ever, John gives his own distinctive account of them. Only one woman, Mary Magdalene, discovers the empty tomb (John 20.1–2). She encounters the risen Jesus and attempts to touch him (John 20.11–17). Jesus later appears twice to the disciples, confirms that he is the crucified one, and commissions them for ministry, conferring on them authority to forgive sins by the gift of the Holy Spirit (John 20.19–29). The Fourth Gospel also records a meeting of the risen Jesus with seven disciples in Galilee, in a narrative that contains several reminiscences of episodes of the Galilean ministry (John 21.1–19).

Noteworthy throughout John's version is the prominence of Peter. He is the first to attest to the real emptiness of the tomb (John 20.6–7), a tradition also found in some texts of Luke (Luke 24.12), and he is the main protagonist in the events at the Sea of Tiberias. There, in a moving dialogue, Jesus grants Peter the supervision of the Christian flock (John 21.15–17). There was a well-attested tradition in the early church that the first appearance of the risen Jesus had been to Peter (Luke 24.34; 1 Cor. 15.5).

letters probably provide the oldest evidence of the early Church's belief in the Resurrection—also lists a number of appearances of Jesus to various individuals and groups (1 Cor. 15.5–7).

Matthew provides a coherent account of the events that followed the discovery of the empty tomb, and displays a clear understanding of their significance. The women meet Jesus and take hold of his feet. This corresponds to the accounts in Luke and the Fourth Gospel of the physical reality of Jesus' resurrection (Matt. 28.9; Luke 24.36–42; John 20.20, 24–27).

For Matthew, and probably also Mark, the true setting for the revelation of the risen Lord is Galilee, where he commands his disciples to travel to meet him (Matt. 28.10; compare Mark 16.7). Jesus appears to them on a mountain, probably to be understood as the place where once he had enunciated the new Law in the Sermon on the Mount (Matt. 5–7; see pp.148–9). There, he delivers his final message: a program for the mission of the future universal Church (Matt. 28.16–20). For Matthew, the Resurrection establishes Jesus as the Lord of the Christian community, which is assured of its ultimate triumph by the power of his continuing presence.

In Luke, the appearances of the resurrected Jesus occur in Jerusalem, and he presents a string of episodes that all take place, somewhat improbably, on the first Easter day. But precise chronology is not Luke's primary

---

concern at this point. His interest is the same as Matthew's: the needs and tasks of the Church, and he already has in mind his second volume, Acts, in which the mission of the Church begins in Jerusalem.

Luke emphasizes that the death and resurrection of Jesus have been foretold in scripture (Luke 24.25–27, 44–45), and this is the major theme of Peter's first sermon (Acts 2.14–36). The disciples are entrusted with preaching to all nations a gospel of repentance and forgiveness of sins (Luke 24.47; Acts 2.38, 5.31). They are to remain in Jerusalem until they receive the gift of the Spirit which will empower them for their task (Luke 24.49; Acts 1.4–5, 8; 2.1–4; see pp.132–3).

THE RISEN LORD AND THE CHURCH

From the very beginning, the Resurrection became the central article of Christian faith. The New Testament books are unanimous in describing it as a genuine historical event, but its significance cannot be fully expressed in merely historical terms. It is a mighty act of divine power, comparable to God's primal act of Creation (Rom. 4.16–24), and like the Creation it was not an observable phenomenon. No one saw Jesus leave his tomb and even the guards who, according to Matthew, were present at the time, only witnessed an angelic visitation (Matt. 28.2–4). There is no description of the actual moment of resurrection: the gospels infer that it took place from the evidence of the empty tomb and the appearances of Jesus afterward.

Many authorities have suggested that the traditions of the empty tomb and of the appearances of the risen Christ originated separately. According to this theory, faith in Jesus' resurrection originally arose from his followers' belief that they had experienced Jesus' continuing presence after the Crucifixion; the story of the empty tomb was a later legend, designed to prove the reality of Jesus' physical resurrection.

It is true that only the evangelists refer to the empty tomb, and not Paul, whose letters predate the gospels. On the other hand, Paul may simply be taking the story of the empty tomb for granted, because it was so well known. Besides, his focal

The Roman Catholic church at Emmaus commemorates the famous encounter between two disciples and the resurrected Jesus described in Luke 24.13–32.

concerns were to validate his own personal experience of the risen Jesus, and to emphasize the truth of the resurrection of all believers, which Jesus' own resurrection guaranteed.

Conversely, if the original version of Mark's gospel ends at 16.8, as many believe (see box, p.129), then this evangelist provided no record at all of the appearances of the risen Jesus and offered only the words of the angelic man at the empty tomb as evidence for the Resurrection. All in all, it is probably best to view the reported experiences of the risen Jesus and of the empty tomb as jointly providing the source for the belief that Jesus rose from the dead.

Another suggestion is that the appearances of the risen Christ in reality represent subjective mystical or visionary experiences of his followers, arising from their own conviction that Jesus would rise from the dead.

However, the source of any such conviction is not clear. There is no firm evidence that contemporary Jews believed that the expected Messiah would die and rise again; and Jesus' own predictions of his death and resurrection, as recorded in the synoptic gospels, are regarded by most scholars as stemming from the evangelists and the early Church rather than from Jesus. In any case, the gospel accounts emphasize that the disciples were unable to understand or accept his words (Mark 8.32–33, 9.10, 9.32; Matt.16.22–23, 17.23; Luke 18.34).

THE ASCENSION

MYSTICAL ASCENT TO HEAVEN
According to the nonscriptural Jewish writings known as the Pseudepigrapha, a whole range of figures from Israel's past ascended to heaven, including Adam, Enoch, Abraham, Moses, and Isaiah. In heaven they were transformed into angelic beings, to whom divine cosmic secrets are revealed. Such accounts probably represent the actual subjective experience of Jewish mystics, as is suggested by some evidence from Qumran and by Paul's account of how he himself was mysteriously "caught up" to heaven and heard divine secrets (2 Cor. 12.1–7).

Some authorities claim that Jesus himself underwent the same kind of experience, and that this is seen notably in the description of his Transfiguration (see p.106). This has much in common with the New Testament references to his ascension, which have probably been shaped in part by mystical tradition.

A view eastward across the Old City of Jerusalem toward the Mount of Olives, also known as Mount Olivet, the scene of Jesus' Ascension (Acts 1.12). Close to the traditional site stands the tall belfry of the 19th-century Russian Orthodox Church of the Ascension.

Of all the writings of the New Testament, only Luke's second volume, Acts, describes Jesus' ascension to heaven as a genuine historical event and a visible phenomenon (Acts 1.2–11). Most often the New Testament speaks of the "exaltation" of Jesus, notably in an early hymn quoted in the letter to the Philippians (Phil. 2.6–11). The same image is dominant in the letter to the Hebrews (Heb. 1.3–4) and elsewhere: after his earthly sufferings, the Son is invested by God with supreme authority over the cosmos (Eph. 1.20–22). He inaugurates the new messianic age, and his followers share in his exalted status (Eph. 2.4–6). All this is achieved because Jesus has been carried into the heavenly realm and seated at God's right hand (Mark 16.19; Rom. 8.34)—that is, Jesus has returned to the divine state he enjoyed, as the agent of Creation, before his incarnation (Col. 1.15–17; Heb. 1.2).

As with Jesus' bodily resurrection (see p.131), the moment of Jesus' heavenly ascent remains largely undescribed. Luke's gospel states that Jesus "withdrew" from his disciples "and was carried up into Heaven" (Luke 24.51). According to Acts, as the disciples watched, Jesus was "lifted up, and a cloud took him out of their sight" (Acts 1.9). In the verses added to Mark (see box, p.129), Jesus is said to have been "taken up into Heaven," where he "sat down at the right hand of God" (Mark 16.19). However, Matthew speaks only of the supreme cosmic authority conferred on Jesus and of his continuing presence (Matt. 28.18–20). In John, Jesus announces to Mary Magdelene his imminent ascension, but its actual occurrence has to be inferred (John 20.17).

THE GIFT OF THE SPIRIT

Only Luke (in Acts) and John record the gift of the Holy Spirit to the disciples (John 20.22; Acts 2.1–13, 33). It represents Jesus' final bequest: the Spirit is to take his place, as it were, after he withdraws to heaven. For Luke, the descent of the Spirit is a public, visible, and dramatic event. In John, the disciples receive the Spirit in secret (John 20.19–23) and it remains known only to them (John 14.17).

In five sayings, John sets out what Christians are to understand about the nature and operation of the Spirit, also termed "the Advocate" (John 14.15–17, 25–26, 15.26, 16.4–11, 12–15). The Advocate will focus on Jesus and his teaching (John 14.26, 15.26, 16.14), and will guide the disciples into "the truth," which is Jesus himself (John 16.13–15; see p.153). The promise of the Spirit in Acts and John corresponds to Jesus' promise in Matthew that he will always be with the disciples (Matt. 28.20).

According to the gospels, the Spirit was involved at key moments throughout Jesus' earthly existence, and indeed directed his entire life and teaching (John 3.34). It was the agent of his conception (Matt. 1.18; Luke 1.35) and descended on him at his baptism (Mark 1.10 and parallels; John 1.32–33); at the start of his ministry, Jesus claimed to be the Spirit-filled prophet foretold in Isaiah (Luke 4.16–21). Through the Spirit, Jesus performed deeds of power, such as casting out demons (Matt. 12.28). Similarly, the gift of the Spirit grants the disciples "power from on high" (Luke 24.49) to exorcise, heal, and perform other "signs" in Jesus' name (Mark 16.17–20).

The Ascension, *by Pietro Perugino (ca. 1448–1523). Jesus ascends amid angels and cherubs, as the apostles gaze up to heaven (Acts 1.9–10). Following an early tradition, the Virgin also appears (center), as does Paul (with sword).*

The special object of the Ascension narrative in Acts is to make clear that the post-Resurrection appearances have come to an end. Jesus leaves the earth, not to be seen again until his second coming at some unknown date. His presence will be replaced by that of the Holy Spirit which will empower and inspire the Church (Acts 1.8). Luke's account appears to be modeled on the ascension of Elijah as described in the Hebrew Scriptures (2 Kings 2.9–12). For example, the forty-day period between the Resurrection and the Ascension on the Mount of Olives recalls Elijah's forty days' journey to Mount Horeb (1 Kings 19.8); and the gift of the Holy Spirit is paralleled by the gift to Elisha of the spirit of Elijah.

The unique feature of Jesus' ascension is its eschatological significance. It symbolizes the end of the old world order and the inauguration of the last age; his final coming will bring into being a wholly new heaven and a wholly new earth (Rev. 21.1).

THE TEACHINGS

How Jesus Taught	**136**
Sayings and Parables	136
Jesus and Scripture	140
Jesus and the Jewish Law	142
Gentiles and Samaritans	144
The Ethics of Jesus	**146**
God the Father	146
Sermons and Discourses	148
The Call of the Kingdom	150
The Teachings in John	154

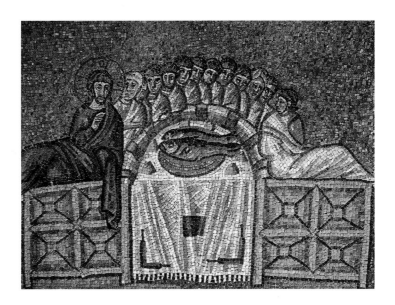

ABOVE: The Last Supper, *a mosaic in the church of Sant' Apollinare Nuovo,
Ravenna, Italy. The gospel accounts of Jesus' final meal are central to
Christian teachings on the Eucharist and the kingdom of God.*
OPPOSITE: Christ the Redeemer *(detail), by Agnolo Gaddi (ca. 1350–96). Jesus
holds open a passage (in Latin) from one of his discourses in John's gospel:
"I am the way, the truth, and the life" (John 14.6).*

SAYINGS AND PARABLES

The gospels clearly present the "parables" of Jesus as central to his message and to the way in which he proclaimed it. What is less clear is how this word (Greek *parabole*) should be defined. Most often, it is used to refer to any of the numerous narratives with which Jesus illuminates his teaching (see sidebar, opposite). But *parabole* covers a variety of other meanings, for example it is used of a metaphorical saying in Mark 7.14–17 and is translated as "proverb" in Luke 4.23. Conversely, Luke records some of Jesus' most famous and characteristic parables—such as the Good Samaritan (Luke 10.30–37) and the Prodigal Son (Luke 15.11–32)—but does not call them parables.

In the Septuagint, the oldest Greek version of the Hebrew Scriptures, *parabole* translates the Hebrew *mashal*, a word that can indicate a proverb, an allusion, a gibe, a riddle, or a prophetic oracle. *Mashal* derives from a root meaning "to be like," and is often found in conjunction with a comparative phrase such as "It is like" and "It may be likened to" in the Hebrew Scriptures (for instance, Ezek. 16.44) and in rabbinical texts. Similar phrases occur in the gospels in association with *parabole* (as at Mark 4.30; Matt. 13.24, 25.1), and may also introduce what is clearly a parable even when the term itself is absent (Matt. 18.23, 20.1).

The Ten Bridesmaids, *by Frans Francken the Younger (1581–1642), illustrating Matthew's parable about the vigilance required of those seeking to enter God's kingdom (Matt. 25.1–13). The five wise bridesmaids (right) have filled their lamps in anticipation of the arrival of the bridegroom (the Messiah), unlike the five foolish bridesmaids (left). When the Messiah's arrival is announced, the foolish bridesmaids must go to buy oil and are shut out of the messianic banquet.*

A mosaic of a grapevine from the church of Santa Maria di Capua Vetere, Italy. The image alludes to Jesus' parable of the Vine and the Branches (John 15.1–10).

NARRATIVE PARABLES OF JESUS

It is possible to list numerous examples of parables in which the element of narrative is characteristic—brief stories that illustrate one or more ideas. Most scholars would accept the following list:

PARABLES IN ALL THREE SYNOPTICS:
A Divided House (Mark 3.23–26 and parallels)
The Sower (Mark 4.2–9 and parallels)
The Mustard Seed (Mark 4.30–32 and parallels)
The Wicked Tenants (Mark 12.1–11 and parallels)
The Fig Tree (Mark 13.28–29 and parallels)

PARABLES COMMON TO MATTHEW AND LUKE:
The Two Builders (Matt. 7.24–27; Luke 6.47–49)
The Yeast (Matt. 13.33; Luke 13.20–21)
The Lost Sheep (Matt. 18.12–14; Luke 15.4–7)
The Wedding Banquet (Matt. 22.1–14; Luke 14.15–24)
Faithful and Unfaithful Slaves (Matt. 24.45–51; Luke 12.42–46)
The Talents or Pounds (Matt. 25.14–30; Luke 19.11–27)

A PARABLE ONLY IN MARK:
The Growing Seed (Mark 4.26–29)

PARABLES ONLY IN MATTHEW:
The Sower of Weeds (Matt. 13.24–30)
The Hidden Treasure (Matt. 13.44)
The Pearl (Matt. 13.45–46)
The Great Net (Matt. 13.47–48)
The Unforgiving Servant (Matt. 18.23–35)
The Vineyard Laborers (Matt. 20.1–16)
The Two Sons (Matt. 21.28–31)
The Ten Bridesmaids (Matt. 25.1–13)
The Judgment of the Nations (Matt. 25.31–46)

PARABLES ONLY IN LUKE:
The Creditor (Luke 7.41–43)
The Good Samaritan (Luke 10.30–37)
The Unexpected Guest (Luke 11.5–8)
The Rich Fool (Luke 12.16–21)
The Barren Fig Tree (Luke 13.6–9)
Choosing a Seat (Luke 14.7–11)
The Lost Coin (Luke 15.8–10)
The Prodigal Son (Luke 15.11–32)
The Dishonest Manager (Luke 16.1–8)
The Rich Man and Lazarus (Luke 16.19–31)
The Widow and Unjust Judge (Luke 18.1–8)
The Pharisee and the Tax Collector (Luke 18.9–14)

"PARABLES" IN JOHN:
The Good Shepherd (John 10.1–18)
The Vine and Branches (John 15.1–10)

So a parable may be defined, in a wide sense, as any figure of speech containing an arresting and illuminating image, allegory, or analogy. In this light it is quite understandable for Mark to describe Jesus' popular preaching as consisting wholly of "parables" (Mark 4.34), which modern scholars would variously categorize as similes, proverbs, metaphors, aphorisms, fables, and so on.

In the Fourth Gospel, Jesus' teaching tends to be less figuratively expressed, but his style of instruction is not so radically different from that in the synoptists as is often supposed. Not only does John contain two passages that have the distinct character of parables as the term is ordinarily understood—the Good Shepherd (John 10.1–18) and the Vine and the Branches (John 15.1–10)—but the gospel also conveys Jesus' message by means of a whole range of metaphors and figurative expressions.

The question arises as to how far it is possible to recover Jesus' actual words and the meaning that he himself attached to his parables. The evangelists present the parables as they were preserved, used, and understood in different circles within the early Church. This is evident from the way in which the same basic parable may vary from one gospel to the next. An example is the parable of the Wedding Banquet, to which the guests choose not to come (Matt. 22.1–14; Luke 14.15–24). In Luke, the story provides a message for the present, a warning against a refusal to accept God's gracious summons. In Matthew, it refers to the future messianic wedding feast for God's own Son and forecasts the coming destruction of Jerusalem.

The gospels tend to group parables (for example, Matt. 13.1–50, 25.1–46; Mark 4.1–34; Luke 6.39–49, 12.35–59). This suggests that the evangelists considered such parables to share the same theme, whether or not this was originally the case. For example, some parables are carefully

BIBLICAL AND RABBINIC PARABLES

An important influence on the parables in the New Testament was provided by the parables in the Hebrew Scriptures. The function of a parable is illustrated by the story told to King David by the prophet Nathan in order to open David's eyes to the depths and consequences of his misdeeds (2 Sam. 12.1–15): to bring home to hearers the reality of their situation and to alert them to the response demanded from them (Luke 10.36–37). Much the same purpose inspired the parable told by King Jehoash in his fiery confrontation with King Amaziah (2 Kings 14.8–10).

In both these instances, the speaker adds an explanation of the thrust of the story, so that it comes close to allegory, a feature that becomes increasingly prominent in the Hebrew Scriptures. For example, Ezekiel's parable of the Eagles and the Vine is specifically described as a "riddle" and an "allegory" (Ezek. 17.1–21).

The way in which the rabbis used parables in their teaching also throws considerable light on the gospel parables.

The Prodigal Son *(detail), by the Master of the Female Half-Lengths (ca. 1490–1540). The parable of the son lost to his father but found again (Luke 15.11–32) draws upon themes in the story of Joseph.*

Most extant examples are later than the time of Jesus or the New Testament, but there are good grounds for believing that they reflect a well-established tradition. Like Jesus, the rabbis drew their examples from the circumstances of daily life, and many of their typical images correspond to those in the gospel parables.

Rabbinic parables frequently illustrate passages of scripture. The only clear parallel to this method in the gospels is the parable of the Wicked Tenants (Mark 12.1–12 and parallels), which begins with a reference to Isaiah 5.2 and ends with the direct quotation of Psalm 118.22–23. But there are also indirect allusions to scriptural themes in Jesus' parables. For example, the story of the Good Samaritan interprets Leviticus 19.18, which is quoted (Luke 10.27), while the role of the Samaritan may recall 2 Chronicles 28.15. The parable of the Prodigal Son echoes the story of Joseph (Gen. 37–47), and the teaching about Choosing a Seat (Luke 14.7–11) is an interpretation of Proverbs 25.6–7.

explained in considerable detail as if they were allegories (Mark 4.13–20 and parallels; Matt. 13.36–43, 49–50). But it has been noted that in the parables unique to Luke, there is an absence of allegory, just a straightforward ethical message. The passages in the Gospel of Thomas (see box, p.59) that parallel the synoptic parables also lack allegorical features.

Consequently, some scholars have attempted to recover the "original" form and significance of Jesus' parables by stripping them of all elements of allegory and eschatology. However, if Jesus was influenced by the Hebrew Scriptures or by contemporary rabbinic practice (see box, above), he may well have used allegory on occasion. Indeed, it is hard to see how such parables as the Sower and the Wicked Tenants are intelligible except as allegories.

It has been suggested that Jesus' parables are primarily concerned with his central theme of the Kingdom (see pp.150–51), but he may have used them for a variety of purposes, sometimes perhaps simply to emphasize moral duties. The gospels imply that Jesus did not expect his parables to be widely understood, and revealed their real meaning only in private to the disciples (Mark 4.10–12 and parallels; Mark 4.33–34). But this may represent an attempt by the early Church to account for the fact that Jesus' public teaching had met with so little response in his lifetime. It seems clear that Jesus did indeed intend his parables as aids to getting his message across, not least because their imagery is overwhelmingly drawn from daily life.

Modern literary studies of the New Testament stress that the parables invite multiple interpretations and applications. The way in which they were transmitted in the early Church should perhaps be viewed, therefore, not as an obscuring or perversion of Jesus' teaching, but as a first witness to the continuing challenge to the Christian community to understand, and assimilate, his words.

The Sower of Weeds, by Domenico Fetti (ca. 1589–1623). Like many of Jesus' parables, Matthew's story about God's kingdom (Matt. 13.24–30) draws upon everyday rural life: "The kingdom of heaven may be compared to someone who sowed good seed in his field; but while everyone was asleep, an enemy came and sowed weeds among the wheat." The weeds represent those who will be judged unworthy to enter the kingdom: "At harvest time I will tell the reapers, Collect the weeds first and bind them in bundles to be burned, but gather the wheat into my barn."

JESUS AND SCRIPTURE

MIDRASH

MIDRASH

Recent study suggests that Jesus' use of scripture may be illuminated by comparison with the methods of biblical quotation and analysis current in the Palestine of his day. In mainstream Judaism, biblical analysis and interpretation were the prerogative of the rabbinical schools, whose wide variety of interpretative systems goes under the general description of *midrash* (from a Hebrew root meaning "to investigate").

Most of the extant rabbinic evidence is later than Jesus' time, but because the background of *midrash* has much to do with the scribes and the Pharisees, it could well have emerged by the first century CE.

The aim of *midrash* was to preserve the relevance and authority of the ancient scriptures in the life of every generation. To meet contemporary needs, additional legal regulations and moral teachings were drawn from the Hebrew Bible. This was done in various ways, for example by interpreting one scriptural passage in the light of another; by referring to oral tradition (see p.30); or by applying general theological or legal principles to extend the scope of a particular passage.

Allusions to the Hebrew Scriptures abound in the gospels, and there are also many direct quotations. As these quotations illustrate, in the first century CE the scriptures existed in a multiplicity of textual forms. Most passages quoted by the evangelists are taken from one or other version of the Septuagint (the oldest Greek version of the Hebrew Scriptures), but some, especially in Matthew, seem to depend more on the original Hebrew, while others do not correspond precisely to any known Greek or Hebrew text. It is possible that the gospel writers may often have quoted inexactly from memory, or felt free to adapt a biblical passage in order to make a particular theological point. Another suggestion is that they may have been influenced by the Targums, the Aramaic paraphrases of scripture that were used in the synagogues at the time for the benefit of Jews who did not understand Hebrew (see p.46).

All the evangelists employ verses from the Hebrew Scriptures in the course of their narrative in order to bring out the significance of Jesus' words and deeds. They do this in ways that have parallels in the Judaism

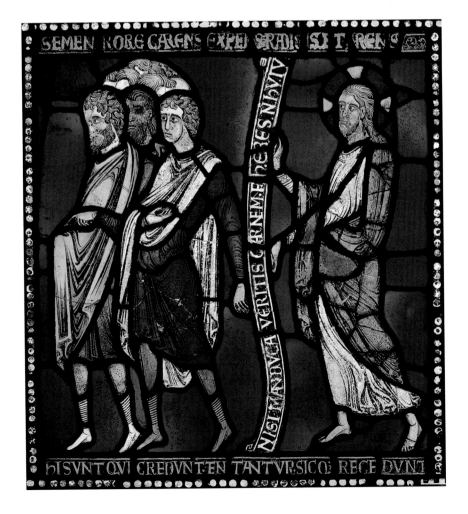

Christ Disputing with the Pharisees, one of a series of 13th-century stained glass panels known as the "Poor Man's Bible" in Canterbury cathedral, England.

of their time (see sidebars), except, of course, when they interpret various biblical prophecies as being fulfilled by episodes in the life of Jesus. The question arises as to whether Jesus himself used scripture in similar fashion in his own teaching—which in turn involves the issue of the authenticity of the words attributed to him.

Jesus was clearly accepted as a teacher (see pp.162–3), and a recognized teacher would have been expected to be familiar with the scriptures and to turn to them in his instruction. The gospels certainly portray Jesus as a person who was generally well versed in the scriptures, and several of his sayings, parables, and prayers contain echoes of biblical phrases and themes. For example, Mark 13.24–26 and parallels allude to Isaiah 13.10 and 34.4 and Daniel 7–13; the conclusion of the parable of the Growing Seed (Mark 4.26–29) echoes Joel 3.13; and the prayer on the cross in Mark 15.34 and Matthew 27.46 quotes Psalm 22.1, while that in Luke 23.46 paraphrases Psalm 31.5.

However, Jesus was an itinerant preacher who did not belong to any of the more "official" Jewish teaching groups, and the chief priests, elders, and scribes (experts in Jewish law; see p.30) are represented as querying his qualifications (Mark 11.27–33 and parallels). The gospels specifically contrast him with the scribes—whose particular expertise was scriptural analysis and interpretation—as one who presents a new teaching that has "authority" (Mark 11.27–28 and parallels). This indicates that Jesus was regarded by his followers as a prophet who, like his biblical predecessors, was delivering a divine message direct from God. Such a message did not require biblical evidence to support it, so it is not surprising that the evangelists present Jesus as appealing to scripture comparatively infrequently in order to authenticate his preaching.

Jesus had recourse to the Hebrew Scriptures to justify his teachings or actions primarily when he was challenged by various learned opponents. He then employed the kinds of argument that would have been familiar to his challengers and so might have been more likely to convince them (Luke 20.39). One technique was that of interpreting a biblical verse in the light of another, which was among the methods of *midrash* (see sidebar, left), as in his controversy with the Pharisees over divorce (Mark 10.2–9, Matt. 19.3–8) and his argument with the Sadducees over the doctrine of resurrection (Mark 12.26–27 and parallels).

Using the technique known as *pesher*, which was also employed by the Qumran sect (see sidebar, right), Jesus could point to events connected with his life as being the fulfillment of biblical prophecy—notably the role of John the Baptist as forerunner of the Messiah (Matt. 11.10; Luke 7.27) and the desertion of the disciples (Matt. 26.31; Mark 14.27). In particular, Jesus announced that he and his entire mission represented the realization of earlier prophetic writings (Matt. 12.39–40; Luke 4.16–21, 11.29–30, 22.37).

Part of the ruins of the settlement at Qumran in the Judean desert. These steps led to the pool used by Qumranites for ritual purification.

QUMRAN AND *PESHER*
Since the discovery of the Dead Sea Scrolls (see sidebar, p.37), scholars have devoted a great deal of attention to the analytical and interpretative techniques of the Qumran sect, particularly as they relate to Jesus' own methods of expounding the Jewish scriptures. The most characteristic method of biblical commentary at Qumran was *pesher* (Hebrew, "interpretation"), whereby a verse of scripture was quoted and then explained in a passage beginning with an introductory formula ("Interpreted, this concerns...").

Any verse thus cited was understood to be a prophecy and was usually taken from the prophetic books of the Hebrew Bible. The prophecies treated in this manner refer to events of the end time, which the Qumran sect believed had arrived. Through *pesher*, the Qumranites sought to identify contemporary persons and events in the life of the Qumran community to which the prophecies might be referring. The inner meaning of the prophecies, they believed, had been divinely revealed to the community's founder, the figure known as the Teacher of Righteousness.

THE LAW AND THE EVANGELISTS
The question must arise as to how far
sayings about the law ascribed to Jesus
represent his own teaching rather than the
ideas of the evangelists and of various
currents within the early Church. For
example, Matthew's gospel contains Jesus'
most positive statements about the law
(Matt. 5.17–19) and even presents him as
approving of the teaching—if not the
actual practice—of the Pharisees (Matt.
23.2–3). Is Matthew here reproducing the
attitude of contemporary Jewish
Christians in Palestine?

By contrast, Mark's comment that
Jesus' teaching "declared all food clean"
(Mark 7.14–19) may reflect the particular
outlook of Pauline Christianity, with its
mission to win over the Gentiles (compare
Rom. 14.14).

JESUS AND THE JEWISH LAW

It is possible to discern in the gospels a reasonably coherent and distinctive
attitude on the part of Jesus toward the Torah, the Jewish law (see p.30). He
is depicted as an observant Jew who regularly attended synagogue. He advocated obedience to the law's precepts, even in matters of ritual, such as sending gifts to the Temple (Matt. 5.23). But he warned against putting too much
emphasis on the precise carrying out of such external regulations. Jesus perceived the deeper religious significance of the law as the means by which people can attain a good life in accordance with the will of God. While he was
not alone in this among the Jewish teachers of his day, he laid special emphasis on it in his own teaching. Above all, Jesus emphasized that what was crucial was the correct intention on the part of the individual.

Much of Jesus' teaching on the Torah finds parallels in Jewish thought
of his time. The concept of the perpetuity of the law was a central dogma
of Judaism, and the gospels may well preserve the authentic words that
Jesus used in supporting that idea (Matt. 5.18; Luke 16.17), although they
appear to modify its absolute character (Matt. 11.13; Luke 16.16). It may
be that Jesus envisaged that the law would continue only for the comparatively brief period before the advent of the new age.

THE LAW IN CONTEMPORARY JUDAISM

All Jews accepted the supreme
authority of the Torah, but
Judaism in the first century CE
was not a monolithic system. By
this time, the ancient law required
interpretation and exposition to
make it relevant to contemporary
social conditions, and there were
a number of different groups (see
pp.34–7) with their own exposi-
tory methods. It is only to be
expected that Jesus, as an independent teacher, would have
had his own distinctive ways of interpreting the law.

At the same time, it has often been pointed out that there
is something of a problem with the term "law" as translated
in the New Testament. The Greek word *nomos*, used in the
gospels, certainly means "law" but in no way conveys the full
sense of the Hebrew word Torah, which means "instruction"

*A stone carving of ca. 400CE from
Capernaum of a wheeled Torah
shrine, in which the scrolls of the
law were kept in a synagogue.*

or "direction." Torah comprises
the whole of God's revelation to
humanity—the entire corpus of
scripture together with associated
religious tenets. For the Pharisees
it included the oral law (the "tra-
dition of the elders"; Mark 7.3, 5; Matt. 15.2), although this
was rejected by other groups, notably the Sadducees (see p.35).

It could sometimes appear that Torah, in this wide sense,
embraced inconsistent teachings, so that it was sometimes
necessary to decide which should take precedence. Such a
procedure is several times attributed to Jesus in the gospels
(see main text). (See also pp.30–31.)

In the Sermon on the Mount there are six sections (Matt. 5.21–48) in which Jesus quotes from the law and apparently contrasts it with his own ruling, for example: "You have heard that it was said, 'An eye for an eye and a tooth for a tooth' [compare Exod. 21.24]. But I say to you, Do not resist an evildoer…"(Matt. 5.38–39). The formula "but I say to you" was also employed by the Pharisees (Matt. 15.4–6; Mark 7.9–13) and does not in itself imply that Jesus was attempting to contradict or supersede the law. Rather, Jesus often aimed to support and bolster the Torah by indicating the interior moral disposition that must be confronted in order to ensure the law's proper observance. Thus anger is the cause of murder (Matt. 5.22); lust is equivalent to adultery (Matt. 5.28); true love must embrace enemies (Matt. 5.43–48). A promise need not be reinforced by swearing to God (Matt. 5.34–35, 23.16–22; Jesus uses common rabbinic paraphrases for the divine name)—the simple word of an honest person is enough (Matt. 5.37). Philo and Josephus record that the Essenes held much the same view.

Elsewhere, Jesus interprets the law within the framework of regular rabbinic methods of interpretation and analysis. His teaching on marriage and divorce (Matt. 19.3–8; Mark 10.2–9) relies on an appreciation that one scriptural text (Gen. 2.24) is of greater weight than another (Deut. 24.1). Similarly, when Jesus is accused of breaking the Sabbath by healing on that day, he points to the generally accepted principle that the need to preserve life supersedes the Sabbath taboos (Mark 3.4 and parallels; Mark 14.5 and parallels). The Pharisees' complaint against his disciples for plucking grain on the Sabbath (Mark 2.23–28 and parallels) seems to categorize the act as "harvesting," which was forbidden on that day. Jesus defends it by appealing, in typical rabbinic fashion, to scriptural precedent (1 Sam. 21.1–7; Matthew also mentions Num. 28.9–10)—which had greater authority than the rules of the Pharisees.

JESUS' SUMMARY OF THE LAW

On various occasions Jesus is represented as summarizing the whole of the law in brief, pithy statements. To this end he quotes the Ten Commandments (Mark 10.17–19 and parallels), pronounces the so-called Golden Rule (Matt. 7.12; Luke 6.31), and teaches that the whole of scripture can be summed up in just two commandments: to love God and one's neighbor (Mark 12.28–34 and parallels). The directness and clarity of Jesus' words, and the manner in which they embrace all the ethical and religious aspects of the Torah, strongly suggest that they embody his particular and authentic teaching.

Within Judaism there was a similar tendency to define the essence of the law in one or more simple statements, and parallels to all three of Jesus' summaries can be found in Jewish authors and early rabbinical sources. For example, Hillel, a great teacher of the first century BCE, is reported to have said: "What is hateful to you, do not to your neighbor. That is the whole Torah. The rest is commentary."

GENTILES AND SAMARITANS

Christ and the Woman of Samaria at the Well, *by Philippe de Champaigne (1602–74). When Jesus asked a Samaritan woman to give him a drink, she was initially wary (John 4.9), since the attitude of Jews and Samaritans was often one of mutual hostility. According to John 4.7–29, Jesus revealed himself to her as a prophet and as the Messiah, declaring that Samaritans would share in the "living water"—the gift of divine spirit that Jesus brought. Samaria was an early destination for the missionary apostles, and Philip is said to have had great success there (Acts 8.5–8). However, whether Jesus himself really sanctioned a mission to the Samaritans is debatable (see p.36).*

Within a few years of Jesus' death, the embryonic Church emerged as an active missionary body centered on Jerusalem. The traditional Christian view is that the Jerusalem leadership agreed to concern themselves with converting Jews, while the apostle Paul and his colleague Barnabas would embark on a mission to the Gentiles (Gal. 2.7–10).

There is considerable evidence to indicate that Jesus himself personally undertook no such mission to non-Jews. He said that he had been sent "only to the lost sheep of the house of Israel" (Matt. 15.24). On occasion he even displayed a distinct antipathy toward Gentiles, for example describing them as "dogs" (Mark 7.27 and parallels), an epithet also employed in rabbinic sources. When Jesus sends out the twelve apostles on their missionary journey, he orders them not to go either to Gentiles or to Samaritans (Matt. 10.5).

Such sayings seem to reflect the authentic attitude of Jesus himself, since they do not chime with the practice of either the Jewish or the Gentile wings of the early Church (see pp.172–3). It is worth noting that the first Christians, in their approach to the Gentiles and the question of circumcision, never appeal to any direct teaching of Jesus on these issues.

However, some words and actions of Jesus point in a different direction. He declared that the twelve disciples would sit on thrones at Judgment Day to judge only the tribes of Israel (Matt. 19.28; Luke 22.28–30), but both gospels also report his statement that those who will sit in the kingdom of God are in fact the Gentiles, who will supplant the Jews (Matt. 8.11–12; Luke 13.28–29). Jesus said that he found more faith in a Roman centurion than anywhere in Israel (Matt. 8.10; Luke 7.9) and recognized the truth of the Canaanite woman's claim that a Gentile might share in Jewish privileges (Matt. 15.27–28; Mark 7.28–29). Jesus is recorded as healing not only Jews but also crowds who flocked to him from non-Jewish areas (Mark 3.7–8 and parallels).

These divergent attitudes toward Gentiles reflect Jewish thought of the time (see box on opposite page). Jesus may well have seen his ministry as preparing

JEWS AND GENTILES IN JESUS' TIME

Most Jews were keenly aware of their separateness from the Gentiles who surrounded them. Condemnations of the Gentiles for idolatry and immorality were frequent, and the regulations of the Torah—especially regarding clean and unclean food and circumcision—served, for Jews, to mark them off as the people chosen and set apart by God.

But there is also much evidence of a positive attitude toward Gentiles. Some were recognized as righteous, and were accordingly expected to observe the seven basic commandments that God is said to have given Noah after the Flood (Gen. 9). There were Jewish thinkers who believed that such righteous Gentiles would be rewarded with a place in the future Messianic age. In the face of much Gentile hostility, some Jewish writers sought to defend and commend their faith to outsiders, to considerable effect. Judaism as a whole was not an active missionary movement, but converts and proselytes were often welcomed and apparently sometimes vigorously sought out (Matt. 23.15). A proselyte had to accept all the requirements of the Jewish law; many Gentiles felt unable to go so far, but remained attracted to Judaism on account of its strict monotheism, ethical concerns, and morality, which they learned about in the synagogues—places that were open to all. Many Gentiles, like the centurion at Capernaum (Luke 7.2–5), enjoyed friendly relations with Jews.

The attitudes toward Gentiles prevalent in Jesus' time find their roots in the Hebrew Bible. On the one hand, it betrays

A relief carving from the synagogue at Capernaum. According to Luke 7.5, the synagogue of Jesus' own day was built by a Gentile benefactor, a centurion in the occupying Roman army.

a strong exclusivist strain, especially in postexilic writings such as Ezra and Nehemiah, which forbid marriages with non-Jews.

Elsewhere, however, there is a note of universalism: Israel is a light to the nations (Isa. 49.6), with a mission to unite with the Gentiles (Isa. 55.5) so that they too become God's people (Zech. 2.11). This is symbolized by the image of peoples converging on Jerusalem (Isa. 60.3, 11; Zech. 8.20–21) to worship the one true God (Zech. 14.6). In this way, according to a verse that Jesus quotes, the Jewish Temple becomes "a house of prayer for all peoples" (Isa. 56.7; Mark 11.17).

Israel for the imminent advent of the perfect rule of God (Matt. 10.23), while conceding that this would also embrace Gentiles and Samaritans.

So even if it is concluded that the idea of a mission to all the nations arose only after the Crucifixion (Matt. 28.18–20; Mark 16.15; Luke 24.47), such a mission can be understood as a legitimate development of Jesus' own words and deeds. There is a pronounced strain of universalism in his teaching, as in the idea that God cares for all men and women equally, and even embraces one's enemies (Matt. 5.43–48; Luke 6.27–28, 32–36). One of the most characteristic features of Jesus' ministry was his fellowship with, and concern for, those rejected by society: tax collectors, sinners who had put themselves outside the Jewish law, Samaritans, and the disabled. Here may be seen the root of the concept of a gospel for the whole of humanity, as expressed by Paul: "For there is no distinction between Jew and Greek; the same Lord is Lord of all and is generous to all who call upon him" (Rom. 10.12).

GOD THE FATHER

God the Father Enthroned, *from the Limoges Missal (late 15th century). The figure of God is depicted wearing the papal tiara; one hand is raised in blessing, while the other holds an orb with a cross, signifying the sovereignty of Christ over the world. He is surrounded by the evangelists and their symbols.*

The concept of God as father is central to the life and teaching of Jesus as presented in the gospels, and the concept was certainly known in the Judaism of his day. It derives from the Hebrew Scriptures, where God is described, for example, as the father of the Israelite nation (Deut. 32.6; Isa. 63.16; Jer 31.9) and of the Israelite king (2 Sam. 7.14).

However, "father" is much less common in the Hebrew Bible than other descriptions and titles of God, whereas Jesus employs "Father" almost without exception (although some examples of his use of the term may well have been shaped by the evangelists or the liturgy of the early Church). Conversely, although "king" is a frequent title for God in the Judaism of the time—and despite the fact that the kingdom of God is another constant theme of Jesus' teaching (see pp.150–51)—only once does Jesus refer to God as king (Matt. 5.35), and even this instance is questionable. There can be little doubt, then, that the notion of God as father is an authentic element in Jesus' thought.

For Jesus, the fatherhood of God means that he is a forgiving deity and forgiveness must be a special mark of true worshipers (Matt. 6.14; Mark 11.25). The description of the Father as "heavenly" or "who is in heaven"—especially frequent in Matthew—points to God's perfection, which again must be a mark of his true followers (Matt. 5.48), who will be aided by his spirit (Matt. 10.20; Luke 11.13).

Above all, Jesus teaches that the heavenly Father actively cares for his whole creation, for all human beings, good and sinful, and such compassion once more must be a pattern for every human life (Matt. 5.43–46;Luke 6.32–36). God's providence extends to the natural world (Matt. 6.25–34, 10.29; Luke 12.6, 12.22–30). He may be compared to a human father who will always seek to give the best to his children (Matt. 7.7–11; Luke 11.9–13) so that the children of the heavenly father, unlike others, can be certain that he will always provide for their needs—if their priority is to seek to enter his kingdom (Matt. 6.31–34; Luke 12.29–31).

The "little ones"—probably not simply infants but all who believe with childlike openness, as an addition in some manuscripts suggests—are always in the father's sight (Matt. 18.10, 14). The secrets of the human heart are known to God, with the result that it is not the outward actions involved in almsgiving, prayer, and fasting at which he looks but the inner intention of an individual that obtains his reward (Matt. 6.2–8, 16–18).

The gospels record five prayers of Jesus in which he addresses God as "Father," the best known of these being "The Lord's Prayer" (see sidebar, right). In his two prayers from the cross recorded in Luke (Luke 23.24, 46) Jesus also addresses his "Father": in the second case the word is added to a quotation from Psalm 31. Of special importance is Jesus' great thanksgiving prayer (Matt. 11.25–27; Luke 10.21–22), which certainly depicts a unique relationship between Jesus and his divine father. This passage characterizes Jesus very much as he is presented in John's gospel, and consequently it has been dismissed as a later addition, influenced by Hellenism (see pp.22–3) or even Gnosticism (see pp.176–7). But the idea expressed in this prayer that a special individual might be admitted to divine secrets and then in turn reveal them to others, is widely attested in Jewish writings such as the books of Enoch and some Qumran texts.

Jesus' fifth "father" prayer is spoken in Gethsemane (Mark 14.36 and parallels). Mark preserves the Aramaic term *Abba* (properly translated as "my father" or "our father"), and most scholars agree that this is the word Jesus would have used, both here and elsewhere. It also occurs twice outside the gospels (Rom. 8.15; Gal. 4.6), where it represents the practice of Greek-speaking churches—a fact that probably shows how deeply Jesus' own usage had embedded itself in Christian tradition.

A great deal has been read into the word *Abba*. Some have claimed that it represents a young child's way of speaking (the equivalent of "Daddy") and therefore indicates a special intimacy on the part of Jesus with his heavenly Father. But there is no real evidence that *Abba* means anything other than simply "father," and its precise significance must be determined by the context. For example, it was the regular title used when speaking to revered rabbinic teachers.

THE LORD'S PRAYER

Jesus' most famous prayer is The Lord's Prayer (Matt. 6.9–13; Luke 11.2–4). It might better be described as "The Disciples' Prayer," since it is intended as a brief and comparatively simple pattern for disciples to follow, in contrast to the "many words" apparently characteristic of Gentile prayers (Matt. 6.7). There is no fundamental difference in content between the versions in Matthew and Luke, and the petitions that come after the initial address reflect Jesus' general teaching about the nature of the heavenly father (see main text).

The clause in Matthew "Your will be done" stresses the need for earthly life to correspond to the heavenly: in Jesus' teaching, those who desire to belong to the Father's family must seek first and foremost to carry out the divine purpose (Mark 3.35 and parallels; Matt. 7.21). The next petition, about "daily bread," probably refers to God's provision for ordinary human needs, of which Jesus speaks elsewhere. Commentators have proposed that the obscure Greek word translated as "daily" actually means "for tomorrow" and refers to the Day of Judgment expected shortly, but the likely Aramaic original suggests that Luke's "each day" gives the true sense—Jesus elsewhere discouraged any concern for "tomorrow" (Matt. 6.34).

Again, the prayer for the remission of debts or sins appeals both to the divine attribute of forgiveness and the requirement that human beings imitate it in their relationships with one another (see also Matt. 18.23–35; Luke 7.41–43, 47). The final petition, whatever its precise significance, reflects Jesus' assurance elsewhere (Matt. 18.14) that the Father will protect believers from harm.

The Lord's Prayer appears in 100 languages on the walls of the Pater Noster Church on the Mount of Olives. The church—the name of which is the Latin for "Our Father"—stands on the spot where Jesus is said to have spoken the prayer.

THE SERMONS: A SUMMARY

MATTHEW'S SERMON ON THE MOUNT:
5.3–12 The Beatitudes
5.13–16 The new community
5.17–48 The fulfillment of the Law
6.1–18 Duties toward God
6.19–7.12 How human life is to be lived
7.13–27 Challenges of choosing the right path

LUKE'S SERMON ON THE PLAIN:
6.20–23 The Beatitudes
6.24–26 The Woes
6.27–36 Love for enemies
6.37–45 Human life and relationships
6.46–49 Challenges of choosing the right path

SERMONS AND DISCOURSES

According to the synoptic gospels, Jesus expressed most of his teaching in short, pithy sayings or in brief parables (see pp.136–9). This contrasts with the Fourth Gospel, in which Jesus' teaching is presented almost entirely in lengthy discourses (see pp.154–5). However, there are examples in the synoptic gospels of extended addresses attributed to Jesus, such as the so-called "Synoptic Apocalypse" (Mark 13.5–37 and parallels). In Matthew's gospel, in particular, there are at least five such discourses, which occupy a prominent place in the structure of the work (see box, below).

Nonetheless, although it is not impossible that Jesus occasionally made orations in the manner of some of the prophets of ancient Israel, internal

JESUS' DISCOURSES IN MATTHEW

New Testament scholars often claim that Matthew's gospel has a five-part structure based around five great discourses attributed to Jesus, each of which is rounded off with the phrase "when Jesus had finished" (Matt. chs. 5–7, 10, 13, 18, 23–25). It has been suggested that this pattern is intended to parallel the Pentateuch, the first five books of the Bible (Genesis–Deuteronomy, the books of the law) and that Matthew's gospel thus has the character of a code of religious instruction—the new law for the Christian community.

However, it is far from clear that there are only five important discourses in the gospel. For example, Matthew 11 is also an extended collection of Jesus' sayings. Also, if Matthew were understood as essentially a lawcode, the narratives of the Nativity, Passion, and Resurrection would fall outside its main structure, which seems very strange.

Other scholars propose that Matthew's framework echoes the Hexateuch, the first six books of the Bible. Thus the birth narratives parallel Genesis, the Passion parallels Deuteronomy (which ends with the death of Moses), and the Resurrection stories parallel Joshua (in which the Israelites enter the Promised Land and reaffirm their covenant with God).

But the evangelist himself provides no indication of any such conscious scheme. It seems better to conclude that Matthew intended to present his work as history: an account of the life and ministry of Jesus.

The Flight into Egypt, *by Gentile da Fabriano (ca. 1370–1427). Claims about the "Pentateuchal" structure of Matthew have been based on stories such as the Holy Family's journey to Egypt (see pp.74–5), which has echoes of the story of Joseph in Genesis.*

This hill near Capernaum, known as the Mount of the Beatitudes, is the traditional site of the Sermon on the Mount. On its crest stands the Roman Catholic Church of the Beatitudes, built in 1936.

evidence suggests that, as they stand, all the discourses in Matthew, Mark, and Luke are actually compilations of individual sayings. For example, sayings that appear in a discourse in one gospel sometimes occur in another gospel in a quite different context.

The best known of such discourses appears in two related versions, traditionally called the "Sermon on the Mount" (Matt. 5–7) and the "Sermon on the Plain" (Luke 6.20–49), which deal with Jesus' challenging ethical demands. A comparison between Matthew's and Luke's versions suggests that they both derive from an earlier collection of sayings, either in oral or written form, which each evangelist has expanded and interpreted in his own way. In both gospels, the discourse is represented as being addressed to a general audience (Matt. 7.28; Luke 6.17, 7.1), but it seems likely that originally it was intended for the disciples alone (Matt. 5.1; Luke 6.20) and that it was preserved as a manual of instruction for the early Church.

In both Matthew and Luke, the discourse essentially represents the proclamation of the kingdom by the Messiah. This is clearer in Matthew, where the sermon opens the section of his gospel that sets out the message and teaching of Jesus (Matt. 4.17–16.20). To view it as primarily law—even as a new law for Israel—is to mistake its character. The moral and ethical teachings it contains represent the demands and obligations made on those who are prepared to accept the gift of the kingdom.

The position of the Beatitudes ("Blessings") at the beginning of the sermons is significant: they provide the keynote for all that follows. Luke has only four of the nine blessings cited by Matthew, and there are differences (probably unimportant) in the wording of those they have in common. The formal structure of the Beatitudes is modeled on similar sayings in the Hebrew Bible and other Jewish writings. For example, there is a sequence of nine blessings in the book of Sirach (Ecclesiasticus) (Sir. 25.7–10).

BLESSINGS OF THE KINGDOM

The Beatitudes in Matthew's Sermon on the Mount and Luke's Sermon on the Plain seem deliberately to reflect the opening verses of Isaiah 61, and this provides the clue to their character. Isaiah 61 was the text upon which Jesus first preached in the synagogue at Nazareth (Luke 4.18–20), and the Beatitudes are prophetic and apocalyptic sayings that express the substance of Jesus' preaching in the synagogues of Galilee, where he proclaimed the gospel of the kingdom (Matt. 4.23). The millenarian connotations are more emphatic in Luke, who to the four Beatitudes adds four "Woes" that depict the fate of those who are deaf to the demands of the kingdom (Luke 6.24–26).

Matthew's first four blessings stress the reversals of fortune that the kingdom will bring to "the poor in spirit," "those who mourn," "the meek," and "those who hunger and thirst for righteousness." The remainder continue the theme of the rewards in a kingdom that is still to be consummated, although both gospels display the conviction that this consummation is close at hand. The discourses reach a climax with a call for people to act on Jesus' words in light of the coming Judgment. This is expressed in the parable of the houses built on rock and sand (Matt. 7.24–27; Luke 6.47–49), which is based on the Israelite idea of "the two ways" of righteousness and wickedness (Deut. 30.15; Ps. 1.6; Prov. 4.10–19).

THE CALL OF THE KINGDOM

Christ Pantocrator *("Ruler of All"),*
a mosaic in the dome of the Byzantine
church at Daphni, Greece (ca. 1200).
Jesus, as God the Son, is portrayed as
king of kings, omnipotent sovereign
of the universe, holding in his left hand
the book of the new law that he brings.

Jesus' preaching in Galilee centered on "the good news of the kingdom" (Matt. 4.23; Luke 8.1), and the synonymous expressions "the kingdom of God" and "the kingdom of heaven" occur around a hundred times in the synoptic gospels. Nowhere is the nature of this kingdom explicitly defined, which suggests that Jesus was talking about a concept familiar to his audience. At the same time, in spite of the many references to the kingdom, Jesus seems never to have spoken of God as "king," and there is a marked absence of royal imagery in his sayings about the kingdom.

Scholarly debate about the kingdom in the gospels has focused mainly on the issue of whether Jesus viewed it as a future phenomenon or as a reality already present. There are certainly passages which suggest that the kingdom has yet to appear, as in the petition "Your kingdom come" in the Lord's Prayer (see p.147), and in Jesus' promise to some of his disciples that they will live to witness the arrival of the kingdom (Mark 9.1 and parallels). At the Last Supper, Jesus says that he will not again drink wine until he drinks it anew in the kingdom of God (Matt. 26.29; Mark 14.25: see pp.112–13), referring to the great banquet that was expected to be held in celebration of the beginning of the messianic age. The banquet is also mentioned in a verse that tells of the future entry of all the nations into the kingdom (Matt. 8.11; Luke 13.29), which echoes ideas in the Hebrew Scriptures (Isa. 2.3; Mic. 4.3). The use of the future tense in Matthew's version of the Beatitudes (see pp.148–9) suggests that the disciples' enjoyment of the kingdom is yet to come.

On the other hand, numerous passages (such as Mark 1.15) speak of the kingdom as already present. Jesus' exorcisms are evidence that this is so (Matt. 12.28; Luke 11.20), and signs of the approach of the kingdom need not be sought, for it is here (Luke 17.21). The parables of the Growing Seed (Mark 4.26–29), the Mustard Seed (Mark 4.30–32 and parallels), the Yeast (Matt. 13.33; Luke 13.20), the Sower of Weeds (Matt. 13.24–30), and the Great Net (Matt. 13.47–50) all view the kingdom as a present reality.

In assessing whether the gospels view the kingdom as here or yet to come, commentators have often simply opted for one or other alternative. However, it is now increasingly recognized that the gospels are not necessarily self-contradictory, because the notion of God's kingdom as

THE KINGDOM IN JUDAISM

The nearest thing to the term "the kingdom of God" in the Hebrew Bible is "the kingdom of the Lord," which occurs once (1 Chron. 28.5) and refers to Israel. But the scriptures regularly refer to God as "king" and as "reigning," and speak of "his kingdom" (Ps. 145.12), "your kingdom" (Ps. 145.11, 13), and "my kingdom" (1 Chron. 17.14). Initially, the God of Israel was conceived, like other Near Eastern national deities, as the divine king of one people. However, as Israelite monotheism developed, God's sovereignty came to be seen as both universal and eternal (Pss. 22.28, 103.19, 145.13; Wisd. of Solomon 10.10). But his rule was not universally recognized, so later Jewish writings developed the idea of God's kingdom as a hope for the future, to be realized either by his direct intervention or through his Messiah.

By the first century BCE, this hope had become particularly fervent, and was coupled with a belief in a present kingdom of evil at war with the kingdom of God. Contemporary disasters for the Jews, which appeared to be multiplying, were interpreted as signs that this conflict was close to its climax, when

The Mount of Olives from the walls of Jerusalem. According to Jewish tradition, the kingdom would be inaugurated by the arrival of God's Messiah on the Mount of Olives. It was here that the accompanying resurrection of the dead would begin—hence the thousands of Jewish graves that cover the hillside.

evil would be defeated and God's kingdom established. This was a central belief of, for example, the Qumran sect (see p.37).

The dual notions of a present and future kingdom also appear in rabbinic thought. The faithful Israelite can enter the kingdom here and now by taking on "the yoke of the kingdom of heaven": submitting to God and observing the law. On the other hand, in the Kaddish prayer, the worshiper asks for God's kingdom to be established "speedily and at a near time." The two concepts come together in a Targum (Aramaic paraphrase) of the Song of Moses in Exodus 15: "The Lord's is the kingdom in this world and his in the world to come."

Christ and the Rich Youth, *by Bartolomeus Breenberg (ca. 1599–1657). A rich young man knelt before Jesus and asked how he could attain eternal life. Jesus replied that, as well as keeping the commandments, he must sell all he owned and give the money to the poor. Crestfallen, the youth departed, prompting Jesus' remark: "It is easier for a camel to go through the eye of a needle than for someone who is rich to enter the kingdom of God" (Mark 10.17–25 and parallels.)*

JESUS' IMAGERY OF COMMITMENT
To drive home the necessity for absolute submission to the will of God, Jesus often employed vivid, even exaggerated images, as with his famous analogy of the camel and the needle's eye (see above). Just as a plowman should always look ahead, so no one entering the kingdom should look back to his or her old life (Luke 9.62). The kingdom even overrides the sacred duty of burying the dead, which must be left to the dead—Jesus' stark description of those who do not enjoy the new life of the kingdom (Matt. 8.22; Luke 9.60).

If a hand, a foot, or an eye "causes you to stumble" on the way to the kingdom, Jesus says, it is better they should be cut off or plucked out than be allowed to hinder one's entry (Matt. 18.8–9; Mark 9.43–48). Similarly, "there are eunuchs who have made themselves eunuchs for the sake of the kingdom of heaven" (Matt. 19.11–12).

both a present and future reality already existed in Judaism (see box, p.151). The thrust of Jesus' teaching is that the kingdom already exists but only becomes properly "activated" by his message and ministry, and this leads to its full and final consummation at some point in the near future. But the ultimate triumph of the kingdom depends upon men and women accepting its demands and devoting themselves wholly to its service (Matt. 6.33), not least as co-workers with Jesus in bringing others to repent and to acknowledge its claims (Matt. 10.7; Luke 9.2).

Most of Jesus' sayings about the kingdom address the religious and moral qualities that individuals require in order to enter it, and these form the core of his ethical teaching. As many people have observed, Jesus says nothing directly about social issues, nor is it possible to attribute any specific political doctrines to him. Rather than constituting a rounded, systematic, and universally applicable ethical system, Jesus' teaching as recorded in the gospels was prompted by *ad hoc* situations, often in response to particular questions put to him. This is not to say that many of his contemporaries did not regard his teachings as having significant social consequences. Jesus' radical demands were often an occasion of conflict in that they broke with convention and were seen to challenge accepted social priorities.

The first requirement that Jesus pressed on individuals was the need for repentance and belief in the good news that the kingdom had arrived. The gospels present this as the essential kernel of his preaching (Matt. 4.17; Mark 1.14–15). Repentance for past sins alone was not enough—and in this it is possible to detect a difference between Jesus and John the Baptist, for whom repentance was central (Matt. 3.6; Mark 1.4–5). Although the idea of turning from sin is certainly present in Jesus' teaching, his central concept is more positive: the turning around of a person's entire life toward the wholehearted service of God. This is the condition for entry into the kingdom, where the believer realizes and enjoys the divine forgiveness that is a leading theme of Jesus' message.

Entry into the kingdom must be complete and unconditional: its demands are overriding and nothing must stand in its way. It involves detachment from possessions and family ties, and a complete reversal of the usual social distinctions (Mark 10.29–31 and parallels). The striking language with which Jesus expressed how an individual should submit to God (see sidebar on opposite page) should not be understood as prescribing specific modes of external behavior. It points to the fact that Jesus' ethical teachings center primarily on one's interior disposition and commitment. Thus the Sermon on the Mount calls not just for the outward observance of the commandments of the law but for obedience to the spirit of those commandments (see pp.142–3).

Along with repentance goes utter trust in God, who, when people renounce everything except service to him, will supply all their needs, freeing them from all anxiety. The model for those hoping to enter the kingdom is the unquestioning trust of a little child (Mark 10.15 and parallels; Matt. 11.25; Luke 10.21). In their own personal behavior the kingdom's children are to exhibit the very nature of their heavenly Father, reflecting his perfection in themselves (Matt. 5.48, 19.21). Just as the Father is loving and merciful to all human beings, irrespective of their merits, so too all humans must practice universal benevolence, even toward enemies (Matt. 5.43–48; Luke 6.27–36), and show mercy toward all in need (Luke 10.29–37). The prime ethical principle of Jesus, therefore, is fundamentally one of love, crystallized in his summary of the law: "You shall love the Lord your God with all your heart, and with all your soul, and with all your mind, and with all your strength" and "you shall love your neighbor as yourself" (Mark 12.29–31 and parallels).

JESUS AND THE END TIME
Jesus' proclamation of the kingdom, according to the gospels, seems to have located that kingdom both in the present and in the future (see main text). Many scholars would say that it was the future kingdom that dominated Jesus' own convictions—that he believed that the present age would shortly come to an end, to be replaced by another inaugurated by God, and that this belief conditioned all his ethical teaching. Jesus very likely did expect an imminent time when the kingdom would be fully realized. Some of his ethical demands reflect this, for example, his teaching about the conduct needed to face the Last Judgment with confidence (Matt. 25.31–46)—although the attribution of this passage to Jesus is widely questioned.

But Jesus was not primarily a prophet of the end of the present world, nor did he teach that such an expectation should be a motive for right conduct. He discouraged speculation—widespread at the time—about "signs" that were thought to herald the advent of the kingdom (Mark 8.11–12; Luke 17.20). In fact, he declared that the hour of its appearance was unknowable, even to him (Matt. 24.36; Mark 13.32), so that people should be ready for it whenever it might occur (Luke 12.39–40).

Jesus' words reveal his belief that he and his followers were already living in the "end time," an epoch quite different from all that had gone before. His demands on men and women are determined not so much by the expectation of the imminent end of the world but by faith in the God who has brought salvation in Jesus and in the divine will that Jesus proclaims. The kingdom is already present, waiting only for individuals to discover it and respond to it (Matt. 13.44–46).

THE TEACHINGS IN JOHN

Jesus' teaching in the Fourth Gospel is conveyed largely through six extended speeches (John 3, 4.7–26, 5.19–46, 6.25–65, 8.12–59, 10), in addition to his farewell addresses to the disciples (John 14–17). Not only is the form of the teaching in John very different from that which characterizes Matthew, Mark, and Luke, but its content is also distinctive. However, such divergences must not be exaggerated, as there are also passages in John in which the evangelist seems to develop themes and concepts that are present in the synoptic gospels. Either the author knew one or more of the other gospels directly or he relied on a shared corpus of traditions.

In the synoptics, Jesus' preaching centers on the kingdom of God and the moral demands that it makes on those who seek to enter it (see pp.150–53). However, in the discourses of the Fourth Gospel, Jesus primarily expounds the real significance of his own person and what is involved in recognizing his true nature. John uses the expression "the king-

FAITH AND BELIEF IN THE FOURTH GOSPEL

The whole of John's gospel is written with the purpose of awakening faith (John 20.31): the evangelist uses the verb "to believe" more often than all the other gospels put together. Belief consists not so much in accepting a body of teaching but in the conviction that Jesus himself is the uniquely authentic revelation of the Father, and the only way to him. Jesus' miracles are not only works of power but, above all, "signs" that indicate who Jesus really is (John 9.3).

This rock in the Franciscan church at Cana (Kafr Kanna) is said to mark the precise spot where Jesus performed his first miracle, according to John 2.1–11.

According to the evangelist's complex theology, the gift that believers receive from Jesus is eternal life (John 10.10). Believers are incorporated into the life and body of Christ, and this concept is expressed in various ways. For example, they are branches of the "true vine" (John 15.1ff.). Incorporation into the life of Jesus is attained by partaking of his flesh and blood (John 6.53–57).

After Jesus has left the earth, the "Spirit of truth" will enter his disciples (John 14.16–17). The truth is Jesus himself (John 14.6), and so the Spirit will lead the disciples to a complete knowledge of Jesus, and thus of God, and enable them to continue to glorify Jesus and to bear witness to him (John 14.26, 15.26–27, 16.13–15).

During Jesus' incarnate life the world is largely in the darkness of error (John 3.19). To believe in Jesus, the "light of the world" (John 8.12), is to turn from darkness. Believers are children of light (John 3.21, 12.35–36, 46).

Above all, believers in Christ form a community distinguished by mutual love. Jesus' only explicit commandment in the Fourth Gospel is that his followers are to love one another (John 13.34, 15.12). This love creates a perfect union (John 17.23), because it is a response both to Jesus' love for his disciples and the Father's love for the Son (John 17.26).

dom of God" only twice, and in the same context (John 3.3, 5), and even then he gives it his own particular interpretation. Elsewhere in the Fourth Gospel, Jesus speaks of "my kingdom" and accepts the title "king" (John 18.36–37). But there are indications in the synoptic gospels, too, that the kingdom is bound up with the person and work of Jesus (Luke 11.20), and he appears as its sovereign in some sayings that Matthew and Luke attribute to him (Matt. 16.19, 16.28, 25.31–46; Luke 22.29).

In the Fourth Gospel, Jesus predominantly refers to himself as the Son and to God as his Father. The synoptists also represent the Father-Son relationship as a central feature in their portrayal of Jesus (see pp.166–7), but the concept is carried much further in John. Here, Jesus is the Son of God in a unique sense: he is himself divine, and is described as such in the gospel's prologue (John 1.1–18), where the main themes of the work are outlined, and in the confession (avowal of faith) of the disciple Thomas (John 20.28), just before what was probably the original end of the gospel (John 20.31).

Jesus repeatedly says that God is unknown and unknowable to human beings (John 5.37, 6.46) but is revealed in his Son, and that this is the whole purpose of his ministry. For John, simply to see Jesus is to realize his identity as the Son of God and to receive his gift of eternal life (John 6.40) (see box, opposite), and the same reward is assured to those who attend to his words (John 5.24). Those who see the Son see also the Father (John 14.8–10); the Father can be approached only through the Son (John 14.6), because the two are in complete and perfect union (John 10.30, 14.11). The work of the Son is not his own and he does nothing of his own volition (John 5.19, 8.28–29), but he simply carries out the Father's will in utter filial obedience (John 5.30, 6.38). The Father entrusts the Son with total authority because he loves him (John 3.35). John's distinctive teaching about the Father and Son may represent the development of a tradition about Jesus that is traceable also in two of the synoptic gospels (Matt. 11.27; Luke 10.22).

It is hardly surprising that the title "Son of God" for Jesus is used more freely in John's gospel than in Matthew, Mark, and Luke. But John also brings out clearly the humanity of Jesus. Whatever is meant by the term "Son of Man" in the synoptic gospels (see pp.168–9), John gives this phrase a particular sense: it expresses the evangelist's distinctive doctrine about the person of Christ in which Jesus is perceived as the heavenly savior who descends from, and ascends to, the Father (John 3.13, 6.62).

The Throne of God ("Mourning Trinity"), by the Master of Flémalle (fl. 1410–1440). God the Father, enthroned in heaven, holds the body of the crucified Son; the Spirit hovers in the form of a dove. John's gospel contrasts the earthly world with the heavenly realm from which Jesus descended (John 3.13) to bring eternal life to believers (John 3.36, 6.47). His heavenly glory belonged to him before creation (John 17.5) and was visible throughout his earthly life (John 1.14). It was revealed in his miracles (John 2.11, 11.40) and was demonstrated supremely not so much in the Resurrection as in the Crucifixion (John 17.1).

INTERPRETATIONS

How Jesus Saw Himself	158	The Patristic Period	174
The Healer of Body and Soul	158	Jesus and Gnosticism	176
The Prophet	160	Founder of the Church?	178
Master, Rabbi, Lord	162	The Apocalyptic Jesus	180
Messiah	164	The Revolutionary	182
Son of God	166	The Mystic	184
Son of Man	168	Jesus and Feminism	186
		Judaism and the Church	188
The Man and the Message	170	Jesus and Islam	190
The Early Church	170	In Search of the Jesus of	
Jewish and Gentile Christians	172	History	192

ABOVE: Christ Giving the Keys to St Peter, *a mosaic (ca. 500CE) in the Church of Santa Costanza, Rome. The scene is based on a disputed passage (Matt. 16.18–19), and the extent to which Jesus can be viewed as the founder of the Church remains the subject of debate (see pp.178–9).*
OPPOSITE: *This chapel in the Church of the Holy Sepulchre, Jerusalem, is said to mark the site of the Crucifixion, an event that has been central to the interpretation of Jesus and his mission.*

THE HEALER OF BODY AND SOUL

Steps leading down to the ancient pool of Siloam in Jerusalem, where Jesus sent a blind man to be cured, according to the Fourth Gospel (John 9.7).

HEALINGS
- Blindness (Mark 10.46–52 and parallels; Mark 8.22–26; Matt. 9.27–31)
- Leprosy (Mark 1.40–45 and parallels; Luke 17.11–19)
- Fever (Mark 1.29–31 and parallels)
- Hemorrhage (Mark 5.25–34 and parallels)
- Withered hand (Mark 3.1–6 and parallels)
- Deaf mute (Mark 7.31–37; Matt. 15.29–31)
- Paralysis (Matt. 8.5–13; Luke 7.1–10; Mark 2.1–12 and parallels)
- Crippled woman (Luke 13.10–17)
- Dropsy (Luke 14.1–6)
- Official's son (John 4.46–53)
- Crippled man (John 5.2–9)
- Blindness (John 9.1–12)

EXORCISMS
- Man at Capernaum (Mark 1.24–28; Luke 4.31–37)
- Gerasene/Gadarene/Gergesene demoniac (Mark 5.1–20 and parallels)
- Mute demoniac (Matt. 9.32–34)
- Blind mute demoniac (Matt. 12.22)
- Syro-Phoenician woman's daughter (Mark 7.24–30; Matt. 15.21–28)
- Boy with a spirit (Mark 9.14–29 and parallels)

Jesus' acts of healing and exorcism (see pp.94–7) formed the major part of his activity and made the greatest impression upon those around him. In the first instance, Jesus' healings were a response to individual suffering— the gospels speak of him being moved with pity in the presence of afflicted persons. This reflects his particular concern for social outcasts, because those with physical disabilities, such as lepers, were often shunned by their fellow citizens.

The distinct structure of each healing story in the gospels (see p.94) represents the form in which such accounts were treasured and passed on in the early Church. To a certain extent they may be influenced by the standard ways in which the miracle cures of other contemporary healers, both Jewish and pagan, were described. Certainly, Jesus would have regarded himself in some respects as one among many charismatic healers and exorcists (see box, p.96) in Palestine, and the gospels indicate that some of his opponents viewed him in that light. He is recorded as recognizing the power of other miracle workers (Matt. 12.27; Mark 9.38–39; Luke 9.49–50, 11.19).

But Jesus was also significantly different from other wonder-working figures, because his healings had a great underlying purpose. When John the Baptist's disciples ask Jesus whether he is the "Coming One"—the Messiah—Jesus replies by referring to his healing miracles in words that are derived from messianic prophecies in the Hebrew Scriptures: "Go and tell John what you hear and see: the blind receive their sight, the lame walk, the lepers are cleansed, the deaf hear, the dead are raised, and the poor have good news brought to them" (Matt. 11.2–6 and Luke 7.18–23, citing Isa. 26.19, 35.5–6, 61.1). Much of what Jesus did, therefore, tended to prove that he was indeed the expected Messiah, and distinguished him from the Baptist, who performed no miracles (John 10.41).

Jesus saw his healings—especially the exorcisms—in an eschatological light. That is, they indicated that the present epoch was nearing its end and a new age was dawning as the kingdom of God was being realized (Matt. 10.7–8,12.28; Luke 10.9; 11.20). The healings and exorcisms were not simply remarkable cures of physical disorders but the means by which individual men and women received the kingdom, brought to them in the person of Jesus, with the consequence that their whole existence was transformed and the reign of God became a reality in their lives. For Jesus, faith in him as God's manifestation and the acceptance, through him, of divine forgiveness were the conditions required of a person who wished to be healed (see box, opposite).

It is remarkable that of all the numerous recorded wonder-workers of the time, none is credited with as many miracles as Jesus. Matthew, Mark, and Luke record a total of some thirteen incidents of healing and six cases of exorcism, covering a considerable range of physical and mental conditions that are summarized—with considerable medical awareness—by Matthew (Matt. 4.24). The narratives that describe the restoring to life of a dead person should perhaps be added to this list (Mark 5.35–43 and parallels; Luke 7.11–17; John 11.1–44; see box, p.95). There are also three accounts of healings in the Fourth Gospel, although John records no acts of exorcism.

Compared with the stories told of other healers, the gospel accounts of Jesus' cures are marked by sobriety and restraint. The evangelists report that Jesus appealed to those whom he healed to keep their cures secret (Matt. 9.30, 12.15–21; Mark 1.41, 5.43, 7.36; Luke 8.56), perhaps indicating that Jesus, unlike other wonder-workers, did not wish to claim personal credit for his miracles.

HEALING, FORGIVENESS, AND FAITH

When Jesus says, in the account of the cure of the paralytic, "Your sins are forgiven" (Mark 2.5 and parallels), he simply means "You are healed." In the gospel accounts, this is regarded by the Jewish religious teachers as an extraordinary and blasphemous claim on his part, since only God could forgive sin. But Jesus would not necessarily have been presuming divine status. The idea that forgiveness of sin was a prerequisite of healing was familiar in Judaism. For example, a text from Qumran called *The Prayer of Nabonidus* relates how a Jewish exorcist cured a Babylonian monarch by forgiving his sins.

More notable is the fact that faith is several times said to be necessary for healing to take place. Either the actual sufferer must have faith, or those concerned for him or her, such as the centurion of Capernaum (Matt. 8.13; Luke 7.9–10) and the friends of the paralytic. At one level, "faith" means confidence in Jesus' ability to heal, but at another it probably means the recognition of Jesus' unique status and character. So the centurion has faith in Jesus' supreme authority, contrasted with the general lack of faith in Jesus among his fellow Jews. By the same token, lack of faith inhibits healing. Jesus is said to have been unable to perform more than a few cures in his own home town of Nazareth because of the unbelief of the inhabitants (Matt.13.58; Mark 6.5–6). This statement may well be reliable, since Christians are unlikely to have invented a tradition that showed Jesus as possessing limited powers.

Jesus Heals the Paralytic, *from the* Bible Moralisée *(French, ca. 1240). Jesus cured a paralyzed man with the words: "Stand up and take your mat [Matt. and Luke: 'bed'] and walk" (Mark 2.9, 2.11 and parallels; compare John 5.11–12).*

THE PROPHET

Peter's confession at Caesarea Philippi
(Mark 8.27–33 and parallels; see pp.106–7)
sets Jesus on a higher plane than all other
prophets. However, it seems that his
disciples venerated him as a prophet for the
most part because of his miracles and his
teachings. Thus the two disciples on the
road to Emmaus following the Crucifixion
described Jesus as "a prophet mighty in
deed and word before God and all the
people" (Luke 24.19), and Peter in Acts
speaks of him as one through whom God
accomplished "deeds of power, wonders,
and signs" (Acts 2.22).

The gospels attest that Jesus was widely regarded as a prophet. It was as
a prophet that the crowds hailed him on his entry into Jerusalem (Matt.
21.11), and his miraculous healings led people to recognize his prophetic
status (Luke 7.16; John 6.14, 9.17).

Such popular acceptance of Jesus as a prophet was something of which
his opponents were very much aware (Matt. 21.46). They sought to dis-
prove his entitlement to such a status by attempting to show that he lacked
the superior knowledge or "second sight" that was believed to characterize a genuine prophet (Matt. 26.68; Luke 7.39, 22.64). Many biblical
prophets had enjoyed this gift—for example, the blind Ahijah was able to
penetrate the disguise of King Jeroboam's wife (1 Kings 14.1–18) when she
asked him to foretell the future. In the gospels, Jesus demonstrates that he
does indeed possess such abilities when he tells the Samaritan woman
things about her past that he could not have known otherwise: she
instantly acknowledges him as a prophet (John 4.16–19). Matthew, Mark,
and Luke all record how, before he entered Jerusalem, Jesus told his disciples that there would be a donkey's colt for him to ride waiting on the
Mount of Olives (Mark 11.2–4).

Although Jesus never explicitly called himself a prophet, the concept

The Transfiguration, *by Duccio di
Buoninsegna (ca. 1260–1318). Jesus
stands between the greatest prophets
of Israel's past, Elijah and Moses, whom he
both succeeds and transcends (see box,
p.106). The disciples Peter, John, and
James look on in awe. (Compare
illustration on p.167.)*

FALSE PROPHETS

There is evidence that the Jewish religious authorities regarded Jesus as a "false prophet" who was corrupting and disturbing the populace. He was accused before Pilate of "perverting" and "stirring up" the people (Luke 23.2, 5, 14), and of being an "impostor" and deceiver (Matt. 27.62–64). A similar charge of deception is leveled at him in the Fourth Gospel (John 7.12, 47). Such an allegation may well have constituted a formal indictment under the Jewish law, based on biblical descriptions of false prophets who entice the nation to apostasy or are otherwise unauthorized by God. Such individuals merit the death penalty (Deut. 13.1–5, 18.20).

Jesus himself is represented as denouncing false messiahs and prophets who would lead the people astray (Matt. 24.24; Mark 13.22). There was clearly widespread concern about such individuals at the time, and with good reason, because a whole string of them appeared in Palestine during the early years of the first century CE. They were a major contribution to the region's troubles: the Jewish historian Josephus mentions that a considerable number of self-styled "prophets"

were in the service of those who led rebellions against the Romans. As well as insisting on the title "prophet," most of these figures foretold the deliverance of the Jewish nation by supernatural means, and claimed to perform prodigious miracles. Josephus labels them unequivocally as "impostors" and names two in particular, who are also referred to in the New Testament: Theudas, who was active sometime between 44 and 46CE (Acts 5.36) and a man known as "the Egyptian," active between 51 and 60CE, for whom Paul was mistaken (Acts 21.38).

These two men enjoyed mass support, and it is not surprising that Jesus' popularity among ordinary people should have led the educated classes to regard him as just one more prophetic troublemaker, who posed a threat to law and order and should therefore be suppressed. To a greater or lesser extent, the high priests, Sadducees, and Pharisees all stood for accommodation with the Roman authorities in the interests of avoiding the national catastrophe that rebellion would inevitably bring—and as indeed it finally did with the great Jewish revolt that began in 66CE.

seems to have been an important element in his self-understanding. Twice, he is clearly referring to himself when he speaks of what a prophet may expect to experience and the ultimate fate awaiting him, (Mark 6.4 and parallels; Luke 13.33). When he rebukes Nazareth, he draws a parallel with the actions of the great prophets Elijah and Elisha (Luke 4.25–27), figures who had come to be revered in Judaism as the supreme wonderworkers (Sir. 48.1–14). Several of Jesus' miracles parallel those performed by these two figures, notably his revival of the widow's son at Nain (1 Kings 17.17–24; 2 Kings 4.18–38; see p.95) and the miraculous feedings of a great crowd with few provisions (2 Kings 4.42–44; see pp.98–9).

Jesus' awareness of himself as a prophet may well have been initiated and confirmed by his association with John the Baptist, another Elijah-like prophetic figure (Matt. 3.4; 2 Kings 1.8). John too had been acclaimed as a prophet (Matt. 11.7–9, 14.5, 21.26; Luke 7.25–26), but the gospels all emphasize that the Baptist's ministry was only preparing the way for the appearance of the even greater figure of Jesus, the final Judge and Savior. This idea probably derives from a passage of Deuteronomy in which God promises to raise up another prophet like Moses, through whom the deity will speak (Deut. 18.17–19). Peter cites these verses in reference to Jesus during his speech to the crowd on the Temple Mount (Acts 3.22–23).

JUDAISM IN THE RABBINIC AGE

Soon after Jesus' time, the word *rabbi* was to become primarily a title, and one that genuinely and almost exclusively denoted a trained and officially authorized interpreter of the law. This was largely the consequence of the destruction of Jerusalem in 70CE, when the Temple and its priesthood came to an end and most of the different sects and parties within the Jewish community (see pp.34–7) ceased to exist.

Only the Pharisees and their scribes (see p.30) survived, and it was they who subsequently were to determine the character of Judaism. They became the sole authoritative religious leaders and delivered binding judgments on a whole range of issues; their authority was accepted on account of their profound knowledge of scripture and their highly respected, and distinctive, tradition of interpretation.

The Pharisees established academies in which legal wisdom and expertise were passed on from one generation of scholars to the next. The interpretative work of successive scholars was eventually collected in the Mishnah (ca. 200CE) and the Talmud (ca. 400–500CE). In this period, commonly referred to as the rabbinic or Talmudic age, the word *rabbi* came to mean a person who had undergone extensive and exhaustive training in the Jewish law and emerged as a recognized teacher and spiritual guide. This status was acknowledged in a formal ordination rite that conferred on them the right and authority to teach.

MASTER, RABBI, LORD

On a number of occasions in the gospels Jesus is addressed by the Hebrew term *rabbi* or its Aramaic equivalent, *rabbouni* (Matt. 26.25, 26.49; Mark 9.5, 10.51, 11.21, 14.45; John 1.38, 1.49, 3.2, 4.31, 6.25, 9.2, 11.8, 20.16). The appearance of such non-Greek words in the gospels suggests that they represent a reliable tradition faithfully preserved by the evangelists. *Rabbi/rabbouni* literally means "my master," and in Jesus' time this was a reverential greeting to a person of authority—the term is also addressed to the Baptist (John 3.26). The Fourth Gospel explicitly translates *rabbi* and *rabbouni* as "teacher" (John 1.38, 20.16), and when Jesus is addressed as "teacher" (Greek *didaskale*, *epistata*) elsewhere in the gospels it probably represents one or other of these Semitic terms.

Like other teachers, Jesus taught in the synagogues, expounded on disputed points of the Jewish law, and gathered around him a body of students—this is the proper meaning of the word "disciple" (Latin *discipulus*, Greek *mathetes*, "pupil"). Commentators have often claimed that Jesus must therefore have been a "scribe," a highly trained and widely recognized interpreter of scripture (see p.30), and have seen evidence for this in the fact that his followers and others addressed him as *rabbi*. Similarly, occasional attempts by scholars to see Jesus as a dissident Pharisee have partly been based on the fact that he was called *rabbi*.

However, in Jesus' day, the term *rabbi* had not acquired the distinct sense it was later to possess of a religious teacher or scribe trained in the Pharisaic tradition (see sidebar, left). The great Pharisaic teachers who were Jesus' contemporaries or near-contemporaries—Hillel, Shammai, and others—were never called *rabbi*. There is also every reason to believe the

The 1st-century synagogue at Masada, a former palace-fortress of Herod the Great destroyed in 73CE (see also p.183). Pharisees and other religious teachers taught most frequently in the synagogues, and Jesus himself is reported as having done so. They would probably have stood in the center of the floor to teach, while the congregation sat either on the ground or on stone benches around the walls.

JESUS THE "LORD"

According to the gospels, Jesus was regularly addressed as "lord" (Greek *kurios*, also transliterated *kyrios*). There is considerable debate over this word, particularly with regard to its use in Acts and the letters of Paul. Influenced by the fact that the title "Lord" came to indicate Jesus' divinity, numerous authorities have concluded that the appearance of the term in the gospels must be attributable to the early Church. According to this theory, the title derives from after Jesus' lifetime: he never thought of himself as "lord" or was addressed as such either by his disciples or others.

However, in the time of Jesus, *kurios* and the corresponding Aramaic term *mar*—the phrase *maranatha* ("come, lord"; 1 Cor. 16.22) was probably an invocation current in the very early Church—both had a wide range of applications. Like *rabbi* and *rabbouni* (see main text), they basically designated a male figure of authority. *Kurios* was a common title for God, but it could also be used of the head of a family (Matt. 21.30), the owner of a large property (Matt. 13.27), or a ruler (Matt. 27.63). The vocative form *kurie*, used in direct address (as in another Christian invocation, *kyrie eleison*, "lord, have mercy"), could be little more than a polite way of addressing a man, and is often translated simply as "sir" (John 4.11, 5.7).

In the miracle stories, Jesus is addressed as "Lord" by his disciples as an expression of awe at his supernatural power (Matt. 8.25, 14.28; Luke 5.8; John 21.7). *Mar* was similarly bestowed on other charismatic Jewish wonder-workers.

The Miraculous Draft of Fishes, from the church of Sant' Angelo in Formis, Capua, Italy. In John 21.7, the disciples declare "It is the Lord!" in acknowledgment of Jesus' miraculous powers.

In the gospels, Jesus only once describes himself as "lord" (John 13.13), but there is no evidence that he actively prevented others from doing so, and other passages suggest that the idea of his "lordship"—however defined—may well have formed part of his self-understanding. Like *rabbi* and *rabbouni*, both *kurios* and *mar* can have the sense of "authoritative teacher" (Luke 12.42, 18.6; John 6.68), and Jesus rebukes those who call him "lord" but are not prepared to obey his teachings (Matt. 7.21–23; Luke 6.46).

gospels' claim that Jesus' methods of teaching were in fact very different from those of the Pharisees. To begin with, there is no evidence that he ever received a scribal education, and contemporaries perceived his teaching to be different from that of the scribes (Matt. 7.29; Mark 1.22). The scribes themselves questioned Jesus' status as a recognized teacher (Mark 11.27–28 and parallels) and considered that his teaching betrayed a lack of formal training (John 7.15).

While *rabbi* eventually came to refer most often to religious scholars and teachers, in Jesus' day it had a wider application and could also be addressed to Jesus as, for example, a great miracle-worker (Mark 10.51; but note NRSV: "my teacher"). Jesus appears to have been happy to be called *rabbi*, and to have regarded the authority it denoted as applying to him in a unique sense. His followers are "not to be called *rabbi*," because there is only one teacher—the Messiah—and they are no more than his students (Matt. 23.8–10).

MESSIAH

Ancient remains on the traditional site of Jesus' trial before the high priest, where he was accused of claiming to be the Messiah, according to the gospels.

OPPOSITE: King David Enthroned, *a late 14th-century French tapestry. Over the centuries, a vast quantity of Christian art has been inspired by the dramatic story of David, the shepherd boy turned great king of Israel (ruled ca. 1000–ca. 965BCE) and traditional author of the Psalms. His revered status in Christianity derives above all from the belief that he was the ancestor, and prefigurement, of Christ (see sidebar, opposite). Thus David's defeat of the giant Goliath (1. Sam. 17.48–51) was held to prefigure Christ's triumph over Satan and his forces, and David's words about the shepherd who protects his flock (1 Sam 17.34–35) were seen as an annunciation of the coming of Jesus, the Good Shepherd.*

It has been a central tenet of the Christian Church from its earliest beginnings that Jesus was the Messiah, or Christ. But nowhere in the gospels does Jesus state "I am the Messiah" or—publicly at least—accept the title. For this reason, commentators have often questioned whether the concept of messiahship formed part of his self-understanding at all, or whether it derives instead from the faith of the early Church.

According to Luke, Jesus perceived himself as one anointed by the Spirit, as set out in Isaiah 61.1–2, which Jesus reads out in the synagogue at Nazareth (Luke 4.16–21). Evidence from Qumran shows that in Jesus' day these verses were strongly associated with the coming Messiah; by using the passage at all, therefore, Jesus was effectively making a messianic claim. In Matthew, Jesus also alludes to Isaiah (Matt. 11.4–6), and the gospel explicitly refers to his deeds as those of the Messiah (Matt. 11.2).

However, Jesus spoke about only one aspect of popular messianic expectation, namely the reign of justice and renewal that the Messiah would bring (Matt. 19.28; Luke 22.30). The idea of the Messiah as a royal and military figure (see sidebar, opposite) are entirely absent from his words, but his followers do appear to have thought of him in such terms (Acts 1.6), and his opponents call him "Messiah" sarcastically, evidently believing that Jesus had falsely claimed that status (Matt. 26.68; Mark 15.32 and parallels).

Jesus seems never to have explicitly rejected the title Messiah, perhaps because people might have understood this as a denial that he was *any* sort of redeemer. But he did not promote its use and sought to discourage most of the expectations associated with it. Thus demons who recognize Jesus as the Messiah (Luke 4.41) are forbidden to speak, and a request for a place of honor in Jesus' "kingdom" (Matt. 20.20–23; Mark 10.35–40) elicits Jesus' refusal of the kingly role (Mark 10.41–45 and parallels). When some people ask him directly if he is the Messiah, Jesus does not give a direct affirmation but points to the testimony of his miracles (John 10.24–25). When Peter confesses his belief that Jesus is the Messiah (see pp.106–7), Jesus acquiesces, but forbids his followers to proclaim him as such. This is because—as Luke, at least, suggests (Luke 9.21–22)—Jesus' destiny as Messiah was not to lead Israel in kingly triumph, but to undergo suffering and death. Peter cannot accept this and receives a severe rebuke.

How Jesus perceived his messiahship perhaps emerges best from the accounts of his trials (see pp.118–21). In Matthew and Luke, Jesus gives an ambiguous answer to the question of whether he is the Messiah (Matt. 26.64; Luke 22.67–70). This is perhaps more likely to be authentic than Mark, who gives Jesus' reply as "I am" (Mark 14.62), because for Jesus either to admit or deny his messiahship outright would be to lay himself open to serious consequences—the wrath of the authorities or rejection by many followers. When Pilate asks if he is the "King of the Jews"—the messianic claim that was of most concern to a Gentile ruler—Jesus' response is again equivocal (Mark 15.2 and parallels).

The Fourth Gospel represents Jesus as explicitly claiming the messianic title on at least one occasion (John 4.25–26), albeit in a private conversation. In John's account of the trial, Jesus once more equivocates about accepting the designation "king." He acknowledges that he has a kingdom, but it is "not from this world"—it was not to be achieved by force, as most Jews would have expected of the Messiah, and as Pilate might have feared (John 18.33–37).

Perhaps the soundest conclusion is that Jesus regarded himself as the fulfillment of the general hope among Jews for a redeemer who would herald a new epoch (see sidebar, right). But he was aware that his own understanding of his person and mission did not truly correspond to any of the concepts of the Messiah then current, and he avoided the public use of the title "Messiah" because of its nationalistic and revolutionary implications. In the volatile political climate of Roman Palestine, anyone suspected of claiming to be the Messiah was unlikely to survive long, and so it proved with Jesus: the inscription affixed to his cross, which all four gospels record, makes it clear that he was crucified as a dangerous messianic revolutionary (see sidebar, p.183).

THE SON OF DAVID

In the first century CE there was a general expectation among Jews that God would shortly intervene to end the present age and usher in a new world of perfect righteousness. Some believed that God would act directly, others that he would send an intermediary: his "Anointed One," or Messiah (Hebrew *Mashiach*, Greek *Christos*). "Messiah" was a title given in the Hebrew Bible to Israelite rulers of King David's dynasty. The Savior was thus seen as a king, a "son" (descendant) of David, who would overcome Israel's oppressors.

The gospel genealogies of Jesus (see pp.62–3) presuppose an early belief that Joseph came from Bethlehem, David's city, and was of David's line. (Matt. 1.20; Luke 1.27, 2.4; Rom. 1.3). Jesus and his close disciples do not use the title Son of David, but others hail him as such (as at Mark 10.46–52 and parallels; Matt. 21.9).

At one point, Jesus apparently denies that the Messiah would be a Son of David (Mark 12.35–37 and parallels), perhaps to counter hopes that the Savior would be a military figure who would end Roman rule.

THE "SON" AS MIRACLE-WORKER
In the gospels, the phrase "Son of God" is also used to mark Jesus out as a worker of miracles, and there is evidence that the title was applied to other charismatic Galilean wonder-workers of the time. When Jesus exorcizes demons, they address him as Son of God in recognition of his miraculous healing power (Mark 3.11, 5.7 and parallels). Satan, too, expected the Son of God to be able to perform miracles, as the Temptation shows (see pp.86–7).

The one occasion on which Jesus' followers address him directly by the title is in the context of a miracle (Matt. 14.33), and the onlookers at Golgotha challenge him to prove his status as Son of God by freeing himself from the cross (Matt. 27.39–40, 42–43). The expression of awe uttered by the centurion at the Crucifixion ("Truly this man was God's Son!") is provoked by the marvels that accompanied Jesus' death (Matt. 27.51–54).

SON OF GOD

To profess that Jesus is the Son of God has been central to Christian faith from the earliest times, as the New Testament shows. Nowhere in the gospels is the title found on Jesus' own lips, but his habit of addressing God as his Father (see pp.146–7) implies not only that he saw himself as *a* son of God but that he perceived himself to be God's son in a special sense.

Twice in the gospels Jesus speaks of himself as "the Son" in reference to God as his Father, but scholars often debate whether these instances can be regarded as authentic sayings of Jesus. In the first passage, Jesus states that "neither the angels of heaven nor the Son" know when "the end" will come, but only the Father (Mark 13.32; Matt. 24.36). These may be genuine words of Jesus, since early Christians are unlikely to have created such an admission of ignorance on Jesus' part, placing himself on a lower footing than God. The phrase "nor the Son" is omitted in many early manuscripts of Matthew, which tends to support this idea.

In the second passage, Jesus says that the Son alone knows the Father and the Father alone knows the Son (Matt. 11.27; Luke 10.22). Although it is likely that the words as we have them are those of the early Church, they may well be based on an authentic expression by which Jesus affirmed his special intimacy with his heavenly Father.

The parable of the Wicked Tenants (Mark 12.1–11 and parallels) reaches its climax when the absentee landowner sends his son to collect his

THE MESSIANIC SON

The term "Son of God" is closely associated with the title "Messiah" (Matt.16.16, 26.63; Mark 14.61; Luke 22.67–70). In the Hebrew Scriptures the reigning monarch was called God's son (Ps. 2.7; 2 Sam. 7.14), but by the time of Jesus, such references were understood to refer to a future descendant of King David: the Messiah (see pp.164–5).

God's declaration in Psalm 2.7 ("You are my Son, today I have begotten you") was particularly significant for the first Christians (Acts 13.33), and Mark and Luke echo these words in their accounts of Jesus' baptism (Mark 1.11; Luke 3.22). It served as a formula whereby God adopted a person as his son and is also reflected in Luke's Nativity narrative, where the future child is to be a royal figure, who will be designated by God as "the Son of the Most High" and "Son of God," and will receive "the throne of his ancestor David" (Luke 1.32, 35).

The title "Son of God" is particularly characteristic of the Fourth Gospel, where it is also linked with the kingship of Israel and other messianic concepts (John 1.49, 11.27, 20.31). But the evangelist also carries the idea much further. Jesus' divine sonship is wholly unique (John 1.18). He is a preexistent entity who has always been with the Father (John 13.3), unknown to the world until revealed in his incarnation (John 6.42). This notion is comparable with some contemporary Jewish beliefs that the Messiah would remain hidden in heaven until he was revealed on Earth.

For John, Jesus is not simply adopted as God's offspring but is literally his son, "equal to God" (John 5.18), sharing his divinity and exercising full divine authority (John 3.35–36, 17.10). Jesus expresses it unequivocally: "The Father and I are one" (John 10.30).

The Transfiguration, *a 14th-century Russian icon (Novgorod School). Eastern depictions of this momentous event (compare the Western version on p.160) typically show Jesus within a* mandorla *(almond-shape) representing the "bright cloud" of heavenly radiance from which the divine voice declared "This is my Son, the Beloved!" The three disciples are shown physically hurled to the ground by the sight. The spearhead-shaped figure represents the mountain peak, but its three points tapering to one also symbolize the three-in-one Godhead of Father, Son, and Holy Spirit.*

dues from the tenants of his vineyard. All commentators agree that the parable is an allegory, and that the landowner represents God, the vineyard Israel, and the son Jesus. Jesus here speaks of himself as God's son in a unique sense. Jesus' followers are to become sons of God (Matt. 5.45; Luke 6.35), but they enjoy this status because they follow the teaching and example of Jesus: he is the first and true Son of God. The Hebrew Scriptures frequently describe the people of Israel as God's sons (Exod. 4.22; Jer. 31.20), and in later writings the righteous Israelite is specifically God's son (Sir. 4.10; Wisd. of Solomon 2.17–18).

Perhaps most significant for Jesus' self-understanding was the occasion of his baptism (see pp.84–5), when he was endowed with the Spirit, and the heavenly voice proclaimed him, for the first time, "My Son, the Beloved." This expression clearly implies uniqueness. In this way, according to the gospels, Jesus' real character and vocation were revealed to him—to be immediately tested and confirmed by his victorious encounter with the devil in the wilderness (see pp.86–7).

OFFSPRING OF THE DIVINE

It has been frequently observed that when people address Jesus as Son of God in the gospels, the title does not necessarily imply divinity in the sense that it was later understood in Christian theology, of a complete sharing in God's nature. In the Judaism of the first century CE, the concept of divinity was quite broad and any heavenly supernatural being could be considered a "Son of God." For example, in the Hebrew Scriptures and other Jewish writings, "Son of God" can refer to angels and other celestial beings (Gen. 6.2, 4; Ps. 29.1; Job 1.6), and it is not impossible that Jesus was viewed in this light.

At his Transfiguration, when the voice of God proclaims Jesus "my son," he is transformed into a heavenly being, like Moses and Elijah (see pp.106–7, 186–7). It is notable that it was the exorcized demons, themselves supernatural entities, along with their leader Satan, who recognized the true nature of Jesus as Son of God (see sidebar on opposite page).

SON OF MAN

THE "SON OF MAN" BEFORE JESUS
It has been claimed that the concept of a messianic figure known as the "Son of Man" existed in Judaism before the time of Jesus. Daniel 7.13–14 speaks of "one like a son of man," who comes on clouds and receives universal dominion. Later rabbis certainly identified this figure with the Messiah, but there is no evidence that they did so as early as Jesus' day—nor did they use the term "Son of Man" as a distinct messianic designation.

Outside the Bible, the apocryphal book 2 Esdras has a passage obviously dependent on Daniel 7.13 that speaks of "something like the figure of a man" rising from the sea and flying on the clouds (2 Esd. 13.3). This being is subsequently identified with the Messiah, and no doubt this represents the beginning of rabbinic interpretation of the figure in Daniel—2 Esdras may date from as late as ca. 100CE. But, again, "something like the figure of a man" does not in itself specifically denote the Messiah.

It is the writings known as the books of Enoch that have attracted most attention from New Testament scholars. Within 1 Enoch is a section called the "Similitudes of Enoch" that refers some sixteen times to a "Son of Man" figure as a divine messianic being. Again, however, this passage also derives from Daniel 7, using the same imagery, and cannot be taken to prove that "Son of Man" was a distinct concept or title. Recent evidence suggests that the Similitudes, too, may be very much later than Jesus' lifetime.

The expression "Son of Man" occurs more than sixty times in the gospels, yet it is found only three times elsewhere in the New Testament (Acts 7.56; Rev. 1.13, 14.14) and is used only in sayings attributed to Jesus. Debate over the significance of the phrase has been, and continues to be, very wide-ranging. The Greek term used by the evangelists does not sound idiomatic and almost all scholars now agree that it represents a literal translation of an original Aramaic phrase. The Semitic background leaves no doubt that "Son of Man" means primarily "the man" or "a man," and it can also be an indefinite pronoun, the equivalent of "one" as in "one does."

It has also been proposed that "the son of man" was employed simply as a circumlocution for "I." There are some complicated linguistic problems connected with this last proposal, but it appears to be gaining acceptance among New Testament scholarship. The Aramaic evidence suggests that a speaker might say "the son of man" instead of "I" out of modesty or

Banias, ancient Caesarea Philippi, where Peter acknowledged Jesus as Messiah (see pp.106–7). The gospel accounts of this episode provide strong evidence that Jesus used the Aramaic phrase "Son of Man" as a way of referring to himself. In Matthew, Jesus asks: "Who do people say that the Son of Man is?" but Mark and Luke give the question as: "Who do people say I am?" (Matt. 16.13; Mark 8.27; Luke 9.18).

JESUS AND THE APOCALYPTIC "SON"

Even if the term "Son of Man" represents a colloquial idiom used instead of "I" (see main text), the question still arises as to whether, in using it, Jesus saw the phrase as holding a special significance. It was the description that he used most commonly of himself, which suggests that this was so.

It has often been asserted that the concept of the "Son of Man" as an apocalyptic figure already existed in some Jewish circles (see sidebar, opposite) and that Jesus employed the expression as a definite messianic title. Whether this is true or not, it is quite likely that Jesus did envisage both a present and a future role for himself, and that his view of his future role was influenced by the "Son of Man" figure in Daniel 7.13. The early Church may be responsible for the actual wording of Jesus' references to this passage—whether explicit (Mark 13.26, 14.62 and parallels) or implicit (Mark

A fresco in the cathedral of Anagni, Italy. The central winged being derives principally from the vision of Ezekiel (Ezek. 1.1–14; compare Rev. 4.8), which may have influenced Jesus' understanding of himself as Son of Man.

8.38 and parallels)—but they may genuinely be founded on Jesus' own view of himself as the coming divine agent in the final Judgment. This is analogous to his teaching of the kingdom of God (see pp.150–51) as both a present and a future reality.

It is also possible that Jesus was aware of God's repeated use of "son of man" (Hebrew *ben adam*; NRSV: "mortal") to address the prophet Ezekiel in the Hebrew Scriptures, and that the phrase therefore contributed to Jesus' awareness of his own role as a prophet. There is considerable evidence, particularly in John's gospel, that the book of Ezekiel influenced the New Testament.

reserve, and this could well be the case with Jesus, who often appears to have been cautious about making claims for himself, as he was with the title Messiah (see pp.164–5). "Son of man" could also be employed to soften an unacceptable or unpalatable statement. So when Jesus foretells his death to his disciples, he almost always refers to the fate of the "Son of Man" (Mark 8.31, 9.31, 10.33 and parallels; Luke 9.22).

According to one relatively recent hypothesis, "Son of Man" occurs in three distinct contexts: Jesus' activity and teaching during his ministry; statements concerning his death and resurrection; and passages dealing with his ascension and apocalyptic return. This categorization, however illuminating, has not convinced everyone. Some scholars continue to doubt whether Jesus himself ever employed the expression "Son of Man," while others view only the apocalyptic utterances as genuine: Jesus proclaimed the coming of the "Son of Man" (see box, above), but did not necessarily identify himself with this figure—this identification was only made later by his followers.

However, the fact that "Son of Man" is confined to the gospels and to the lips of Jesus, that it represents an original term in his own language, and that it rapidly fell out of use in Christian circles, tells against the view that it was a theological concept that developed in the early Church.

THE EARLY CHURCH

Crosses placed by worshipers outside the Church of the Holy Sepulchre, Jerusalem, revered by Christians as the traditional site of the Crucifixion.

Paul states that if Christ had not risen again, all Christian faith and teaching would be in vain (1 Cor. 15.12–19). Certainly, all the documents that make up the New Testament are written in the light of the firm conviction that Jesus rose from the dead, but it is the writings other than the gospels that most clearly express the early Church's belief in the resurrected Christ. The Acts of the Apostles and the Letters contain the first stages of what is known as "Christology": the continuing task of interpreting the significance of the person of Jesus Christ to the faith of the Church.

The New Testament authors use a wide range of titles and concepts to express this significance. One of the most basic themes is that the Resurrection was an act of divine exaltation, by which God had vindicated Jesus and conferred on him a position of supreme authority in the universe. Jesus had risen and been taken up to heaven, and would eventually return to restore all things (Acts 3.20–21; 1 Thess. 1.10). Jesus' Resurrection therefore both revealed and proclaimed him definitively as Messiah, Lord, and the Son of God (Acts 2.36; Rom. 1.4).

In interpreting the person of the risen Jesus, the early Christians naturally also turned to the Hebrew Scriptures. Paul compares Jesus with Adam:

HEBREWS AND CHRIST CRUCIFIED
The letter to the Hebrews provides the fullest interpretation of Jesus' death, depicting it throughout in terms taken directly from the Hebrew Scriptures. It was an atoning sacrifice (Heb. 2.17) and the fulfillment of Jeremiah's prophecy of a new covenant (Heb. 8.6–13). Above all, it showed Jesus to be the true high priest according to the order of Melchizedek (Heb. 5.6–10).

Hebrews compares Christ's saving work with the great annual ritual of the Day of Atonement (Yom Kippur), the occasion when, in ancient times, the high priest entered the Holy of Holies of the Temple with the atoning blood of sacrificial victims (Lev. 16.11–17). The equivalent exaltation of Jesus occurs when he enters heaven to come before the presence of God with his own atoning blood (Heb. 9.12, 9.24, 10.12). Jesus' self-offering is the perfect, once for all, sacrifice for sin—an act that entirely supersedes the need for the sacrifices of the old Israel (Heb. 7.26–28).

"WISDOM CHRISTOLOGY"

The New Testament writers identified Jesus with the biblical concept of Wisdom (1 Cor. 1.24, 30). In the Hebrew Scriptures and later Jewish texts, Wisdom is personified as the expression of the inner being of God and as his sole agent in the work of Creation. Wisdom is also the revelation of God and the means of salvation for human beings (Wisd. of Sol. 7.22–27). These characteristics are applied to Jesus Christ in several New Testament passages that are probably quotations from early Christian hymns. He is the visible image of the invisible God, the one through whom all things were created, who sustains all creation, and who, by his triumphal ascension to heaven, finally reconciles the world to the Father (1 Cor. 8.6; Col. 1.15–20; Heb. 1.2–4).

Wisdom Christology also inevitably meant that the early Church recognized its Lord as a preexistent divine being, who had been "with God" from before the Creation. This is most clearly expressed in the Fourth Gospel (John 1.1–18), but it is attested elsewhere in the New Testament, most notably in a hymn quoted by Paul, which describes Jesus as originally being "in the form of God" but then "taking the form of a slave, being born in human likeness" (Phil. 2.6–11). Similarly, Jesus—the exact imprint of God's being, superior to all angelic beings (Heb. 1.3–4)—was for a time "made lower than the angels" by sharing in ordinary human nature (Heb. 2.9, 14–17).

but while the disobedience of Adam had brought death into the world, the perfect obedience of Christ brought eternal life for believers (Rom. 5.12–21). Again, Paul describes Jesus as "the last Adam": the first Adam was "a man of dust," a physical being made from the dust of the ground, but the resurrected Christ is a man "from heaven" and "a life-giving spirit"—a spiritual being who transmits this character to his followers. Just as every human bears "the image of the man of dust," he or she will be resurrected through Christ "to bear the image of the man of heaven" (1 Cor. 15.45–49).

If the early Church saw Jesus as an exalted heavenly figure, its members also knew that he had first suffered the shameful death of crucifixion. Despite the fact that such a death was seen as humiliating by both Jew and Gentile (1 Cor. 1.23), its significance was central to the thought of all the New Testament writers—especially Paul, who saw the crucified Christ as the essence of the whole gospel (1 Cor. 2.1–2). In what may be examples of the earliest Christian preaching, Jesus' execution is represented as Israel's rejection of its true Messiah, with the Resurrection as God's reversal of that judgment (Acts 2.23–24, 3.13–15, 10.39–40). But there are already suggestions of the developed Christian idea that the death of Jesus had a broader saving purpose for humans—it is said to be part of God's plan (Acts 2.23) and foretold in Scripture (Acts 3.18).

Most simply, it could be said that Christ died to atone for the sins of humanity (Rom. 3.25; 1 Cor. 15.3; 2 Cor. 5.14; Gal. 1.4; 1 Pet. 3.18). The faithful interpreted this basic conviction in various ways, mainly through the use of images and concepts from the Hebrew Bible. The blood that Christ shed is compared with the blood ritual of the annual Jewish sacrifice of atonement, through which God is able to wipe away sins (Rom. 3.24–25; 1 John 2.2). The New Testament letters present Jesus as the true Passover lamb (1 Cor. 5.7; 1 Pet. 1.19), and portray his suffering in the same language used in Isaiah 53 to describe the figure of the "Suffering Servant," a figure who, in his death, bore the sins of many (1 Pet. 2.21–25; Isa. 53.5–12).

The idea of Jesus' death as a sacrifice on behalf of others is especially developed by Paul. On the Cross, Jesus took upon himself the curse of the old law (Gal. 3.10–14). In a paradoxical statement, Paul says that the wholly sinless one was made sin (2 Cor. 5.21)—taking on the sins of others and making them "righteous" in God's sight. Not only did the Cross annul the divine penalty for human sin but it also marked a decisive victory over the cosmic powers of evil (Col. 2.13–15), a triumph to be finally realized at Christ's second coming (1 Cor. 15.23–25).

The Last Judgment: Christ Enthroned and the Resurrection of the Dead, *from the Ingeborg Psalter (French, ca. 1210).*

PAUL AND THE JESUS OF HISTORY
It has sometimes been asserted that Paul fundamentally transformed what had been the earliest Christian faith, substituting for the historical Jesus a heavenly redeemer on the model of similar figures in the religions of the Greco-Roman world. In support of this assertion, it has been pointed out that Paul's letters show little knowledge of Jesus' life and teachings. But this claim is exaggerated. Apart from the fact that he lays great emphasis on the Cross—acknowledging the climactic historical event of Jesus' career (see main text)—Paul knows of Jesus' human birth (Gal. 4.4), his betrayal, and the Last Supper (1 Cor. 11.23–26), and also refers to examples of his teaching (1 Cor. 7.10, 9.14).

OPPOSITION TO PAUL

In his letters to the churches of Corinth, Philippi, and especially Galatia, Paul writes about various groups who oppose his mission. A number of commentators have suggested that this opposition represented a united Jewish Christian assault on Paul's teaching, but the situation was in fact more complex and it is far from clear in every instance that his adversaries were Jewish Christians. This does seem to have been the case in Galatia—although again Paul's opponents there probably represented only one particular Jewish Christian group.

This 12th-century French reliquary of wood, silver gilt, semiprecious stones, and glass, portrays Stephen, a prominent member of the Hellenist group in the early Church, who is revered as the first Christian martyr.

JEWISH AND GENTILE CHRISTIANS

Christianity began as one movement among the numerous currents within first-century Judaism (see pp.34–7). The first Christians regularly attended Temple worship (Acts 2.45) and some Pharisees who joined the Church continued to observe the provisions of the Jewish law (Acts 15.5). Peter's first sermons were addressed to Jews (Acts 2.14, 3.12). What distinguished the Christians from other Jews was their conviction that Jesus was the expected Messiah (Acts 2.36, 3.20) and that he had fulfilled the messianic prophecies addressed to Israel in the Hebrew Scriptures (Acts 3.22–26).

Within the Christian community, the Church in Jerusalem—headed by James, the brother of Jesus (see p.80)—was accorded special preeminence and authority. But tensions arose early on, and there emerged a distinct group of "Hellenists" (Acts 6.1), Greek-speaking Christians who probably began as members of a synagogue for Diaspora Jews (Acts 6.9). One member of this group, Stephen, was executed by stoning for speaking against the Temple and the Jewish law (Acts 6.14, 7.44–50), and his views provoked a wave of persecution by the Temple authorities. This seems to have affected only the Hellenists, who were expelled from Jerusalem. The apostles and other Aramaic-speaking Christians appear to have been left undisturbed (Acts 8.1), presumably because they were still considered to be within the fold of Judaism.

The dispersal of the Hellenists took the Christian mission beyond the boundaries of Israel, beginning with the preaching of Philip to the Samaritans (Acts 8.4). But the real crisis was brought about by the extensive and successful evangelization of Gentiles by Paul, who had begun as a Pharisee (Acts 23.6, 26.5) and a zealous persecutor of Christians (Acts 8.1–3). Paul held that his new converts were not required to observe the full Jewish law—especially with respect to circumcision—and his teaching of universal salvation through the death and resurrection of Jesus represented a markedly new development of the Christian gospel.

The New Testament indicates that the split between Jewish Christianity and Gentile Christianity, as advocated by Paul, was formalized by a pact whereby the Jerusalem Church took responsibility for evangelizing Jews, while Paul undertook to convert Gentiles (Gal. 2.9). Under this agreement, according to Acts 15, Gentile converts would have to obey only the "Noahide laws"—seven basic commands said to have been handed by God to Noah after the Flood. Jews had to obey the whole Torah, but any non-Jew who observed the Noahide laws (for example, the rules quoted in Acts 15.21, 25) was counted among "the righteous of the nations of the world."

JEWISH CHRISTIAN SECTS

The destruction of Jerusalem by the Romans in 70CE was the principal cause of the decline in Jewish Christianity, and determined that in future the Church would be a predominantly Gentile body. One source reports that the Christians of Jerusalem migrated to Pella in Transjordan, and from this time Jewish Christianity was increasingly marginalized and fragmented. Various sects survived until at least 300CE in different parts of the Near East. What little is known about them comes from references in the works of the Church Fathers (see p.174). They sometimes quote from Jewish Christian gospels, many of which were based on Matthew, the most "Jewish" of the canonical gospels. The Fathers regarded most of these groups as heretics, so their reports cannot always be wholly relied upon. But they convey a reasonable picture of three groups.

Ruins of ancient Pella in present-day Jordan, where the Jewish Christians are said to have fled following the destruction of Jerusalem by the Romans in 70CE.

The best-known Jewish Christian group, the Ebionites, lived in Transjordan, and their name probably means "the poor." Their Greek gospel was a reworking of Matthew, but omits the nativity and infancy narratives because Ebionites rejected the virgin birth. They were "adoptionists," believing that Jesus became Messiah and Son of God only when the Spirit entered him at his baptism. While Ebionites observed many Jewish rites, as vegetarians they rejected the sacrifices of the Temple.

The group that produced the gospel of the Hebrews appears to have originated in Egypt in the early second century.

Their distinctive gospel echoes Gnostic ideas (see pp.176–7) and at its core is the Holy Spirit—a female figure like the Gnostic Sophia ("Wisdom"). Again, the Baptism is the key moment in Jesus' life, when the Spirit descends on the pre-existent Son and finds ultimate rest and fulfillment in him.

The Nazarenes, based at Aleppo in Syria, were not considered heretics. Their gospel, written in Aramaic in the second century CE, was also based on Matthew, with the inclusion of picturesque elaborations and popular legends.

Scholars disagree on whether the Christian mission really was formally divided up in this way. In any event, it did not settle the issue of the relationship between Jewish and Gentile Christians. Even within the Church at Jerusalem, some members were apparently prepared to compromise, while others insisted that Gentiles "be circumcised and ordered to keep the law of Moses" (Acts 15.5). The eventual dominance of Gentile Christianity—and this should not be considered simply as a synonym for the teachings of Paul—was largely the result of external factors rather than internal strife (see box, above). The Christian movement as a whole preserved, in its scriptures, several texts of a clearly Jewish Christian character, such as the gospel of Matthew (see box, p.53), the letter of James, and Revelation.

THE PATRISTIC PERIOD

THE CHURCH FATHERS
The eminent theologians known as the "Church Fathers" include Clement of Rome, Ignatius of Antioch, and Polycarp of Smyrna in the first century CE; Justin Martyr and Athenagoras of Athens in the second century; Clement of Alexandria, Origen, and Cyprian of Carthage in the third century; and Ambrose, Athanasius, Augustine of Hippo, Basil, Gregory of Nyssa, Gregory Nazianzus, Jerome, John Chrysostom, and Cyril of Alexandria in the fourth and fifth centuries.

The Church Fathers determined Christian orthodoxy and rejected other ideas and doctrines as heretical. They also established the final form of the New Testament, the authoritative canon of Christian scripture (see p.51).

From the first century CE until around the middle of the fifth century, the Church was engaged in a constant debate on the nature, character, and significance of Jesus. The great (male) thinkers who contributed to this debate are known as the "Church Fathers" (Latin *Patres Ecclesiae*; see sidebar, left) and the era of their activity is known as the Patristic period.

The key issue in the early Patristic period was Jesus' relationship to God. How could New Testament statements implying the divinity of Christ be reconciled with the Judaic belief in one God accepted by most Christians? The Apologists, a group of influential second-century writers who defended Christianity against pagan and Jewish attacks, perceived Jesus as the Wisdom of God and the Son of God, but above all as the creative Word (Greek *Logos*) that "was with God" and "was God" (John 1.1) (see sidebar, opposite).

The achievement of the Apologists was to present Jesus as both identical with, yet distinct from, the one God, much like the figure of Wisdom in Proverbs 8 and Sirach (Ecclesiasticus) 24. But this view was open to challenge on two fronts. Some strict monotheists held that Jesus the Logos was simply a human being on whom the power of God rested, or that he was one of a succession of temporary (not eternal or preexistent) "modes of operation" on the part of the unique Godhead. Others, such as Arius of Alexandria (ca. 250–336CE) claimed that Jesus could not properly be called God, because he was created by God like all other things in existence, although Jesus was the first and greatest of creatures and the agent

Remains of the 2nd-century walls of the city of Nicea in Asia Minor (present-day Iznik, Turkey). A Church council met at Nicea in 325CE to counter the Arian heresy and formulate the Nicene Creed, the statement of belief that forms part of Christian liturgies to this day.

JESUS AS GOD AND MAN

The second great debate in Christianity during the Patristic period was over the problems raised by the Incarnation. If God had assumed human nature in the man Jesus, how were divinity and humanity to be viewed together in the one person? Arius (see main text) had used the numerous references in the gospels to Jesus' human weaknesses to argue that he could not be truly divine. Some thinkers were apparently content to affirm the doctrine known as Nestorianism—that there were two separate personalities in the incarnate Son, one divine, the other human. Thus the miracles of Jesus could be ascribed to the former, his human fallibilities to the latter.

Opponents countered with the claim that Christ had one personality, but that his human nature was confined to the "flesh" while the divine element, the Logos, replaced his human soul or mind. It was objected that, if this were true, Jesus would lack the most significant elements of human nature and therefore could not be fully human. This in turn

Christ [*right*] with Abbot Mena, *a Coptic (Egyptian Orthodox) icon of ca. 600CE. The Coptic Church was one of several groups that rejected the two natures of Jesus. It adhered to Monophysitism, the belief that Christ had one, divine, nature.*

effectively nullified the purpose of the Incarnation: to restore humanity's true nature, lost by the fall of Adam and Eve in Eden. To quote one key Patristic phrase, Christ "became what we are in order that we might become what he is."

The subtle, complicated, and sometimes confused debate achieved a resolution at the Council of Chalcedon in 451CE. The Chalcedonian Definition, which was generally—but not universally—accepted, does not explain precisely how two natures operate in the one being of Jesus. Rather, it essentially states that a Christian must believe in the reality of a Christ who is inseparably human and divine: "one and the same Christ...recognized in two natures, without confusion, without change, without division, without separation."

through whom everything else was made. Arius pointed to passages of scripture that seemed to uphold his view that the Logos was indeed a created being and thus subordinate to the Father (for example, Prov. 8.22; John 14.28; Sir. 24.8).

Arius' teaching—Arianism—caused a crisis in the Church, not least because Arius' opponents failed conclusively to make their point: that universal salvation was not the work of a supernatural being distinct from the Father, but the revelation of God himself in the life of Jesus (2 Cor. 5.19). Unfortunately for the supporters of traditional Logos Christology, passages of scripture used to support their doctrine could also all too easily be given an Arian interpretation.

Arianism was finally condemned as heretical at a great ecclesiastical council held at Nicea in Asia Minor (325CE), at which the Church settled on the nonscriptural formula that Jesus was "of one substance with the Father"—that is, they shared the same essential being. This formula was incorporated into the Nicene Creed, the fundamental statement of Christian belief, and thereafter became the orthodox doctrine of the Church.

THE LOGOS

The concept of the divine Logos as a kind of "world soul," a universal creative force, was common to much Greek philosophy and was also influential among some speculative currents within first-century CE Judaism. By identifying Jesus with the Logos, the Apologists were able to represent him as an expression of the innermost being of God, the Deity's reason projected into speech, the agent of both creation and revelation. He was close to the Father's heart and God's Son in that he was the only being that the Father had "begotten." In this way, the Father was the sole source of Jesus the Logos, who existed before the Creation and was the directing reason of the whole universe.

GNOSTICISM AND THE NEW TESTAMENT

Concepts resembling those of Gnosticism appear in the New Testament, especially in John's gospel and the letters of Paul. For example, John regularly uses the verb "to know" and Paul the noun "knowledge." The frequent contrasts that both writers make between light and dark, flesh and spirit (Rom. 8.1–13) can be interpreted with reference to Gnostic dualism.

In reality, it is very doubtful how far these and other ideas in the New Testament have the same meaning as in the Gnostic systems, because such concepts were common in the general religious and intellectual climate of Jesus' time, both Hellenistic and Jewish. Moreover, the New Testament shows evidence of deliberately setting out to combat Gnostic beliefs. For example, it strongly asserts the reality of Jesus' bodily humanity (1 John 1.1–4; 1 Tim. 3.16; 2 Tim. 3.8), against the Gnostic view that, because all matter and flesh were evil, Jesus was human only in appearance.

The later New Testament letters rebut Gnosticism most clearly and strongly, indicating how serious a threat it was perceived to be to the emergent Christian orthodoxy. They denounce false myths (1 Tim. 4.7; 2 Tim. 4.3–4; 2 Pet. 1.16); the practice of asceticism and celibacy to avoid contamination by the evil material world (1 Tim. 4.1–5); and the Gnostic genealogy of "eons" (1 Tim. 1.4; Tit. 3.9). Jesus is unique, superior to all other spiritual beings (Heb. 1.1–14) and justly called "God" (Tit. 2.13).

JESUS AND GNOSTICISM

"Gnosticism" is the modern term for a major religious movement of the early centuries CE. It existed in a bewildering variety of forms that collectively provided the principal challenge to the development of mainstream Christianity in the era of the Church Fathers (see pp.174–5). From at least the second century CE, Gnosticism was regarded by leading Christian theologians as a highly dangerous heresy.

The word Gnosticism derives from the Greek *gnosis* ("knowledge"), and a Gnostic is thus one who is considered to have attained to true knowledge. This concept was a basic feature of all the different Gnostic systems: an initiate had first to understand the condition in which human beings find themselves, and this understanding became in turn the means of deliverance from the human predicament.

In Gnosticism, humanity is akin to the divine. Every person represents a "divine spark" imprisoned in a material body. Salvation is the freeing of that divine element so that the individual may realize his or her heavenly nature. The basis for this doctrine is a radical dualism between "spirit" and "matter," whereby the material world is a realm of evil from which the individual needs to escape. Because the world is evil, the being that created it cannot be the one true God. Above this creator-being, or "demiurge," and sharply distinguished from it, there must be an unknown transcendent Deity.

The "knowledge" to which the Gnostic attains takes the form of an elaborate creation myth. This is recounted differently in the various Gnostic systems, but they all speak of an ultimate divine figure, the Father, from whom

Christ Giving the Word of God to the Apostles Paul [left] and Peter, a mosaic of ca. 500CE in the Church of Santa Costanza, Rome. Paul's letters have been said to echo Gnostic dualism, for example the contrast he makes between flesh and spirit. But this is better compared with the rabbinic doctrine of the good and evil inclinations within a single person. In reality, the early Church strenuously opposed Gnostic speculation.

The Nile at Nag Hammadi in Upper Egypt. A cache of documents discovered here in 1945 provides firsthand evidence for Gnosticism, and has clarified references in the New Testament letters to "cleverly devised myths" (2 Pet. 1.16) and other aspects of Gnostic thought.

emanates a genealogy of spiritual beings known as "eons," who together constitute the *pleroma*, the "fullness" of divinity. The eons progressively move away from the divine center until one or other of them "falls," carrying spirit into the lower realm of matter. When this happens, the visible world comes into being (sometimes through the work of a demiurge) at the same time as the evil powers ("archons") that govern it.

According to this understanding, human beings are so enmeshed in matter that they can realize their authentic spiritual nature only through a supernatural revelation. Where Jesus appears in Gnostic speculation, this is the role he fulfills. He is a heavenly figure who descends to reveal to humanity the true and redeeming *gnosis*. He is not incarnate as a real human being, as Christian orthodoxy insists (although Gnostic texts are not consistent on this point), because that would corrupt him with the material world. The "Gnostic gospels" relate nothing of the ministry, death, and resurrection of the human Jesus but instead are either meditations on his message or collections of his sayings. His teaching is sometimes described as "secret words," hidden knowledge not granted to ordinary believers.

Until the twentieth century, knowledge of Gnosticism was largely confined to the hostile accounts of Church Fathers and such extracts as they reproduced from Gnostic writings. This situation was transformed by the discovery in 1945 of a quantity of Gnostic texts at Nag Hammadi in Egypt. Gnosticism can now be viewed not simply as a distortion of the true faith, but as a belief system in its own right that was widely attractive because it appeared to offer the hope of deliverance from humanity's sad condition. The Nag Hammadi documents, which include the Gospel of Thomas (see box, p.59), seem to indicate the existence of a pre-Christian Gnosticism that became largely Christianized while retaining its original basic outlook.

CHRIST THE REDEEMER

A central issue between the Church and Gnosticism was the uniqueness of Christ and the understanding of his redemptive work. The Gnostic Jesus was only one in the evolving succession of divine emanations known as "eons," and, since he was not viewed as physically human, there was no place in Gnostic thought for the notion of salvation through Jesus' bodily death and resurrection. By contrast, for the Church, the whole divine *pleroma* (see main text) was contained in Jesus (Col. 1.19, 2.9): he is *the* one through whom the universe came into being (John 1.3), the sole mediator between God and humankind (1 Tim. 2.5), who "was handed over to death for our trespasses and was raised for our justification" (Rom. 4.25).

FOUNDER OF THE CHURCH?

The Catholic Church of the Primacy of St. Peter was built in 1934 on the foundations of a Byzantine church near Tabgha. The rock, called "Christ's Table," is traditionally where the disciples shared a meal with the risen Jesus, who designated Peter as the head of the body of believers with the words: "Feed my lambs" and "Feed my flock" (John 21.9–17). Whatever the authenticity of this scene, the New Testament certainly shows that Peter enjoyed a special position of leadership in the early Church.

It is often asserted that Jesus had no intention of founding a Church in the sense of an enduring body of followers. Jesus, it is claimed, expected the imminent end of the present age, but was mistaken in this expectation and the Church and its mission came into being to meet a situation for which he had provided no guidance. The creation of the Church may be explained by the sociological theory known as "cognitive dissonance," according to which a group faced with the failure of its accepted beliefs retains their form—in this case Jesus' predictions of a speedy end of the world—but reinterprets their substance. Thus Jesus' anticipation of the impending end was replaced by the future hope of his Second Coming, the *Parousia*.

However, many scholars would still wish to claim that the foundation of the Church was central to the purpose of Jesus. The Greek word translated as "church" is *ekklesia*, which originally meant just "gathering" or "assembly." But the usage of the term in the New Testament seems to be derived from the Septuagint, the Greek version of the Hebrew Scriptures, where, as well as denoting popular assemblies of various kinds, *ekklesia* frequently also denotes the Israelite nation. The first Christians, therefore, saw themselves as the continuation and true realization of Israel, God's chosen people (Rom. 9.6–8; Gal. 6.16; Phil. 3.3; 1 Pet. 2.9).

It would seem that in calling the twelve leading disciples, Jesus aimed to set up a group that, with him as its head, would constitute the new twelve tribes of Israel at the renewal of all things (Matt. 19.28; Luke 22.28–9). In Jesus' preaching, the kingdom of God is both present and to come; those who enter it now will constitute a "little flock" (Luke 12.32), a society of the redeemed, when the kingdom is fully and finally realized. If Jesus identified himself with the "Son of Man" in Daniel 7 (see box, p.169), he may also have envisaged the creation of a new community of "the people of the holy ones of the Most High" (Dan. 7.27). The foundation of a community may also be implied in Jesus' conception of himself as Messiah (see pp.164–5).

It is possible to draw too sharp a distinction between Jesus' views on the imminence of the end of the world and those of the early Church. If the "Synoptic Apocalypse" (see pp. 180–81) is to be trusted, Jesus said that he did not know the exact time of the end (Matt. 24.36; Mark 13.32). He envisaged a community in a state of constant watchfulness for the unexpected appearance of the Son of Man (Mark 13.33–37 and parallels), and warned this community to take steps to survive the catastrophes that will usher in the final end (Mark 13.14–20 and parallels).

The members of the very early Church had much the same outlook and expectation: they believed that Jesus would return to establish his kingdom soon (1 Thess. 4.15–18), but the precise time was hidden from them, so all they could do was watch and wait (Acts 1.7; 1 Thess. 5.1–6).

It seems likely that Jesus understood his followers to constitute a distinct group within Judaism, a new synagogue that alone embodied the true Israel. The early Church can be viewed as an organic development of this idea. The Qumran community (see p.37) provides an interesting parallel. It considered itself the only authentic representative of Judaism and its members believed that they were living in the last days, awaiting God's imminent intervention at an unknown time. The Church of the New Testament probably understood itself in the same way, as a body awaiting—in accordance with the teachings of Jesus—the divine consummation of all things.

A FOUNDATIONAL RITE: THE LORD'S SUPPER

Jesus' institution of the Lord's Supper, or Eucharist, can be seen as the formal foundation of the Church. In their accounts of the Last Supper, Mark and Matthew make no mention of the continuation of the rite, and difficult textual problems in Luke's version make it uncertain as to whether or not Jesus envisaged it. But Paul, an earlier witness than the evangelists, certainly knows the Supper as the central sacramental act of worship in the Church: it is what unites believers into a single body (1 Cor. 10.16–17, 11.23–26).

In any event, the gospels agree that Jesus' actions at the Last Supper were a rite of covenant-making, referring back to the covenant with Israel in the Hebrew Scriptures. That covenant designated Israel as God's chosen people: the covenant in Jesus' blood designated his Church as the new Israel. The Lord's Supper prefigures a great messianic banquet in heaven to celebrate Jesus' return—but it is also a sacrament to be respected continually by his followers on earth in remembrance of him.

The words and actions of Jesus can also be seen to replace the sacrificial cult of the Jerusalem Temple, which was the very heart of the religious life of Judaism. A new community is given a new mode of worship: a simple meal replaces the sacrificial food of the Temple, perhaps specifically the Passover meal (1 Cor. 5.7–8). (See also box, p.112.)

The Last Supper, *by Andrea del Castagno (1421–57), a fresco in the refectory of Sant' Apollonia monastery, Florence, Italy. The scene has long been a popular subject for the dining halls of Christian religious communities (compare illustration, p.113).*

THE APOCALYPTIC JESUS

The apocalyptic character of Jesus' message is revealed most clearly in the passages known as the "Synoptic Apocalypse" (Matt. 24.4–25.46; Mark 13.5–37; Luke 21.8–36). All three versions of this discourse are founded on the same basic tradition: Jesus predicted the destruction of the Temple and, in response to his disciples' question as to when this momentous event would happen, revealed that it would herald his second coming and the end of the age (Matt. 24.3).

Speaking in private to his closest disciples (Mark 13.3), Jesus told of the universal catastrophes that would mark the onset of the end of time (Mark 13.7–8 and parallels); these tribulations are described in language that recalls apocalyptic predictions in the Hebrew Bible and the Apocrypha (Dan. 2.2.8; Isa. 19.2: 29.6; Ezek. 5.12; 2 Esd. 13.31–32, 16.18–19). The climax of these calamities would be a profanation of the Temple, a "desolating sacrilege" (Matt. 24.15; Mark 13.14)—this term refers to the pagan

THE REVELATION TO JOHN

Jesus as an apocalyptic figure features most prominently in the book of Revelation. Like many Jewish writings of the apocalyptic genre, it claims to be the vision of a seer who has been vouchsafed heavenly secrets. Its author, traditionally identified with the writer of the Fourth Gospel, draws on the Hebrew Scriptures, the gospels, and a wide range of other sources, such as the books of Enoch, astrology, and myths current in the Greco-Roman world. His primary thematic starting point is the Synoptic Apocalypse (see main text).

Revelation is not just a vision of the future, a view that has often led to a misunderstanding of its character and purpose. Like the book of Daniel, it addresses a particular historical situation of persecution, which is viewed as a prelude to the end of the world and the vindication of the faithful. It opens with

A Byzantine mosaic from Carthage, Tunisia. On either side of the cross, alpha *and* omega *(ΑΩ), the first and last letters of the Greek alphabet, denote Christ as the eternal God, an image derived from Revelation 1.8.*

messages from the risen Christ to the churches of Asia Minor (Rev. 1.11, 2–3), exhorting them to endurance in the face of persecution (compare Mark 13.9–13 and parallels). Calls for watchfulness occur throughout the work (Rev. 13.9–10, 13.18, 14.12, 16.15).

According to Revelation, Jesus was exalted to heaven by his death in order to assume universal authority. He alone controls the course of history and can open the seals on the scroll of destiny (Rev. 5.1–10). The birthpangs of the messianic age will be marked by war, famine, and pestilence (Rev. 6–11) and the appearance of false Christs and prophets (Rev. 12.13). But the forces of evil will soon be overcome by the victory of angelic beings (Rev. 14–18), heralding the return of Christ, the Last Judgment, a new heaven and earth, and a new Jerusalem (Rev. 19–21).

CERUBIN TRONYM SERAFIN

ANGELI·BONIA·TENENTES

The Adoration of the Lamb, *from an 8th-century Spanish manuscript of the* Commentary on the Apocalypse *by Beatus of Liébana. The image is drawn from the vision in Revelation 5.6–14 of elders, angels, and "four living creatures" worshiping the divine Lamb (Christ). The description of the four creatures (Rev. 4.7) derives from apocalyptic writings in the Hebrew Scriptures (compare Ezek. 1.10).*

THE SYNOPTIC APOCALYPSE AND THE TEACHINGS OF JESUS

The Synoptic Apocalypse is closely linked with the eschatology of other New Testament writings, especially Revelation (see box, opposite), and differs in many respects from what the gospels generally record of Jesus' teachings. As it stands, it no doubt reflects the concerns of the evangelists and the communities for which they wrote, but the key question is whether it wholly misrepresents the thought of the historical Jesus, as many scholars have asserted.

While the language of the Synoptic Apocalypse resembles that of other apocalyptic writings, its outlook and content differ considerably. In typical apocalyptic texts, the "signs" enable the reader to predict the time of the end, but in the Synoptic Apocalypse this time is said to be unknowable (Matt. 24.36, 25.13; Mark 13.32). Jesus will return when least expected (Matt. 24.44), and his followers must not be misled by those who claim that he has already reappeared (Matt. 24.23–25; Mark 13.21–23).

Similar teachings are found on the lips of Jesus elsewhere in the gospels (as at Luke 17.20–23). His message is as much for the present as the future, as is shown by the admonitions to be watchful (Mark 13.33–37; Luke 21.34–36), driven home in Matthew by a series of parables (Matt. 24.37–25.30), most of which are found (in different contexts) in Luke. The demand for faithful discipleship and a readiness to accept wholeheartedly the demands of the kingdom are at the core of Jesus' entire teachings (see pp.150–51) .

altar of Zeus erected in the Temple by the Hellenistic king Antiochus Epiphanes in 164BCE (Dan. 9.27, 12.11; 1 Macc. 1.54). In Jewish thought, the Temple represented the universe, and any interference with its rituals brought a cosmic catastrophe. Instead of the profanation of the sanctuary, Luke substitutes a siege of Jerusalem (Luke 21.20). This is generally taken to refer to the events of 70CE, although Luke may have been inspired by similar biblical prophecies (Isa. 29.1–3; Ezek. 4.1–8).

These woes are the prelude to the final deliverance, the coming of the Son of Man (Mark 13.26 and parallels), as prophesied in the book of Daniel (Dan. 7.13–14). His appearance is marked by further cosmic upheavals (Mark 13.24 and parallels), which also echo a number of biblical passages (Ps. 65.7; Isa. 13.10, 24.23, 27.13, 34.4; Zech. 12.12–24). Those who carry out the Son of Man's redeeming mission are the angels (Matt. 24.31; Mark 13.27), who play a central role in Jewish apocalyptic speculation. Matthew concludes his version of Jesus' discourse with a vision of the Son of Man enthroned at the Last Judgment (Matt. 25.31–46).

THE REVOLUTIONARY

"LIBERATION THEOLOGY"
The idea of Jesus as an essentially revolutionary figure is important for the modern phenomenon known as "liberation theology," a movement which emerged in the 1960s in Latin America and has been especially influential there. In liberation theology, a fundamental characteristic of God is that he takes the side of those, in particular the poor, who are oppressed or marginalized by the dominant social structures. The whole Bible is viewed as the record of God's action on their behalf— seen for example in the deliverance of Israel from Egyptian bondage and in the protests of the prophets against social injustices.

The life and teaching of Jesus stand in the same line. Jesus, it is claimed, deliberately chose an "option for the poor" and his message was primarily directed to them. Liberation theologians see Jesus' central proclamation of the kingdom as a message of liberation for the oppressed and downtrodden, and the promise of a free and just society. The response to Jesus today must take the form of a continuation of his struggle to establish this kingdom, through actual social and political activity—from which violence is not always excluded.

Opponents of this kind of theology have objected that it is unduly preoccupied with political activism, often of an avowedly Marxist brand, to the detriment of wider spiritual concerns. Perhaps, above all, it can be criticized for neglecting the work of biblical scholarship and viewing the historical figure of Jesus too exclusively in the light of present-day needs and concerns.

Since the end of the eighteenth century, some scholars have claimed that Jesus advocated armed resistance to free the Jews from Roman rule, and that he was linked with one or more groups that were actively engaged in such a struggle. The New Testament sometimes appears to suggest that Jesus may have been connected, directly or indirectly, with contemporary revolutionary groups. For example, one explanation of the mysterious name "Iscariot" given to the disciple who betrayed Jesus (see p.115) links it with the Sicarii, or "Dagger Men," Jewish fanatics who assassinated those they suspected of being Roman sympathizers or collaborators.

One of the disciples is referred to as Simon the Zealot (Luke 6.15; Acts 1.13). The Zealot party was behind the great Jewish revolt of 66–70CE, and may have existed earlier (Zealot leaders included sons of Judas the Galilean, who had led a rebellion in Galilee in 6CE in protest at a Roman census; see p.61). It has been claimed that some sayings of Jesus reflect Zealot thought, such as his statement that he had not come to bring peace but division (Luke 12.51), and his instruction to his followers at the Last Supper to buy a sword (Luke 22.36). But the Zealots and others held that humans had to assist God in establishing the messianic kingdom, whereas the general tenor of Jesus' teaching was that the kingdom would be brought about by God alone. The term "zealot" applied to a disciple may imply no more than that he was a zealous adherent of the Jewish law.

Perhaps the strongest evidence for Jesus' alleged revolutionary tendencies

The Kiss of Judas, *a 6th-century* CE *mosaic in the church of Sant' Apollinare Nuovo, Ravenna. Judas identifies Jesus for the armed men (left) sent to arrest him. The disciple Peter (John 18.10) draws a sword with which he subsequently cuts off the ear of one of the arresting party. In Matthew, Jesus rebukes this act of violence with the words: "Put your sword back in its place; for all who take the sword will perish by the sword" (Matt. 26.52).*

is the fact that the Roman prefect sentenced him to death on a political charge, namely of claiming to be "King of the Jews," a messianic pretender. According to Luke, the Sanhedrin accused Jesus before Pilate of "perverting our nation, forbidding us to pay taxes to the emperor, and saying that he himself is the Messiah, a king" (Luke 23.2). The charge that Jesus had claimed to be a king is no doubt authentic, as the inscription on his cross indicates (see sidebar, right). But this does not mean that the accusation was justified, any more than the charge that Jesus had forbidden payment of Roman taxes, which was certainly false (Matt. 22.17–21). The inscription may indicate only that Pilate went along with the Sanhedrin's claim that Jesus was a royal pretender who might spark political unrest (see pp.120–21, 164–5). A Roman prefect had to remain on good terms with the Jewish establishment, which could easily cause trouble for him at Rome.

The gospels' picture may have been influenced by later disputes between Christians and Jews, but even allowing for this it seems clear that Jesus' attacks were not political but religious. He was not concerned with how and by whom the Jews were governed, but with those fellow Jews—especially in the Temple authorities—who accused him of laxity in religious observances, and finally took the lead in arresting him. The Cleansing of the Temple (see pp.110–11) was not a signal for a political uprising, as some have suggested, but a symbolic prophetic act of opposition to the Temple as an institution. It was an opposition that Jesus expressed elsewhere and which he shared with other Jewish groups of the time.

The Zealots, with whom Jesus has been linked, held out for 3 years after the end of the 1st Jewish War (66–70CE) in the fortress of Masada. The Romans broke the siege by building a huge ramp (bottom left); most of the defenders committed suicide.

THE INSCRIPTION ON THE CROSS
According to the gospels, the inscription on Jesus' cross—the *titulus* (see p.158)—recorded that Jesus had been found guilty of a political offense: claiming to be "King of the Jews" (Mark 15.26 and parallels). It is generally accepted that Mark's simple wording of the inscription ("The King of the Jews") is probably authentic. However, Matthew's version, "This is Jesus the King of the Jews" (Matt. 27.37), parallels the wording of the placard of a Christian martyr at Lyons, France, in 177CE: "This is Attalus the Christian." John's account (John 19.19) may also contain good historical information. He stresses the official nature of the inscription ("Jesus of Nazareth, King of the Jews") as being authorized by Pilate, with the words "of Nazareth" added to identify the victim more precisely.

THE MYSTIC

To describe someone as a "mystic" implies that he or she regularly enjoys an individual religious experience of peculiar intensity, an intimate communion with the divine. Jesus would certainly seem to have been conscious of an especially close relationship with God (see pp.146–7, 166–7), which the gospels suggest was expressed and confirmed through his own practice of prayer.

Jesus' customary mode of prayer was essentially private and personal: he may have joined in the regular prayer sessions at the Temple (as mentioned in Acts 3.1) from time to time, but the gospels do not explicitly state this. He tended to withdraw to pray alone in isolated places, especially mountains (Mark 1.35, 6.46; Luke 4.42, 5.16, 6.12, 9.18, 9.28, 11.1). The

JESUS AND THE HOLY SPIRIT

The New Testament clearly portrays Jesus as one endowed with the Spirit of God. The synoptic gospels contain comparatively few references to the Spirit in the earthly life of Jesus, but these occur at significant moments in his career, while elsewhere in the New Testament he is the source of the gift of the Spirit to believers (Gal. 4.6).

In the Hebrew Scriptures, the Spirit is primarily a supernatural force that empowers individuals to perform heroic deeds or to voice prophetic utterances. Traces of this concept are evident in the gospels. Thus Jesus comes to Galilee filled with the power of the Spirit (Luke 4.14). After his baptism, he was driven out into the wilderness (Mark 1.12), recalling the way in which the Spirit physically transported prophets such as Elijah or Ezekiel (1 Kings 18.12; 2 Kings 2.16; Ezek. 3.14, 11.1, 37.1, 43.5). Such Spirit possession was usually only temporary and partial, but in later writings prophets increasingly came to be viewed as the permanent bearers of the Spirit (Isa. 11.2, 61.1). In much Jewish thought, the future Messiah was similarly pictured as the bearer of the Spirit.

Jesus is represented as claiming to fulfill those passages in the scriptures that depict the prophet as the bearer of the Spirit (Matt. 12.18–21; Luke 4.18–19). The descent of the Holy Spirit at Jesus baptism constituted a permanent endowment (John 1.32–33). Jesus possessed the Spirit in a unique and complete manner, and did so as the result of his personal relationship with the Father, who gave him the Spirit "without measure" (John 3.34)—fully and not in part, as was the case with earlier prophetic figures. His possession of the Spirit is identical with his divine sonship (John 3.35).

Jesus' whole ministry and preaching were authenticated by the power of the Spirit (Matt. 12.28), and those who failed to recognize the Spirit at work in him and blasphemed against it risked eternal damnation (Mark 3.28–30 and parallels).

The Judean wilderness, where the Spirit drove Jesus (Mark 1.12). His 40-day sojourn in the desert recalls the duration of Elijah's journey to Mount Horeb (1 Kings 19.8).

The Agony in the Garden, *by Andrea
Mantegna (ca. 1430–1506). The artist
depicts Jesus' anguished solitary prayer in
the Garden of Gethsemane shortly before
his arrest (Mark 14.32–42 and parallels;
see pp.114–15). According to Luke, "an
angel from heaven appeared to him and
gave him strength" (Luke 22.43). The
disciples Peter, James, and John lie sleeping
a little way away; in the background, Judas
leads the arresting party from Jerusalem
toward the garden.*

gospels' repeated references to such acts of private devotion show how significant they were felt to be for a proper understanding of Jesus. According
to Christian tradition, intense and dramatic experiences such as Jesus'
prayer in Gethsemane (most vividly portrayed in Luke 22.42) were a regular mark of his life on earth (Heb. 5.7).

One characteristic of mystical experience is the reception of visions of the
supernatural world, the revelation of divine secrets. In the gospels, Jesus
tells of such a vision, in which Satan falls from heaven like a flash of lightning
(Luke 10.18), although this passage may have been influenced by Jewish
myths that were in turn inspired by Isaiah 14.12–15).

At least one authority has recently claimed that Jesus' spiritual experience can be linked with a tradition of Jewish mysticism. Some Jewish
teachers of his time entered a trance-like state in which they claimed to
"ascend to heaven" into the very presence of God. It seems likely that Paul
had such an experience (2 Cor. 12.2–4), although the clearest picture of the
mystical ascent to heaven is found in the nonscriptural writings concerning
the figure of Enoch (see sidebar, p.168). In these, Enoch ascends to the
throne of God, where his whole being is transformed. He is clothed in shining garments of glory and then returns to earth as a heavenly messenger.

Such a tradition may well underlie the description of the person and mission of Jesus at the beginning of Revelation (Rev. 1.1–16), and there are striking parallels with the Transfiguration (see box, p.106). A passage in the
Fourth Gospel (John 3.31–33) can be interpreted as a declaration that Jesus'
gospel was true because it contained what he had seen and heard in heaven.
Other sayings of Jesus in John have been interpreted as providing a glimpse
of his own awareness of a mystical ascent to heaven (John 3.13, 6.42, 8.23).

JESUS AT PRAYER IN LUKE

Luke's gospel especially emphasizes the role
of prayer in the life of Jesus. Two references
are particularly significant. After Jesus'
baptism and the opening of heaven, Luke
adds that Jesus was praying (Luke 3.21);
and at the Transfiguration the appearance
of Jesus is transformed as he prays (Luke
9.29). In both instances, the evangelist may
be suggesting that the heavenly voice which
proclaimed Jesus as God's Son at the
Baptism and the Transfiguration was a
mystical confirmation of his true nature,
revealed to Jesus following his communion
and union with the Father through the
intimacy of prayer.

JESUS AND FEMINISM

A chapel on the shore of Lake Galilee at Migdal, ancient Magdala, the hometown of Mary Magdalene, who always appears first in the list of female followers.

Feminist theory shares with liberation theology (see sidebar, p.184) a concern for a marginalized group, namely women, whom it sees as continually ignored and oppressed throughout history by a male-dominated society. Although all feminist writers would share this outlook, there are considerable differences in their approach to the New Testament and to the ideas and intentions of Jesus in particular.

The gospels make clear the important place of women in Jesus' life and ministry. The names of some of those who accompanied him and provided for him on his Galilean mission (Matt. 27.55–56; Mark 15.40–41; Luke 8.1–3) are preserved, and it was also remembered that women had been the first witnesses of the Resurrection (Mark 16.1–8 and parallels; see pp.128–9). There is a marked emphasis on Jesus' healing of women, for whom he shows a special compassion: he healed a "daughter of Abraham" who had been crippled for eighteen years (Luke 13.10–17); a Syro-Phoenician Gentile (Matt. 15.21–28; Mark 7.24–30); and a woman whose condition made her unclean and a social outcast (Mark 5.25–34 and parallels). Strikingly, Jesus was accepting even of prostitutes, opening the kingdom of God to them (Matt. 21.31–32) and receiving their homage (Luke 7.36–50). Again, images drawn from the world of women and their occupations

THE "ANDROGYNOUS JESUS"

To quote one feminist writer, "where God is male, the male is God." For some radical feminists, Jesus' manhood and the masculine language he employed in speaking of God mean that he cannot be seen as a savior for women. His message, they claim, excludes women, as the mainstream Judeo-Christian tradition has always done. Hence women must reject Christianity in favor of a religion that directly expresses female religious experience.

Other feminist scholars have sought to address this claim by arguing that the New Testament figure of Jesus is to be understood as both male and female. Their view is influenced by the revived interest in Gnosticism (see pp.176–7), which they would see as an authentic Christian movement, the significance of which was obscured as Christian theology became increasingly patriarchal in outlook. Many Gnostics, following ideas current in some Jewish circles, held that the first

human being was androgynous. Christ, the second Adam, restores in his own person the primitive sexual unity of all humanity. This teaching is attributed to Jesus in some of the apocryphal gospels with a Gnostic background, such as the Gospel of Thomas and the Gospel of Philip.

Central also to many Gnostic systems is the figure of Sophia, or Wisdom, the female aspect of deity. In the Hebrew Bible, the personified figure of Wisdom is also described in female terms. Sophia is a mother and identified with the Holy Spirit; the Gospel of Thomas calls her the true Mother of Jesus, and Luke's account of Jesus' conception by the Holy Spirit can be understood in this light (Luke 1.35). In the New Testament, Jesus is sometimes described as the Wisdom of God, and can thus be viewed as the incarnation of Sophia—in whom the fundamental feminine and masculine natures are united—and as her prophet to all human beings, both women and men.

JESUS AND FEMALE DISCIPLESHIP

Feminist scholars seek to read the gospels from the distinctive standpoint of women, and this approach has often produced novel and illuminating results, uncovering aspects hitherto unappreciated in the texts. For example, Jesus' honoring of the woman who anoints him—in the face of his disciples' disapproval—can be seen as affirming a central place for women in the life of the future Church (Matt. 26.6–13; Mark 14.3–9).

In the story of Martha and Mary (Luke 10.38–42), Mary listens to Jesus while her sister Martha busies herself with household tasks. When Martha complains of this to Jesus, he says that Mary "has chosen the better part." This episode may reflect a dispute about the proper role of women in the Christian community, with the favoring of Mary confirming the right of women to full discipleship.

Women in the gospels can be seen as those who humbly and faithfully accept the teaching of Jesus—in contrast to the frequent doubts and questionings of the male disciples. Much interest has focused on the figure of Jesus' mother, and feminist theologians have shown that she is not to be understood just as a passive recipient of the divine purpose but as an active proclaimer of liberation and a model of discipleship for all humanity.

occur in Jesus' parables and teaching (Matt. 13.33, 24.41; Luke 13.20, 15.8–10, 17.35). He also shows concern for widows, whose position in society was often an unfortunate one (Mark 12.42–44; Luke 18.2–8, 21.2–4).

Such facts would be recognized by all New Testament scholars, whether feminist or not, but caution is needed in assessing their significance. It is often suggested that Jesus' attitude marked a radical break from the subordinate position of women in contemporary Judaism. However, comparatively little is known of the place of women in first-century Judaism and they may have enjoyed a higher status than is often supposed. On the other hand, feminists would point out that all the gospels were written by male authors and that their outlook as a whole remains firmly patriarchal. They are therefore unlikely to have portrayed women playing such a special part in Jesus' career unless their role was indeed exceptional for the time.

"JESUS THE JEW"
Recent appreciations of the person of the historical Jesus on the part of both Jewish and Christian writers (see pp.178–9) have opened the way for a new climate of understanding between Christianity and Judaism. Since at least the eighteenth century, New Testament scholarship has increasingly recognized the essential Jewishness of Jesus, and that his life and teaching must be interpreted from within the context of the Judaism of his day.

Similarly, some strands of Jewish scholarly opinion, while obviously continuing to reject belief in Jesus' divinity, and resurrection, have come to view him in a more positive light. Some Jewish scholars—a very small minority, it must be stressed—would say that Jesus revealed what lies at the heart of the Law, the existential relationship between human beings and God, and that his identification with the outcast and oppressed constituted a universal challenge to all humanity.

JUDAISM AND THE CHURCH

The early Church in Jerusalem saw its mission as directed towards Israel, but all the evidence suggests that it gained only limited penetration among Jews, especially in Palestine. Jewish Christians—those who continued to observe the Torah while believing in Jesus and his mission—occupied a precarious position between Judaism and mainstream Christianity and were acceptable to neither. They fragmented following the dispersion of the Jerusalem Church in 70CE and ultimately disappeared (see pp.172–3).

One issue dividing Christians and Jews was of course the Jewish rejection of Jesus as the awaited Messiah. The Judaism of Jesus' day had no concept of a suffering, dying, and resurrected Savior such as Christianity proclaimed. For Christians, Jesus was the prophet foretold in the Hebrew Scriptures, and anyone who did not heed his message would be held accountable by God (Deut. 18.18–19). In Acts, this warning is intensified: "everyone who does not listen to that prophet will be utterly rooted out by the people" (Acts 3.23). Thus the refusal by Jews (or anyone else) to accept Jesus and his teaching inevitably incurred divine judgment against them. However, in Judaism, it is not in itself unacceptable to claim to be the Messiah, and Jewish history has produced many messianic claimants (such as Simon bar Kokhba in the second century CE and Shabbetai Zvi in the seventeenth). What most offended mainstream rabbinic Judaism was the Christian belief in the Incarnation, the idea that Jesus was God made flesh. In Judaism, it has been said, the human cannot be divine and hence the divine cannot be human.

As a result of Paul's teaching that Christ had superseded the Jewish law (Rom. 10.4), Christians no longer felt bound by the full requirements of the Torah. This was a decisive and fundamental break with Judaism, and it meant that the new faith could be preached to Gentiles. The Church soon became, and remained, an overwhelmingly Gentile body.

The break was further widened during the reorganization of national life after the catastrophe of 70CE, when Jewish religious leaders—essentially the Pharisees, since the Temple and its priesthood had ceased to exist—demanded strict observance of the law, under rabbinic authority and teaching. The pluralism that had existed hitherto within Judaism (see pp.34–7)

The Synagogue, an allegorical figure of ca. 1230 from Strasbourg Cathedral, France. Her eyes are bound, to indicate the "blindness" of the Jews to the gospel, and she carries a broken lance (one of the instruments of the Crucifixion, for which Jews were blamed), and a closed book (representing the Jewish law, which Jesus was considered to have superseded).

was greatly reduced. Increasingly, Christians were arraigned before local Jewish tribunals and expelled from synagogues, as the gospels indicate (Matt. 10.17; Mark 13.9; Luke 12.11, 21.12). Paul believed that the Jewish rejection of Jesus would only be temporary (Rom. 11.26), but his hopes were not realized. The breach became ever wider, and the early Church understood the success of its mission to the Gentiles as a sign that Judaism had indeed been superseded (Acts 13.46–47, 18.6).

The further mainstream Christianity became distanced from its roots in Judaism, the less Christians understood the Jewish context in which Jesus had operated, and the more they came to see him and his disciples in contradistinction to "the Jews." In particular, Christians increasingly came to put responsibility for Jesus' death not on Pilate, nor on the Temple authorities and other Jewish groups that had opposed Jesus' teachings, but simply on "the Jews"—the entire Jewish people.

Early on, Peter could say that "the Jews" and their rulers had acted only through ignorance (Acts 3.17), but what Christians saw as the Jews' continued obduracy and refusal to acknowledge the truth about Jesus soon led to a hardening of attitudes. This is to be seen most starkly in the Fourth Gospel, where "the Jews"—here clearly meaning the whole nation—are pictured as seeking to destroy Jesus from the outset. The Jews' rejection of Jesus showed that they were not God's elect, not the children of Abraham, but the offspring of the devil (John 8.31–44).

Over the succeeding centuries, whatever sociological or economic factors may also have been involved, there can be little doubt that the widespread Christian belief that the Jewish people as a whole bore the guilt for Jesus' death lay at the root of Christian anti-Judaism, and of its baleful nineteenth-century racialist offspring, anti-Semitism. As a consequence, Judaism tended to see Jesus as the cause of its persecution and to depict him in the most unfavorable light (see sidebar, right).

Opposition between the two groups varied in its bitterness at different periods, but there was always a link between them in that the Church appealed to the authority of the Hebrew Scriptures, the Christian Old Testament. In medieval Europe there were frequent formal public disputations between learned rabbis and Christian teachers. These were staged by the Church in order to "prove" the superiority of its message, and centered on the Church's belief that various passages in the Hebrew Scriptures referred to Jesus, and on Christian claims that statements in the Talmud expressed a belief in Jesus' messiahship.

The Virgin and Child, *a panel from an Ethiopian Coptic icon diptych of the early 18th century. The infant Jesus holds the book of the new law, which renders obsolete the old law of Judaism.*

JESUS IN THE TALMUD

The Talmud contains brief references that may demonstrate Jewish attitudes toward Jesus in the early centuries CE. A prayer that probably dates from the first century CE petitions for the destruction of heretics, which may be a veiled reference to Christians. It is also alleged that Jesus had been hanged as a criminal for practicing sorcery, and that he had enticed Israel to apostasy. Both charges are reflected in the gospels, notably the sorcery accusation (Mark 3.22–27 and parallels). But the notion that Jesus had attempted to lead Israel astray was undoubtedly strengthened by the Church's abandonment of the full requirements of the Torah.

Another passage in the Talmud speaks of one who, though born of a woman, sought to make himself God—a fairly clear attack on the belief in Christ's divinity.

JESUS AND ISLAM

In the Qur'an, Jesus (Arabic, Isa) is one of a succession of individuals to whom God revealed his Word, beginning with Adam, Noah, and Abraham. The last and greatest of these figures was the Prophet Muhammad, who has no successor and is thus "the Seal of the Prophets." Between Abraham and Muhammad there were many other prophets (*nabi*s), of whom twenty-eight were selected to bear and propagate the divine Word. These special prophets are known as *rasul*s and include Moses and Jesus, who brought the Word to two specific communities, the Jews and the Christians respectively. As "Peoples of the Book"—those to whom God (Allah) has vouchsafed scripture—Jews and Christians thus possess a special status in Islam.

Jesus' distinguished position in the line of prophecy is reflected in the considerable range of titles and descriptions applied to him in the Qur'an, such as "Messiah" and "God's Word and Spirit." He is described most frequently as "Son of Mary," and the virgin birth is strongly emphasized. The Qur'an also has the story of the birth of John the Baptist, whose mission is to confirm Jesus as God's Word.

On his mission (see box), Jesus was strengthened by the Holy Spirit and raised to the highest rank among the prophets. He performed miracles by the power of Allah, healing the blind and the leprous and raising the dead, with the apostles as his helpers. Jesus was given the Gospel by God, and set about teaching its truths. All the "People of the Book" will come to believe in the truth of Jesus, and he will witness against their errors at the Last Judgment.

On the other hand, the Qur'an firmly rejects any notion of Jesus' divinity. Jesus is not God's son, only his servant and prophet—a "Messenger of God," a creature of dust, like Adam. Only those who lack true belief would say that the Messiah, the Son of Mary, is God. The Qur'an particularly condemns the doctrine of the Trinity, although mainstream Christianity would probably argue with the way in which the Qur'an represents Trinitarian doctrine: "They are unbelievers who say, 'God is the Third of Three.' No god is there but One God" (*Sura* 5, "The Table").

The Birth of Jesus, *a Persian miniature of ca. 1700. According to the Qur'an (Sura 19, "Mary"), the pregnant Mary withdrew to a "distant place," where she gave birth to Jesus next to a palm tree. At the behest of the newborn child (right), Mary shook dates from the tree to eat, while a refreshing stream flowed from its roots.*

The Qur'an also denies the Crucifixion. It says that although "the Jews" claim to have executed Jesus, they did not actually slay or crucify him but only his double, who was put to death in his place, while Jesus was "raised up" by God to be with him. Later Muslim traditions speak of Jesus' future return to earth, when he will kill the Antichrist and inaugurate an age of harmony and prosperity under the true religion.

The components of this picture of Jesus reflect the canonical gospels, some of the apocryphal gospels, and debates in which Muhammad engaged with Christians. Christian scholars generally agree that Muhammad probably had no firsthand acquaintance with the four New Testament gospels. His own personal contact with Christians was probably restricted to wandering monks and ascetics, who had penetrated into southern Arabia largely from the adjacent region of Syria, and for whom the Qur'an shows considerable regard. Such people propagated what was essentially a popular form of Christianity, which over the course of time had acquired many legendary and folkloric features and was sometimes at variance with strict Church orthodoxy.

THE LIFE OF JESUS AND THE QUR'AN

The passages about Jesus in the Qur'an echo the New Testament and often also traditions found in some apocryphal gospels, which were evidently well known in southern Arabia, since they exist in numerous early Arabic translations.

In the Qur'an, the Annunciation to Mary is made by an angelic being in human form, to whom Mary responds as in Luke. Jesus' birth takes place under a palm tree (see illustration, opposite): a virtually identical account occurs in the apocryphal "Gospel of Pseudo-Matthew."

The Qur'an mentions Jesus' miracles of healing. He is also described as making birds of clay and bringing them to life, an episode found in many apocryphal sources (see illustration, p.207). In another miracle, Jesus, at the request of the apostles, causes a table laid with a festival banquet to be sent down from heaven for them. This may contain a reference to the Christian Eucharist or perhaps to the miraculous feedings recorded in the gospels.

There are also many allusions to Jesus' teachings. Jesus is said to confirm the Torah, but relaxes some of its prohibitions—this is reminiscent of Jesus' attitude to the law as portrayed in the New Testament (see pp.142–3). Parables of Jesus are also alluded to, such as those of the Sower and of the Ten Bridesmaids, and many Qur'anic phrases recall the language of the canonical gospels.

Several sayings and miracles of Muhammad recorded in the Hadith (Muslim traditions about the life of Prophet) are very similar to words and deeds that the New Testament ascribes to Jesus. Later Muslim historians and theologians often show a good knowledge of the gospels, not least in their debates with Christian opponents, and there are many sayings attributed to Jesus in the writings of Muslim mystics (sufis).

THE GOSPELS IN THE QUR'AN

In the Qur'an, the Gospel is a book given by God to Jesus, in the same way that the Torah was given to Moses. Muslim scholars who knew the four canonical gospels frequently claimed that they represented a corruption of this original Gospel. Part of the corruption, it was claimed, was the removal of Jesus' prophecy of the coming of Muhammad, which appears in the Qur'an:

> "And when Jesus son of
> Mary said, Children of
> Israel, I am indeed the
> Messenger of God to you,
> confirming the Torah
> that is before me, and
> giving good tidings of
> a Messenger who shall
> come after me, whose
> name shall be Ahmad [Muhammad]."

(From *Sura* 61, "The Ranks," translated by Arthur J. Arberry, first published by Allen and Unwin Ltd, 1955; © HarperCollins Publishers; quoted with permission).

IN SEARCH OF THE JESUS OF HISTORY

The Church's doctrine, as formalized in the Patristic age (see pp.174–5), recognized the true humanity of Jesus and viewed him as a real historical person. His deeds and teachings, as recorded in the gospels, were accepted as authentic and authoritative for theology, and were taught to the people at large through preaching, art, and popular drama. In the Churches of East and West, the gospels were believed to be divinely inspired and thus of unquestioned accuracy: their apparent contradictions and variations were harmonized or virtually ignored. Belief that Jesus embodied the perfect union of divinity and humanity meant that there was no difficulty in accepting all the miracles attributed to him in the New Testament. He was seen very much as unique, set apart from Judaism and the world of his time, about which relatively little was known.

A substantial change in this situation began only with the rise of rational ideas and the beginnings of modern science in the seventeenth century. Science revealed a world that seemed to operate through autonomous laws. Assuming that God had ordained these laws at the Creation, questions arose as to the need for further divine interventions, such as miracles, which could appear to violate the laws of nature. Since the gospels record miracles, this inevitably led thinkers such as the English Deists (who sought a faith founded only on rational thinking), to raise fundamental questions as to the nature and origin of the gospels.

It is usually agreed that the modern search for the historical Jesus began with the work of the German scholar Reimarus (1694–1768). Although he was much indebted to his predecessors, such as the Deists, his work was marked by two original, and influential, contentions. First, in sharp contrast to orthodox Christianity, he differentiated between what Jesus really said and taught and what his later followers believed about him—that is, he distinguished between the "Jesus of history" and the "Christ of faith." Secondly, he held that Jesus could only be understood within the context of the Judaism of his day. Jesus, he proposed, was a typical Israelite prophet who had proclaimed the imminence of the messianic and political kingdom for which the Jews had long hoped.

Another important scholar, D. F. Strauss (1808–1874), made the same distinction between the real Jesus and the Church's Redeemer, but perceived this in the gospel texts themselves. Many of the individual stories

The entrance of an ancient tomb at Bethany near Jerusalem, traditionally said to be that of Lazarus, whom Jesus raised from the dead, according to John 11. The Fourth Gospel was formerly considered to provide little reliable historical information relating to Jesus. But this view is now seriously questioned, partly owing to the identification by archaeologists of hitherto undiscovered sites mentioned in John.

about Jesus, he suggested, are mythical interpretations that reveal the significance that Jesus possessed for his followers. Here, to some extent, Strauss anticipated the views of later "form criticism."

At the same period, a further impetus was provided by the rise of historical criticism of the gospel texts, with particular reference to their dating and chronological order. The result included a general acceptance that Mark, not Matthew, was the earliest gospel and that John was comparatively late and of thus little historical value (see p.57). In consequence, Mark came to be regarded as providing the most authentic account of Jesus' life and ministry, one that presented him very much as a human figure, with a basically simple ethical message, in contrast to the dogmatic faith of the Church. Taking this view as a starting point, the later nineteenth century saw the appearance of numerous "lives" of Jesus, which sought to reconstruct his real personality and essentially reflected the dominant liberal Protestant theology of the time.

However, by the early twentieth century, fresh developments in New Testament scholarship appeared to signal the collapse of the whole search for the Jesus of history. The very influential work of Albert Schweitzer (1875–1965), author of *The Quest of the Historical Jesus* (1906), showed that the various liberal lives of Jesus were largely projections of their authors' own ethical ideals. The real Jesus, he claimed, was an apocalyptic prophet whose own ethical teaching was only intended for the brief period before the imminent advent of God's kingdom. It also became clear that Mark's gospel was not just a straightforward objective account of Jesus' life and ministry, but a highly theological work reflecting the beliefs of the early Church.

Above all, the methods of form criticism (see pp.50–51) led many to conclude that the gospel writers had no intention of producing a life of Jesus and that their work provides no material for any such undertaking. Rudolf Bultmann (1884–1976), the dominant form critic, dismissed works attempting to reconstruct Jesus' life, personality, and spiritual development as "fantastic and romantic."

However, interest in the Jesus of history was not seriously weakened by the findings of form criticism. Indeed, some of Bultmann's own followers embarked on what has come to be called the "New Quest" of the historical Jesus. The New Quest sought evidence of continuity between the real Jesus and the Christ of the Church's faith, pointing out that all the New Testament writers had assumed without question the identity of the earthly Jesus with their glorified Christ. The proclamation of Christ by

The Transfiguration, *from the Ingeborg Psalter (French, ca. 1210). While the dramatic accounts of Jesus' Transfiguration (Mark 9.2–8 and parallels) can be viewed in their present form as largely constructs on the part of the evangelists, it has recently been argued that this event may be rooted in a genuine mystical experience of Jesus (see p.185).*

RECOVERING THE "REAL" JESUS"

Three criteria have assumed considerable importance in modern New Testament scholarship. The first criterion is known as "ecclesiastical embarrassment": sayings attributed to Jesus that could have caused embarrassment to early Christians—such as his confession of ignorance of the date of the End Time (Matt 24.36; Mark 13.32)—are highly unlikely to have been made up and the fact that the young Church felt obliged to preserve them is a strong argument for their authenticity.

The second criterion is that of "multiple attestation": sayings that are attributed to Jesus in several strands of the traditions represented by the gospels should be given considerable weight. Behind the different gospels and the material peculiar to each of them lie what was remembered of Jesus and his ministry in several different Christian communities. It is hard to imagine that each of them would have independently invented the same traditions about him.

The Sower, *a window in Canterbury Cathedral, England. Jesus' parable of the Sower is likely to be authentic according to the criterion of multiple attestation: it is is found in all three synoptic gospels.*

The third criterion, that of dissimilarity, has proved the most contentious. According to this, if a saying or practice attributed to Jesus appears to be very dissimilar to anything in the teachings and customs of the Judaism of his day, or diverges significantly from the beliefs of the early Church, it may be accepted as good historical evidence for the distinctive outlook of Jesus himself.

This procedure may well demonstrate the genuineness of certain sayings of Jesus, but it carries the danger of isolating Jesus from his Jewish background, so that anything in his teaching that conforms to Judaism tends to be regarded as inauthentic. Also, our knowledge both of first-century Judaism and of the primitive Church is still very limited and debatable. Without a fuller picture, it is hard to be sure how far some of the sayings of Jesus identified as "genuine" by the dissimilarity criterion really did or did not conform to the beliefs of his fellow Jews or of the first Christians.

the early Church was based, it was claimed, on the ministry and teaching of the historical Jesus, as presented in the gospels.

The problem remained of how far it was possible to discover a body of teaching that could confidently be accepted as representing Jesus' authentic outlook. Various criteria have been suggested for establishing authenticity (see box, above), but more recent scholarship prefers instead to rely on the general yardstick of "historical plausibility" that historians adopt towards all ancient texts. This places Jesus firmly within his Jewish context: traditions about him are likely to be historical if they fit into the known Jewish background of his ministry (see pp.168–9). Here, modern sociological studies have shown that much of what the gospels record of Jesus' activity mirrors conflicts and tensions in first-century Judaism. The approach of historical plausibility also involves a greater appreciation of the direct links between Jesus and the Christ of the early "Jesus movement." The group that Jesus formed around him during his lifetime preserved traditions of what its original members had actually learned from Jesus, and these formed the basis of the Church's mission and its preaching.

Historical plausibility on its own can never become historical fact, and even if an outline of the historical Jesus could be produced that was acceptable to most scholars, the real significance of the details would continue to be debated. Some writers would even question the whole attempt at a search for the "authentic" Jesus in favor of a concentration on the abiding religious value of the gospel stories, whatever their historical origin.

Yet Christianity has always claimed to rest on the life and teaching of a real figure in a particular time and place and it is unavoidable that every age should seek to discover more about Jesus with the investigative tools at its disposal. The great expansion of so many areas of knowledge and the appearance of new scholarly disciplines during the last two hundred years no doubt make the search for the historical Jesus ever more complicated and diverse. But accepted positively, and rigorously tested, this quest can only add to our understanding of Jesus of Nazareth, a figure whose fascination, for so many men and women, continues undiminished.

THE "MYTHICAL" JESUS

Since at least the nineteenth century, there have been claims that Jesus never really existed and that the picture of him in the gospels is wholly fictional and mythical. The supporters of this view generally hold that the Jesus venerated by the early Church was essentially the creation of Paul: a heavenly figure who appeared in ecstatic visions to Paul and his fellow apostles.

To account for the wide acceptance of Paul's preaching, it has been suggested that his congregations were Essenes (see sidebar, p.37) who already revered a "Teacher of Righteousness," the founder of the Qumran community. Paul, it is claimed, identified the Jesus of his visions with this Teacher.

Such claims have failed to find favor with the consensus of New Testament scholarship. They depend heavily on speculative and hypothetical arguments and often seem to ignore evidence which tells against them. For example, while Paul did not know Jesus personally, he clearly had knowledge of Jesus' life and teaching (see sidebar, p.171). His letters offer no hint that his congregations were predominantly Essenes, and nor do the Qumran texts ever suggest that the Teacher of Righteousness was an object of worship.

Above all, if Jesus was really just a supernatural figure, it is difficult to understand how the gospels ever came to be written or why early Christians should have wished to produce such an elaborate fiction of a human being active in a very particular time, place, and society.

The Presentation in the Temple, *by the Master of St. Severin (French, fl. ca. 1485–1515). Luke 2.22–24 records that Jesus' parents observed the Jewish rite of Presentation, although the evangelist endows the event with a Christian significance (see p.77). Modern scholars of the historical Jesus must look behind such theological layers in order to set him more firmly in his Jewish context.*

JESUS IN ART

Early Christian Art	198
The Nativity	200
Madonna and Child	202
Scenes from Childhood	206
The Ministry	210
The Passion	212
The Resurrection	218
Christ Triumphant	220

ABOVE: The Savior, *a 14th-century Russian icon. The austere majesty of the face of Christ epitomizes the Orthodox Church's vision of Jesus as Pantocrator, ruler and redeemer of the universe.*
OPPOSITE: Pietà: Angels Support the Wounded Body of Christ, *by Antonello da Messina (ca. 1430–79). Associated with the theme of the "Man of Sorrows," such images were revered in the late Middle Ages as focusing on Christ's great suffering to redeem fallen humanity.*

EARLY CHRISTIAN ART

The earliest period of Christian art is commonly defined as the time from the mid-first century until the emperor Constantine's Edict of Toleration of 313CE, which ended the persecution of Christians in the Roman empire. The most significant surviving examples of this period date mainly from the third century and come from the catacombs (underground cemeteries) of Rome and the remains of a Christian "house church" (a private house used for Christian worship) at the Greco-Roman city of Dura-Europos on the Euphrates in present-day Syria. Strikingly similar themes and images are found in both these places, suggesting that by this time there was already a common Christian artistic tradition throughout the empire.

Before Constantine's edict, Christianity's nascent artistic expression was largely an adaptation of existing models. It drew in large measure on the motifs and conventions of Greco-Roman art, which furnished Christians with numerous templates—many of them clearly pagan in origin—for the representation of Jesus. Third-century mosaics in a small mausoleum under St. Peter's basilica in Rome include, as well as a depiction of Jonah and the Whale—interpreted at one level as a metaphor of the resurrected Christ—the unmistakable figure of the Classical sun god Helios (or Apollo) riding in his chariot in the sky. This can perhaps be understood as representing Jesus in the terms of the biblical prophecy of the coming Messiah: "For you who revere my name, the sun of righteousness shall rise, with healing in its wings" (Mal. 4.2).

The other main influence on Christian artistic expression at this time was probably Jewish synagogue art. Early Christian decoration is dominated by motifs from the Hebrew Bible, some of which, such as Jonah and the Whale, were considered to prefigure aspects of Jesus.

Christian artists went on to develop representations of incidents from Jesus' life, of which some half-dozen occur frequently in the oldest catacombs: the visit of the Magi; the Baptism; the healings of the paralytic and the woman with a hemorrhage; the Samaritan woman at the well; and the raising of Lazarus. In addition, the Dura-Europos church has scenes of Christ walking on water and the visit of the three women to the tomb.

The earliest representations of Jesus himself are in the catacomb of Priscilla, dating from the mid-second century, and at Dura-Europos, from the first part of the third century. In these and other early depictions, Jesus appears as an ordinary human being, without any distinguishing marks, young, beardless, and shorthaired, wearing the regular dress of the time. Perhaps most striking in what has been preserved of early Christian art is the absence of any depiction of the Nativity or the Crucifixion, so central to the Christian art of all later centuries (see pp.200–201, 212–217).

THE ΠATIVITY

The elements of the Nativity scene so familiar today came together only gradually during the centuries following Constantine's Edict of Toleration. An early representation of the swaddled baby lying in the manger between Mary and Joseph appears on a gospel-book cover (402CE) in Milan cathedral. The ox and ass were also shown from the start, in fulfillment of Isaiah's words: "The ox knows its owner, and the donkey its master's crib" (Isa. 1.3). They bear witness that the child is no ordinary baby but the divine manifested in human form.

Apart from the ox and ass, the main features that appear in depictions of the Nativity in both the Eastern and Western Churches derive from the gospels of Matthew and Luke (see pp.64–75). The Magi (Matt. 2.1–12) were a separate motif in early Christian art, but by ca. 600CE they appear

All the elements of the classic Orthodox depiction of the Nativity are present in this 16th-century Russian icon, for example the setting of a cave rather than a stable. The three kings are shown traveling and arriving at the scene. The foreground is dominated by two apocryphal motifs that are not derived from the canonical gospels: the Devil prompting Joseph (left) to disbelieve in the Virgin Birth; and midwives preparing a bath for the Child.

with the angels and shepherds (Luke 2.8–20) on *ampullae*, small flasks for holy oil, made in the Holy Land as souvenirs for Christian pilgrims. Magi, angels, and shepherds all became regular elements in Nativity scenes.

The Eastern Church took other Nativity motifs not only from the canonical gospels but also from apocryphal gospels and other writings. For example, following the Protevangelium of James (see p.58), Orthodox icons set the Nativity in a cave. The black cave symbolizes the darkness of the material world that the Godhead has entered; it also foreshadows Christ's tomb, while the swaddling clothes prefigure his shroud.

In the medieval West, texts focusing on the mystery of the God taking human form encouraged the naturalistic depiction of the baby. The Revelations of a fourteenth-century visionary, St. Bridget of Sweden, greatly influenced the depiction of the Christ Child in late medieval and Renaissance art. Among her visions was one of the painless birth of Jesus, in a sudden blaze of light, to Mary as she prayed.

The Adoration of the Shepherds, *by Georges de la Tour (1593–1652). A sturdy ordinariness characterizes Mary, Joseph, and their rustic visitors, who are dramatically lit, apparently by Joseph's candle. But the scene recalls the words of St Bridget of Sweden, who saw a vision of the Christ Child "surrounded by a light so brilliant that it completely eclipsed Joseph's candle." The shepherds have brought the gift of a lamb, which prefigures Jesus' sacrificial role as the paschal lamb (see pp.112–13).*

MADONNA AND CHILD

The composite image of the infant Jesus with his mother, the Virgin Mary, forms a particularly rich vein in Christian iconography. The Virgin's central significance in Christian theology was defined at the ecclesiastical council of Ephesus in 431CE, which formally bestowed on her the title *Theotokos* (Greek, "God-Bearing"), an epithet still employed in the Greek Orthodox Church. Artistic conventions then had to be devised for depicting Jesus' mother in a manner befitting her awesome role in mediating the incarnation of God on earth.

To begin with, the imperial imagery of the Byzantine court at Constantinople, inspired images of Mary seated on a jeweled throne in the manner of an empress, with Jesus posed formally on her lap. Although Jesus is represented as the size of a baby in relation to his mother, his features are those of an older child, and his future role as lawgiver is symbolized by the scroll that he holds in his left hand. This tradition persisted

The date of this Russian icon of the Virgin and Child is uncertain, but the upright, full-face pose of the Child and the inclined head of the Virgin are hallmarks of the widespread Russian icon type known as "The Mother of God of Kazan" (see p.204).

OPPOSITE: Madonna and Child, *by William Dyce (1806–64), a Scottish artist whose profound reverence for 14th- and 15th-century Italian sacred art anticipated that of the English Pre-Raphaelites. In this simple but refined portrait, the Virgin's book—a traditional symbol of wisdom—and the infant Jesus' extraordinarily intent concentration upon it, are the only hints that the subjects are more than just a young woman and her child.*

OPPOSITE: Madonna of the Rose Bower, *by Martin Schongauer (1440–91). The predominance of red in this richly symbolic work refers to Christ's sacrifice and, as a royal color, to Mary's role as Queen of Heaven. The roses denote her as the sinless "rose without thorns."*

BELOW: Virgin and Child, *a 12th-century French silver-gilt statuette. Jesus raises his right hand to command attention and in his left holds the new law, inscribed with the Greek contraction of his name (IHS XRS, more correctly IHC XPC).*

into the Romanesque art of the early medieval West. The Eastern Church went on to develop a range of conventions for depicting the Virgin and Child. Some icons show Mary standing full-length, but the majority show her half-length, or just head and shoulders, with the Child in various hieratic (priestly) poses. Usually, Jesus has the domed head of an infant, but his face and posture are those of an adult.

Some individual icon paintings gave their names to whole classes of image. Of these, the most famous was the Virgin Hodegetria, named for the Hodegetrion church at Constantinople (Istanbul) where it was kept, and also known as "The Virgin who shows the way." In this painting and those based upon it, the Virgin holds the Child on her left arm and gestures towards him with her right hand; Jesus sits upright holding a scroll in his left hand and blessing with his right. Another widespread image is "The Mother of God of Kazan" (see illustration, p.202), which is based on a 16th-century Russian original at Kazan on the Volga River that was believed to possess miraculous properties.

In the West, the depiction of Jesus and Mary is commonly known as the Madonna (Italian, "My Lady") and Child. The holy mother and her baby are shown either by themselves or with saints, a type known by the Italian term *sacra conversazione* ("holy gathering"). Early medieval Madonnas retain much of the formality of their Byzantine counterparts, but from the fourteenth century onward the natural human bond was increasingly emphasized; Jesus and his mother became engrossed in each other, the child no longer engaging with the world through his priestly gesture of blessing.

Another ancient image is of Jesus being breastfed by Mary, a type known as the Virgo Lactans (Latin, "Suckling Virgin"). This is believed to derive ultimately from ancient Egyptian depictions of the goddess Isis—whose cult was widespread in the ancient Greco-Roman world—suckling her son, the god Horus. The Virgo Lactans won a new lease of life in the later medieval period, partly as a result of the many places of Christian pilgrimage that claimed to possess a phial of the Virgin's milk, among them Eton and Walsingham in England. The Virgo Lactans is sometimes combined with the image known as "The Virgin of Humility": the Virgin seated on the ground with the infant Jesus on her lap.

Artists established the sacred character of the Virgin and Child through their portrayal of the objects associated with them, such as the scroll or book held by Jesus, which represents the new law that he brings. The surroundings may also be of significance. A favorite late medieval type was the Virgin of the Rose Garden, in which the *hortus conclusus* (Latin, "enclosed garden": see Song of Solomon 4.12) symbolizes Mary's virginity.

SCENES FROM CHILDHOOD

Our Savior Subject to his Parents at Nazareth, *by John Rogers Herbert (1810–90). Luke records that Jesus went missing on a visit to Jerusalem, but after he had been found, in the Temple, he returned home with Mary and Joseph and thereafter "was subject [obedient] unto them" (Luke 2.51, KJV). He goes quietly about his work, but Mary's intent gaze recalls the rest of Luke's verse: "His mother kept all these sayings [Jesus' momentous words in the Temple] in her heart" (KJV). The heap of wood on the ground prefigures the shape of the Cross.*

"And the child grew, and became strong, filled with wisdom" (Luke 2.40). Beyond this simple statement the gospels have virtually nothing to say of Jesus' childhood and youth at Nazareth. The only incident narrated is the visit to the Temple at Jerusalem when he was twelve years old (Luke 2.42–50: see box, p.76). Over the centuries, therefore, artists seeking to depict Jesus' early years have eagerly seized upon the smallest pieces of information, such as the reference to the adult Jesus as a carpenter (Mark 6.3) and the son of a carpenter (Matt. 13.55), which inspired them to portray Jesus as an apprentice in Joseph's workshop.

Apocryphal texts attempted to make good the silence of the canonical gospels, and the infancy gospels recount a sequence of wonders performed by the boy Jesus. Artists depicted many of these apocryphal acts, although

The illuminator of this late 15th-century Spanish manuscript presents the Holy Family as a model of domestic industry, paying detailed attention to Joseph's tools in his carpentry workshop and Mary's needlework. The bird may allude to an apocryphal story, recounted in the Infancy Gospel of Thomas, in which the 5-year-old Jesus modeled sparrows from clay and brought them to life.

some of them are hardly attractive, such as legends that he caused children to drop dead because they had angered him. Renaissance painters developed a type of group portrait known as the Holy Kinship, comprising the Holy Family (Mary, Joseph, and Jesus) with all or some of their close relatives, such as Elizabeth and the infant John the Baptist, as well as Anne (Anna) and Joachim, the—entirely legendary—parents of Mary.

The early nineteenth-century Nazarenes, a group of mainly German painters based in Rome, treated the Holy Family and other sacred themes in a naturalistic way that influenced the English Pre-Raphaelites. The portrayal of Jesus and his parents as, for example, a simple working family outraged those who expected an exalted academic style for religious subjects.

THE MINISTRY

Scenes from the ministry of Jesus were part of Christian art from its beginnings. Healing miracles were among the earliest subjects of catacomb art, and appeared with episodes such as the wedding at Cana and the multiplication of the loaves and fishes on fourth-century sarcophagi.

In the later Roman period, the decoration of churches assumed a more or less standard pattern, with certain images appearing at particular places within the building. Sequences of scenes from Jesus' ministry are found in mosaic or fresco on the walls of the nave or narthex (porch), such as the thirteen small mosaics above the windows on the north wall of the church of Sant' Apollinare Nuovo, Ravenna, Italy, which date from 500–520CE. In these, Jesus has a halo inscribed with a cross, which was first depicted about a century earlier; it persisted in Byzantine, Romanesque, and Gothic art as the form of halo particularly associated with Christ. Also in the fifth

The Healing of the Man Born Blind (John 9.1–7), part of the 11th-century Romanesque fresco cycle in the Basilica of Sant' Angelo in Formis at Capua, southern Italy. Jesus smears clay mixed with spittle on the blind beggar's eyes. Jesus' instruction, "Go, wash in the pool of Siloam," led to this miracle being interpreted as an allegory of baptism.

century, Jesus was portrayed for the first time with shoulder-length hair and beard, an image that eventually superseded the Roman-style, clean shaven Jesus of late antiquity.

The healing miracles retained perennial appeal, but other events from the ministry that were charged with symbolic significance were also frequently depicted. The turning of water into wine at Cana and the miraculous feedings could, for instance, be seen as foreshadowing the Christian Eucharist. The two scenes are sometimes juxtaposed in such a way as to make the connection plain, as in the fourteenth-century mosaics in the church of St. Savior in Chora (Kariye Camii mosque) in Istanbul, where they face each other across the entrance to the church.

In his *Painter's Manual*, which codified earlier iconographical traditions and is still relevant to Orthodox iconographers today, the early eighteenth-century Greek monk Dionysius of Fourna gave minute instructions on how to paint several dozen episodes from Jesus' ministry. In practice, in both the

The Calling of Peter and Andrew, *an early 6th-century mosaic in the church of Sant' Apollinare Nuovo, Ravenna. Jesus summons the brothers from their task of fishing to be his disciples and "fish for people" (Matt. 4.18–20). At this period Jesus was still often represented beardless, and his formal stance and gesture recall the traditional pose of teachers or orators in Greco-Roman art.*

The Raising of Lazarus, *a northern Greek icon of 1611. Jesus, striding forward to perform the miracle, dominates the crowded scene. Lazarus' vertical rock tomb is a convention of Orthodox icons, as are the suppliant figures of his sisters Martha and Mary. Behind Jesus, the disciples, led by the white-bearded Peter, gesture their amazement, as does the crowd in the background, one of whom covers his face against the expected stench from the tomb.*

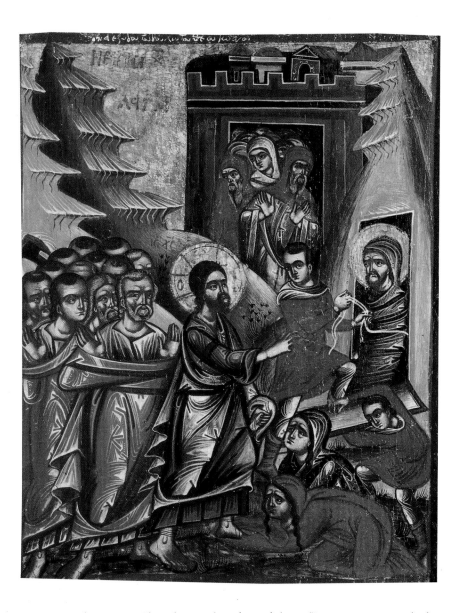

OPPOSITE: The Raising of Lazarus, *by Juan de Flandes (ca. 1465–1519), part of an altarpiece for the church of San Lazaro in Palencia, Spain. The disciples, crowd, and Lazarus' sister Mary all feature in this intensely emotional composition. But the astonished gaze of Lazarus directs the viewer's attention to the true focal point of the picture: the calm, undramatic figure of Jesus.*

Eastern and Western Churches, only a few of these scenes appear regularly. Along with the miracles, the most favored episodes have a strong narrative and symbolic content, such as the summoning of the apostles; the Samaritan woman at the well; Jesus walking on the water and stilling the storm; and Jesus with the woman taken in adultery. These also appear in other media and as individual panel paintings.

The raising of Lazarus (John 11.1–44), Jesus' final miracle before the Passion, combines strong narrative with potent symbolism. It is a drama of suspense and emotional power, which foreshadows Jesus' own resurrection. Its frequency in Orthodox iconography is due to the commemoration of the miracle as one of the twelve great feasts of the Orthodox Church (Lazarus Saturday, the eve of Palm Sunday). The icon depicting the scene is displayed on the iconostasis, the "icon screen" that divides the nave from the sanctuary in an Orthodox church. It appears in the upper level of the screen, which is devoted to festival icons.

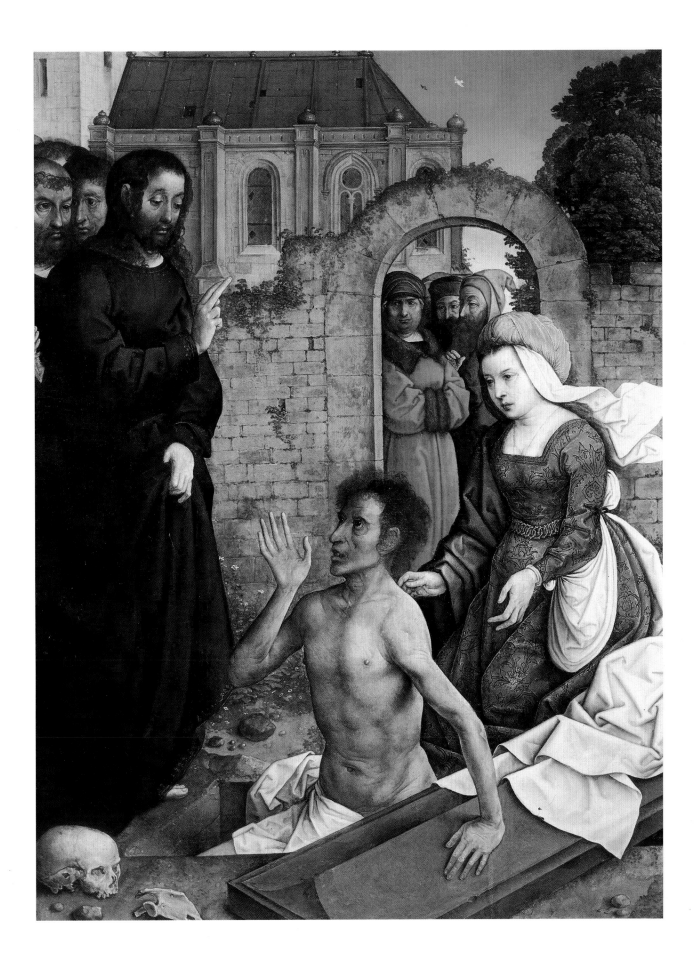

THE PASSION

The Betrayal of Christ, *a fresco in the Scrovegni Chapel, Padua, Italy, by Giotto (1366–1337). The dignified profiled head of Jesus expresses stillness and serenity amid a frenzied tumult of activity, during which Peter (left) cuts off the ear of one of the arresting party.*

The travails that marked the end of Jesus' earthly life are collectively known as the Passion (Latin *passio*, "suffering"). The importance of the Passion to Christian teaching is reflected in the vast range of artistic representations, in almost every medium, of the events following the Last Supper, from Jesus' arrest to his entombment. The climactic event of the Passion is the Crucifixion, but this scene, so common in later centuries, is absent from very early Christian art. The reasons are complex, but one factor was the preference for themes relating to the paradisial afterlife (which often found

LEFT: The Mocking and Crowning with Thorns, *by Hans Holbein the Elder (ca. 1460–1534), from the Passion altarpiece painted in 1500–1 for the Dominican church of Frankfurt-am-Main, Germany. The soldiers are caricatures of brutish cruelty, while Jesus' face looks directly out at the onlooker, invoking pity at his suffering.*

BELOW: The Road to Calvary, *by Simone Martini (ca. 1284–1344). Outside the gates of Jerusalem, Jesus looks back sorrowfully at his mother, who is threatened by a guard. Following behind, Mary Magdalene (identifiable by her long red hair) makes a gesture of grief.*

iconographical precedents in Greco-Roman art); the shameful nature of Jesus' execution was another. The earliest known attempts at the Crucifixion date from the fifth and sixth centuries and perhaps reflect doctrinal uncertainty about how this scene should be handled. Other early Passion scenes feature on an ivory casket at Brescia, Italy (ca. late fourth century), and in miniatures in sixth- and seventh-century gospel books. The Last Supper appears in early sixth-century manuscript miniatures and as part of a mosaic Passion cycle in Sant' Apollinare Nuovo, Ravenna.

The Passion story begins with Judas' betrayal of Jesus in Gethsemane. From the medieval period, this scene might form part of a virtuoso nightpiece, complete with attendant crowd and Peter cutting off the ear of the high priest's servant; or it might consist simply of the two central figures embracing. The ensuing trial of Jesus could be handled similarly. Pilate's showing of Jesus to the crowd with the words "Here is the man!" (John 19.5)—usually known under its Latin title Ecce Homo—was commonly depicted by Renaissance artists with Pilate, the crowd, and others; otherwise the image might consist solely of the purple-robed Jesus wearing the crown of thorns (Mark 15.17 and parallels).

The gospels say little concerning the carrying of the cross to Calvary (Latin Calvaria = Golgotha) beyond recording that Simon of Cyrene was compelled to carry the cross for Jesus, and that Jesus spoke on the way to

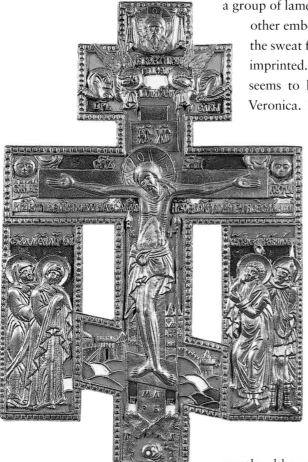

A 19th-century Russian Crucifixion in brass and enamel is surmounted by the image known as the Mandylion. According to an ancient tradition, Jesus himself made the original Mandylion by miraculously imprinting his face on a cloth which he sent to King Abgar of Edessa (modern Urfa, Turkey).

OPPOSITE: The Crucifixion, attributed to Hubert van Eyck (died 1426). The tau (T-shaped) cross towers over a fantasy Jerusalem cityscape. Jesus is already exalted above the mortal emotions and concerns of the grieving Virgin and St. John, the anguished women, and the indifferent men chatting and riding back to the city.

a group of lamenting women. These details were supplemented by, among other embellishments, the medieval tradition of a woman who wiped the sweat from Jesus' face with a cloth on which his likeness remained imprinted. The *vera icon* ("true image") of Jesus upon the fabric seems to have been the origin of this woman's traditional name, Veronica. Famous relics that claimed to bear the true imprint of Christ's features include the controversial Shroud of Turin (see p.126) and the Holy Mandylion of Edessa; the iconography of both of these promoted the now conventional image of Jesus as a bearded man.

The traditions surrounding Jesus' progress to Golgotha and the incidents that occurred on the way evolved in the late Middle Ages into the elaborate sequence known as the "Stations of the Cross," promoted especially by the Franciscans. Beginning with Jesus' condemnation and ending with his burial, the stations now usually number fourteen. They are represented in paintings, sculptures, or tableaux placed at intervals along the route to a church—most famously along the Via Dolorosa ("Way of Sorrows") in Jerusalem, the traditional route taken by Jesus to his place of execution—or inside, around the nave.

The treatment of the Crucifixion itself varies greatly, although certain elements nearly always occur. The way in which Jesus was to be depicted on the cross was a matter of debate throughout the early Byzantine centuries. At issue was how to convey the balance between the suffering humanity and impassive divinity that was believed to coexist in the person of Christ. One tradition, long maintained in the Romanesque art of the West, shows Jesus very much alive, open-eyed and with head erect, and clothed in a tunic (*colobium*). This was superseded around the ninth century in Constantinople by the convention of showing him naked except for a loincloth, with body bent and head slumped.

Around the eleventh century, the Crucifixion became the subject of the special festal icon for Good Friday in the Eastern Church. The icon usually depicts the Virgin and St. John the Apostle (traditionally identified as the "beloved disciple" of John 19.26 and as the evangelist himself), perhaps accompanied by another woman and the centurion (Matt. 27.54). As in Western treatments, a skull lies at the foot of the cross, a reference to the name of Golgotha ("Place of a Skull") as well as a symbol of Jesus' ultimate triumph over death.

In their portrayal of the crucified Jesus, Byzantine artists laid less emphasis on the extremes of physical suffering than was usual in the medieval West. Orthodox icons show Jesus' feet nailed to a slanting footboard with two separate nails, rather than with a single nail to the upright

Pietà, by Michelangelo (1485–1564). The naturalistic portrayal of the dead Christ and the poignant youthfulness of his mother are combined in a marble sculpture that the artist's biographer, Condivi (1553), described as "of so great and rare beauty that no one sees it without being moved to pity."

of the cross, imparting a less contorted form to the body. The overall impression reflects the language of Orthodox liturgical texts that speak of Jesus as "falling asleep" rather than dying upon the cross.

In the post-Romanesque West, a concentration on the physical torments of the Passion aimed to elicit powerful emotions of horror and sympathy in the onlooker. From the fifteenth century onward, a growing observation and understanding of anatomy in the West brought to the near-naked body of Jesus on the Cross a disturbing realism completely absent from the stylized torsos and musculature in Eastern icons.

A similar realism was displayed in Western depictions of the Deposition, or Descent from the Cross (the taking down of Jesus from the cross), and the Lamentation (the scene of mourning over the body). Although the Deposition is described by Dionysius of Fourna (see p.208), the fully elaborated form of the scene is a relative latecomer to Orthodox iconography, being based on Western prototypes of the sixteenth century. Earlier Eastern versions of the subject tend to limit the number of mourners to Joseph of Arimathea, Nicodemus, St. John the Apostle, and the Virgin, and to be more in the nature of a Lamentation. Since the fourteenth century these scenes, with the dead body of Jesus laid out on a cloth or slab, have been embroidered on the *epitaphios* (bier-cloth) used in the Holy Saturday ritual of the Orthodox Church.

The Lamentation and Entombment, the final stages of the Passion narrative, are often combined, and the mourners depicted are usually the same in both scenes. The Lamentation is related to one of the most powerful of all Christian devotional images, the Pietà (Italian, "Pity"), which developed in the thirteenth century. In it, the Virgin holds the dead body of her son in a tragic echo of the Madonna and Child. Associated with the Entombment is the scene referred to as the Man of Sorrows, known in Greek as the Akra Tapeinosis ("Peak of Humiliation"); both titles come from the description of the Suffering Servant in Isaiah 53.1–9. The dead Jesus, usually wearing the crown of thorns, stands in an open sarcophagus; only the naked upper part of his body is visible, often displaying the wounds in his hands and side.

The Avignon Pietà, *attributed to Enguerrand Quarton, or Charreton (fl. 1444–66). Absorbed in grief, the Virgin prays, while Mary Magdalene weeps, and John gently removes Jesus' crown of thorns. The stylized gold background and heavy draperies make a striking foil for the pallid, unnaturally curved body of Christ and the delicate, expressive faces of the mourners. The man who commissioned the work is depicted in the left foreground.*

THE RESURRECTION

The Supper at Emmaus, by Caravaggio (1570–1610) captures the disciples' surprise at the instant when they recognized Jesus (Luke 24.31). The head of the standing man casts a shadowy halo on the wall behind the youthful Christ, whose dramatic gesture of blessing has the two disciples starting from their seats.

Christ's resurrection is not described in the gospels, and the artistic traditions of East and West differ considerably in how they present this event. In early art it was alluded to symbolically, for example by a cross combined with the monogram of Christ to represent his triumph over death. The Western tradition of Jesus rising from his tomb, holding aloft the banner of the Resurrection (a red cross on a white background), did not appear until the eleventh century. The Eastern form of the Resurrection (Greek *Anastasis*) is the scene known in Western art as the "Harrowing of Hell," and depicts the resurrection of the righteous dead by the risen Jesus. The

ΗΑΝΑΣΤΑΣΙΣ

scene is suggested by passages of the New Testament (Matt. 27.52–3; Eph. 4.9, 5.14; 1 Peter 3.18–19) and the Psalms (Pss. 24.7–9, 107.16), although its details derive from apocryphal texts. It first appeared in the eighth century, but it was only in the eleventh that it attained its classic form: the risen Christ, holding the Cross as the symbol of his triumph over death, tramples down the gates of hell and reaches out to the resurrected figures of "saints who had fallen asleep." Foremost among them are Adam and Eve, usually with David and Solomon. John the Baptist is also sometimes shown, and more elaborate compositions include biblical patriarchs and prophets.

The events of the forty days from the Resurrection to the Ascension provided artists with several subsidiary subjects, drawn from episodes related in the gospels. Two have in common the dramatic twist in which the disciples' initially fail to recognize their master, and these became popular in the Renaissance and later. The first is the meeting between Mary Magdalene and the risen Jesus in the garden near the empty tomb (John 20.11–18), known under the Latin title of Noli Me Tangere ("Touch me not"; NRSV: "Do not hold onto me") (John 20.17). The second is the journey to, and supper at, the village of Emmaus (Luke 24.13–35).

The Resurrection (Anastasis). The mosaics of the monastery church of Hosios Loukas in central Greece, include an early version of the classic Anastasis (ca. 1020). Christ, standing on the scattered doors, locks, and bolts of hell, plucks Adam from his sarcophagus. Awaiting their turn are Eve (whose hands are respectfully veiled according to Byzantine imperial protocol) and kings David and Solomon (who are crowned like Byzantine princes).

CHRIST TRIUMPHANT

Christ Pantocrator, a mosaic in the apse of the cathedral at Cefalù, Sicily (1148). Craftsmen working in the Byzantine tradition created this dominating apse mosaic of Christ as judge and ruler of all things. His countenance is stern, but he raises his right hand in blessing and proffers words of comfort and hope from John's gospel: "I am the light of the world. Whoever follows me will never walk in darkness but will have the light of life" (John 8.12).

The issues posed by the representation of Christ after the Ascension, when he takes his place in heaven in triumph as part of the glory of the Trinity, are bound up with the whole question of how, if at all, the Trinity should be represented. Standard Orthodox iconography portrays the three Persons of the Trinity only indirectly, under the guise of the three angels entertained by the patriarch Abraham at Mamre (Gen. 18.1–8).

The symbols associated with Christ triumphant appeared early: a relief carving (ca. 430CE) on a door from Santa Sabina, Rome, shows him standing within a victory wreath, holding a scroll and with the Greek letters Alpha and Omega (AΩ; see Rev. 1.8) inscribed beside him. The scroll (later book) is a constant element, symbolizing Christ as the Logos, the eternal divine Word (John 1.1ff.), and bringer of the New Law. The Greek title Pantocrator ("All-Ruling") appeared from the twelfth century onward in

half-length representations of Christ as ruler and judge of the world. The Pantocrator embodies the attributes of both Father and Son—power, justice, mercy, and love. As a mosaic or fresco, it occupies a dominant position in a church, in the main dome or apse, or over the principal entrance.

The Western Church evolved different conventions for the depiction of the Trinity. Biblical hints were elaborated to produce the archetypes of God the Father as a robed, white-bearded old man ("the Ancient of Days," as Dan. 7.9), while the Holy Spirit takes the form of a dove (Matt. 3.16). Typically, the spatial arrangement of the three Persons is in descending order with the Father at the top, as in Raphael's *Disputà* (see above). A widespread form of northern European Gothic Trinity shows the Father crowned and enthroned, holding a figure of Christ on the Cross with the dove over Christ's head; less common is the Father and Son as crowned figures side by side, with the dove between them.

In the West, the book of Revelation (especially 4.2–10) inspired a subject popular in Romanesque sculpture: Christ crowned and enthroned between the four symbols of the evangelists and surrounded by the twenty-four elders (Rev. 4.4). An example is the tympanum at the abbey of Moissac in southern France, dating from before 1115.

Disputà, by Raphael (1483–1520). This fresco for the Camera della Segnatura in the Vatican, Rome (1508–11) is a huge panorama representing the Church triumphant on earth and in heaven. God the Father (top) stands over the enthroned figure of Christ in glory showing his wounds, flanked by the Virgin and John the Baptist. Around his throne are seated Peter (far left), Paul (far right) and the other Apostles. The Holy Spirit in the form of a white dove becomes present on earth in the Blessed Sacrament of the Eucharist, which stands on the central altar, surrounded by figures from the Church's history.

GLOSSARY

Apocrypha Sacred writings not universally regarded as part of the canon of scripture. For the most part originally in Greek, they include Jewish apocrypha, such as the books of Judith, Tobit, and the Maccabees, which stand outside the Jewish canon and the Old Testament canons of some Christian denominations. In the Roman Catholic Church many of these writings are "deuterocanonical," that is, distinct from the canon but considered of spiritual value. Among Christian apocrypha are the various gospels and letters not included in the canon of the New Testament.

apocryphal Of or pertaining to, or derived from, the Apocrypha.

Christology Doctrine or teaching pertaining to the person of Christ, in particular the union of his human and divine natures.

Davidic Of or pertaining to King David, ruler of Israel ca. 1000–ca. 965BCE.

eschatological Of or pertaining to the "last things" (the apocalypse, the end of the world, the day of judgment, the dawn of a new age, etc.); from Greek *eskhatos*, "last."

eschatology Doctrine or teaching about the "last things."

Fourth Gospel The gospel of John, in contradistinction to the three synoptic gospels (see below).

Hebrew Bible, Hebrew Scriptures The Hebrew writings constituting the Jewish Bible. The Old Testament, the first part of the Christian Bible, consists of the Hebrew Scriptures (ordered differently from the Jewish Bible) with or without the Apocrypha, depending on denomination.

Josephus Flavius Josephus (37–ca. 100CE), a Jewish historian and a key source for our knowledge of Judaism around the time of Jesus. His four extant works are *The Jewish War*, *The Antiquities of the Jews*, *Against Apion* (a riposte to an anti-Jewish tract), and the autobiographical *Life*.

law In the present book, the term "law" almost always refers to the Jewish (Mosaic) law, or Torah.

Mishnah A compilation of, and commentary on, those Jewish legal traditions not found in the Bible. Produced ca. 200CE by the great rabbi Judah the Prince, the Mishnah in turn gave rise to a wealth of commentary and interpretation that was collected and codified in the Talmud (see below).

Mosaic Of or pertaining to Moses, used especially in reference to the Jewish law, or Torah (see below).

Pentateuch The first five books of the Hebrew Bible: Genesis, Exodus, Leviticus, Numbers, Deuteronomy. Also referred to as the Torah, the books of Moses, and the books of the law.

Philo Philo of Alexandria (ca. 15BCE–50CE), a Jewish philosopher whose writings, in particular on the Logos concept (see pp.174–5), were very influential in the early Church.

postexilic Of or pertaining to the period following the sixty-year exile of the Jews in Babylon (597–539BCE).

Pseudepigrapha Religious writings outside the Jewish and Christian canons, Apocrypha, and the corpus of rabbinic works. They are often attributed to a biblical figure, such as Enoch.

rabbinic, rabbinical Of or pertaining to the rabbis (Jewish teachers and interpreters of the law) and their teachings.

rabbinic age, rabbinic era The term given to an era (generally taken to be from the late first century CE to the early seventh century CE) in which the great rabbis (religious teachers) of Judaism, such as Yohanan ben Zakkai, Akiva, and Judah the Prince, were active. The rabbinic age saw the production of the Mishnah (see above) and the Talmud (see below).

Septuagint The Greek translation of the Hebrew Bible, made at Alexandria, Egypt, in the second century BCE. It also includes writings regarded as noncanonical in Judaism and as apocryphal (see above) or deuterocanonical in Christianity. The Septuagint is the Old Testament of the Greek Orthodox Church.

synoptic gospels (synoptics) The gospels of Matthew, Mark, and Luke. "Synoptic" (Greek *sunoptikos*) literally means "seen together": these three gospels share so many textual similarities that they may be set out in parallel and fruitfully compared.

synoptists The authors of the synoptic gospels (see above).

Talmud The Mishnah plus the corpus of rabbinic commentary on it. There are two versions, one produced in Palestine ca. 400CE (the "Jerusalem" Talmud) and one in Mesopotamia ca. 500CE (the "Babylonian" Talmud).

Temple The Temple of Jerusalem, the focus of Jewish religious life until 70CE. The First Temple was built by King Solomon and destroyed by the Babylonians ca. 587BCE; it was rebuilt following the exile in Babylon and lavishly refurbished by King Herod the Great. This Second Temple, the one Jesus knew, was destroyed by the Romans in 70CE and never rebuilt.

Torah Hebrew, "instruction, direction." In a strict sense, the first five books of the Hebrew Bible, containing the 633 commandments (*mitzvot*) that form the basis of the Jewish law, transmitted by God to Israel through Moses. It is supplemented by the "oral Torah," various regulations not found in the Bible and codified in the Mishnah and Talmud.

ABBREVIATIONS

The following abbreviations are used in this book:

General Abbreviations

CE	Common Era (the equivalent of AD)
BCE	Before the Common Era (the equivalent of BC)
ca.	*circa* (about)
ch./chs.	chapter/chapters
ff.	and following

fl.	*floruit* (flourished, active)
p./pp.	page/pages
v./vv.	verse/verses
NRSV	New Revised Standard Version (1989)
KJV	King James (Authorized) Version (1611)

Quotations from Scripture and other Ancient Writings

Books of the Hebrew Scriptures, New Testament, Apocrypha, and Deuterocanonical writings are referred to according to the list of short forms and abbreviations below. Abbreviations are used only in parentheses within the text. Chapter and verse are separated by a period (.) and a sequence is indicated by a dash (–). Thus, Matt. 9.24 = chapter 9, verse 24 of the gospel of Matthew; Matt. 3.7–10 = chapter 3, verses 7 to 10 of Matthew; Matt. 5–10 = chapters 5 to 10 of Matthew.

Short form	Abbreviation
Acts of the Apostles	Acts
Amos	Amos
Baruch	Bar.
Bel and the Dragon	Bel
1 Chronicles	1 Chron.
2 Chronicles	2 Chron.
Colossians	Col.
1 Corinthians	1 Cor.
2 Corinthians	2 Cor.
Daniel	Dan.
Deuteronomy	Deut.
Ecclesiastes	Eccles.
Ephesians	Eph.
1 Esdras	1 Esd.
2 Esdras	2 Esd.
Esther	Esther
Exodus	Exod.
Ezekiel	Ezek.
Ezra	Ezra
Galatians	Gal.
Habakkuk	Hab.
Haggai	Hag.
Hebrews	Heb.
Hosea	Hos.
Isaiah	Isa.
James	James
Jeremiah	Jer.
Job	Job
Joel	Joel
John *or* Fourth Gospel	John
1 John	1 John
2 John	2 John
3 John	3 John
Jonah	Jon.
Joshua	Josh.
Jude	Jude
Judges	Judg.
Judith	Jth.
1 Kings	1 Kings
2 Kings	2 Kings
Lamentations	Lam.

Short form	Abbreviation
Letter of Jeremiah	Let. Jer.
Leviticus	Lev.
Luke	Luke
1 Maccabees	1 Macc.
2 Maccabees	2 Macc.
3 Maccabees	3 Macc.
4 Maccabees	4 Macc.
Malachi	Mal.
Mark	Mark
Matthew	Matt.
Micah	Mic.
Nahum	Nah.
Nehemiah	Neh.
Numbers	Num.
Obadiah	Obad.
1 Peter	1 Pet.
2 Peter	2 Pet.
Philippians	Phil.
Philemon	Philem.
Prayer of Azariah and Song of the Three Young Men (Jews)	Song of Thr.
Prayer of Manasseh	Pr. of Man.
Proverbs	Prov.
Psalm(s)	Ps(s).
Revelation	Rev.
Romans	Rom.
Ruth	Ruth
1 Samuel	1 Sam.
2 Samuel	2 Sam.
Sirach (Ecclesiasticus)	Sir.
Song of Solomon	Song of Sol.
Susanna	Sus.
1 Thessalonians	1 Thess.
2 Thessalonians	2 Thess.
1 Timothy	1 Tim.
2 Timothy	2 Tim.
Titus	Titus
Tobit	Tob.
Wisdom of Solomon	Wisd. of Solomon
Zechariah	Zech.
Zephaniah	Zeph.

BIBLIOGRAPHY

GENERAL STUDIES

Bornkamm, G. *Jesus of Nazareth*. New York: Harper and Row; London: Hodder and Stoughton, 1960.

Bowden, John. *Jesus: the Unanswered Questions*. London: SCM Press, 1988.

Bultmann, R. *Jesus and the Word*. New York: Scribner; London: Collins, 1934, 1958.

Charlesworth, J.H. *Jesus within Judaism*. New York and London: Doubleday, 1988.

Conzelmann, H. *Jesus*. Philadelphia: Fortress Press, 1973.

Crossan, J.D. *The Historical Jesus: the Life of a Mediterranean Jewish Peasant*. San Francisco: Harper; Edinburgh: T. and T. Clark, 1991.

Harvey, A.E. *Jesus and the Constraints of History*. Philadelphia: Westminster; London: Duckworth, 1982.

Moule, C.F.D. *The Origin of Christology*. Cambridge: Cambridge University Press, 1977.

O'Collins, G. and D. Kendall. *Focus on Jesus*. Leominster, England: Gracewing (Fowler Wright Books), 1996.

Sanders, E.P. *The Historical Figure of Jesus*. London: Penguin, 1993.

Schillebeeckx, E. *Jesus: an Experiment in Christology*. New York and London: Collins, 1979.

Stanton, G.N. *The Gospels and Jesus*. Oxford: Oxford University Press, 1989.

Theissen, Gerd and Annette Merz. *The Historical Jesus: a Comprehensive Guide*. London: SCM Press, 1998.

Wright, N.T. *Jesus and the Victory of God*. Philadelphia: Fortress Press, 1996.

Wright, N.T. *The New Testament and the People of God*. Philadelphia: Fortress Press, 1992.

Vermes, Geza. *Jesus the Jew*, 2nd ed. London: SCM Press, 1983.

Vermes, Geza. *Jesus and the World of Judaism*. London: SCM Press, 1983.

Vermes, Geza. *The Religion of Jesus the Jew*. London: SCM Press, 1993.

THE SETTING

Bahat, D. *The Illustrated Atlas of Jerusalem*. New York: Simon and Schuster; London: Macmillan, 1990.

Downing, F.G. *The Christ and the Cynics*. London: SCM Press, 1988.

Hengel, Martin. *The "Hellenization" of Judaea in the First Century after Christ*. Philadelphia: Trinity Press International; London: SCM Press, 1989.

Jeremias, J. *Jerusalem in the Time of Jesus*. Philadelphia: Fortress Press; London: SCM Press, 1984.

Jones, A.H.M. *The Herods of Judaea*. Oxford: Clarendon Press, 1938.

Josephus, Flavius, *Works*. Ten vols., Trans. and ed. by H. StJ. Thackeray, R. Marcus, and L. Feldman. London and Cambridge, Mass.: Loeb Classical Library, 1926–65.

Nickelsburg, George W.E. *Jewish Literature between the Bible and the Mishnah*. Philadelphia: Fortress Press; London: SCM Press, 1981.

Pfeiffer, R.H. *History of New Testament Times*. New York: Harper and Brothers, 1949.

Rousseau, John. J, and R. Arav. *Jesus and His World*. Philadelphia: Fortress Press; London: SCM Press, 1996.

Sanders, E.P. *Jesus and Judaism*. London: SCM Press, 1985.

Schürer, E., G. Vermes, F. Millor, and M. Black. *The History of the Jewish People in the Age of Jesus Christ*. 3 vols. Edinburgh: T. and T. Clark, 1973–87.

THE LIFE

Borg, M.J. *Jesus: A New Vision*. San Francisco: Harper and Row, 1987.

Burridge, Richard. *A. Four Gospels, One Jesus?* London: SPCK, 1994.

Catchpole, D. *The Trial of Jesus*. Leiden: Brill, 1971.

Craig, W.L. *The Son Rises: The Historical Evidence for the Resurrection of Jesus*. Chicago: Moody, 1981.

Finegan, J. *Handbook of Biblical Chronology*. Princeton, NJ: Princeton University Press, 1964.

Hengel, M. *Crucifixion in the Ancient World and the Folly of the Message of the Cross*. Philadelphia: Fortress Press; London: SCM Press, 1977.

Hengel, M. *The Charismatic Leader and his Followers*. Edinburgh: T. and T. Clark, 1981.

Hoehner, H.W. *Chronological Aspects of the Life of Christ*. Grand Rapids, Mich.: Zondervan, 1977.

Jeremias, J. *The Eucharistic Words of Jesus*. New York and London: Scribner, 1966.

Kee, H.C. *Miracle in the Early Christian World*. New Haven: Yale University Press, 1983.

Klasser, William. *Judas: Betrayer or Friend of Jesus?* London: SCM Press, 1997.

Légasse, Simon. *The Trial of Jesus*. London: SCM Press, 1997.

Ludemann, Gerd. *The Resurrection of Jesus*. London: SCM Press, 1996.

Lunny, W.J. *The Sociology of the Resurrection*. London: SCM Press, 1989.

Marxsen, W. *The Resurrection of Jesus of Nazareth*. Philadelphia: Fortress Press; London: SCM Press, 1970.

Metzger, B.M. *The Canon of the New Testament*. Oxford: Oxford University Press, 1987.

Millard, A.R. *Discoveries from the Times of Jesus*. Oxford: Lion, 1990.

Sanders, E.P., *Jesus and Judaism*. London: SCM Press, 1985.

Sanders, E.P., and Margaret Davies. *Studying the Synoptic Gospels*.

ᵉ

Philadelphia: Trinity Press International, 1990.

Sherwin-White, A.N. *Roman Society and Roman Law in the New Testament.* Oxford, Clarendon Press, 1963.

Spong, J.S. *Born of a Woman.* San Francisco: HarperCollins, 1992.

Stanton, G.N. *Gospel Truth? Today's Quest for the Jesus of Nazareth.* San Francisco: HarperCollins, 1995; London: Fount, 1997.

Twelftree, G.H. *Jesus the Exorcist.* Tübingen, 1993.

Van der Loos, H. *The Miracles of Jesus.* Leiden: Brill, 1965.

Vermes, G. *The Dead Sea Scrolls.* Sheffield, England: JSOT, 1987.

Webb, Robert. *John the Baptist in the Gospel Tradition.* Cambridge: Cambridge University Press, 1968.

Wenham, David, ed. *The Jesus Tradition outside the Gospels.* Sheffield, England: JSOT, 1984.

Wenham, D. and C.L. Blomberg, eds. *The Miracles of Jesus.* Sheffield, England: JSOT, 1986.

Wink, W. *John the Baptist in the Gospel Tradition.* Cambridge: Cambridge University Press, 1968.

Winter, P. *On the Trial of Jesus.* Berlin and New York: De Gruyter, 1974.

THE TEACHINGS

Banks, R.J. *Jesus and the Law in the Synoptic Tradition.* Cambridge: Cambridge University Press, 1975.

Beasley-Murray, G.R. *Jesus and the Kingdom of God.* Grand Rapids, Mich.: Eerdmans, 1986.

Davies, W.D. *The Setting of the Sermon on the Mount.* Cambridge: Cambridge University Press, 1964.

Dodd, C.H. *The Interpretation of the Fourth Gospel.* Cambridge: Cambridge University Press, 1953.

Evans, C.F. *The Lord's Prayer.* London:

SCM Press, 1963.

France, R.T. *Jesus and the Old Testament.* London: Tyndale Press, 1971.

Jeremias, J. *Rediscovering the Parables.* London: SCM Press, 1966.

Jeremias, J. *The Prayers of Jesus.* Naperville, Ill., Allenson; London: SCM Press, 1967.

McArthur, H.K. and R.M. Johnston. *They Also Taught in Parables: Rabbinic Parables from the First Centuries of the Christian Era.* Grand Rapids, Mich.: Zodervan, 1990.

Manson, T.W. *Jesus and the Non-Jews.* London: Athlone Press, 1955.

Perkins, P. *Jesus as Teacher.* New York and Cambridge: Cambridge University Press, 1990.

Perrin, N. *The Kingdom of God in the Teaching of Jesus.* Philadelphia: Westminster; London: SCM Press, 1963.

Strecker, G. *The Sermon on the Mount: on Exegetical Commentory.* Nashville, Tenn.: Abington; Edinburgh: T. and T. Clark, 1988.

INTERPRETATIONS

Altizer, Thomas, J.J. *The Contemporary Jesus.* Albany, N.Y.: State University of New York Press, 1997.

Bammel, E. and C.F.D. Moule, eds. *Jesus and the Politics of His Day.* Cambridge: Cambridge University Press, 1984.

Barker, Margaret. *The Risen Lord: The Jesus of History as the Christ of Faith.* Edinburgh: T. and T. Clark, 1996.

Bonino, J.M. *Faces of Jesus: Latin American Theologies.* London: Orbis Books, 1984.

Borsch, F.H. *The Son of Man.* Grand Rapids, Mich.: Eerdmans; London: SPCK, 1983.

Brandon, S.G.F. *Jesus and the Zealots.* Manchester: Manchester University

Press, 1967.

Buber, Martin. *Two Types of Faith: A Study of the Interpenetration of Judaism and Christianity.* New York: Harper Torchbooks, 1961.

Cullmann, O. *Jesus and the Revolutionaries.* New York: Harper and Row, 1970.

Daniélou, J. *A History of Early Christian Doctrine,* vol. 1: *The Theology of Jewish Christianity.* London, Burns and Oates, 1964.

Dodd, C.H. *The Founder of Christianity.* London: Collins, 1971.

Fiorenza, Elizabeth, S. *Jesus: Miriam's Child, Sophia's Prophet.* London: SCM Press, 1995.

Grillmeier, A. *Christ in Christian Tradition,* 2 vols. London, 1965, 1975.

Hahn, F. *The Titles of Jesus in Christology.* New York: World; London: Lutterworth Press, 1969.

Hagner, D.A. *The Jewish Reclamation of Jesus: an Analysis and Critique of Modern Jewish Study of Jesus.* Grand Rapids, Mich.: Zondervan, 1984.

Hamilton, William. *A Quest for the Post-Historical Jesus.* London, SCM Press, 1993.

Kramer, W. *Christ, Lord, Son of God.* London: SCM Press, 1966.

Leivestad, R. *Jesus in His Own Perspective.* Minneapolis: Augsburg Press, 1987.

Linders, B. *Jesus, Son of Man.* Grand Rapids, Mich.: Eerdmans; London: SPCK, 1983.

Meier, J.P. *A Marginal Jew: Rethinking the Historical Jesus,* 2 vols. New York and London: Doubleday, 1991, 1994.

Pagels, Elaine H. *The Gnostic Gospels.* London: Penguin Books, 1982.

Parrinder, G. *Jesus in the Qur'an.* London: Sheldon Press, 1976.

Reiser, M. *Jesus and Judgement.* Minneapolis: Augsburg Press, 1967.

Rudolph, K. *Gnosis: the Nature and*

History of Gnosticism. San Francisco: Harper and Row; Edinburgh: T. and T. Clark, 1983.

Riches, J.K. *Jesus and the Transformation of Judaism*. London: Darton, Longman and Todd, 1980.

Stanton, G.N. *Jesus of Nazareth in New Testament Preaching*. Cambridge: Cambridge University Press, 1974.

Sweetman, J.W. *Islam and Christian Theology*, 4 vols. London: Lutterworth Press, 1945–1967.

Witvliet, Theo. *The Way of the Black Messiah*. London: SCM Press, 1987.

JESUS IN ART

Baggley, J. *Doors of Perception: Icons and their Spiritual Significance*. London and Oxford: Mowbray, 1987.

Dionysius of Fourna *The Painter's Manual*, trans. by P. Hetherington (1974). Redondo Beach, Calif.: Oakwood Publications, rev. ed., 1989.

Every, G. *Christian Mythology*. London: Hamlyn, rev. ed., 1987.

Kuryluk, E. *Veronica and her Cloth*. Cambridge, Mass., and Oxford: Basil Blackwell, 1991.

Meer, F. van der, and Mohrann, C. *Atlas of the Early Christian World*, trans. by M.F. Hedlund and H.H. Rowley. London: Nelson, 1966.

Ouspensky, L. and Lossky, V. *The Meaning of Icons*, trans. by G.E.H. Palmer and E. Kadloubovsky. Crestwood, N.Y.: St Vladimir's Seminary Press, 1989.

Robinson, S.I. *Images of Byzantium: Learning about Icons*. London: Loizou Publications, 1996.

Schiller, G. *Iconography of Christian Art*, 2 vols., trans. by J. Seligman. London: Lund Humphries, 1971.

Speake, J. *The Dent Dictionary of Symbols in Christian Art*. London: J.M. Dent, 1994.

Tudor-Craig, P. "The Iconography of Corpus Christi" in S.E. Porter, M.A. Hayes and D. Tombs (eds.), *Images of Christ: Ancient and Modern*, Roehampton Institute London Paper 2. Sheffield, England: Sheffield Academic Press, 1997.

Weitzmann, K. *The Icon: Holy Images, Sixth to Fourteenth Century*. London: Chatto and Windus, 1978.

REFERENCE

Achtemeier, Paul J., ed. *Harper's Bible Dictionary*. San Francisco: Harper and Row, 1985.

Buttrick, George A., and K. Crim, eds. *The Interpreter's Dictionary of the Bible*. 5 vols. Nashville, Tenn.: Abingdon, 1976.

Coggins, R.J. and J.L. Houlden. *A Dictionary Interpretation*. Philadelphia: Trinity; London: SCM Press, 1990.

Freedman, David Noel, et al. *The Anchor Bible Dictionary*. 6 vols. New York: Doubleday, 1992.

Kittel, Gerhard, and Gerhard Friedrich, eds. *Theological Dictionary of the New Testament*. Grand Rapids, Mich.: Eerdmans, 1985.

Metzger, Bruce M., and Michael D. Coogan. *The Oxford Companion to the Bible*. New York: Oxford University Press, 1993.

Peake, A.S. *Commentary on the Bible*. Edinburgh: Thomas Nelson, 1962.

Roth, Cecil, ed. *Encyclopaedia Judaica*. New York: Macmillan, 1972.

INDEX

References to main text, boxed text, and margin text are in roman (plain) type; references to picture captions are in *italics*.

A

Aaron, 63
Abba, 46, 147
Abraham, 62, 72, 75, 132, 190
Acts of the Apostles, 53 *and see* Luke, Gospel of
Adam, 63, 86, 132, 170–71, 190, *219*, 219
Adoptionists, 173
Adoration, *67*, *181*, *201 and see* Nativity
Adultery, 44, 68, *100*, *143*, 143, 189
Advocate *see* Holy Spirit
Aenon, 14
Agony, *114*, *185 and see* Arrest; Gethsemane
Agrapha, 58, 59
Agriculture, 17, 39, 40–42, *42*, 70
Ahijah, 160
Aleppo, 173
Alexander of Cyrene, 123
Allegory, 138, 167, *208 and see* Parables
Alphaeus, 91
Ananus, 80
Anastasis 218, *219 and see* Resurrection
Andrew (disciple), 17, 43, 47, 91, *209*
Androgyny, 186
Angels, *9*, *114*
  and the apocalypse, 181

and death of Herod, 73
and flight to Egypt, 73, 75
and the Nativity, 74, 201
promising a child, 66
and the Resurrection, 129, 131
and the Temptation, 86
and the Trinity, 220
warnings from, 74
and see Gabriel; Prophecy
Anna (Anne), *58*, 77, 78, 207
Annas (Ananos), 28, 119
Annunciation, 64, *65*, *69*, *70*, 191
  and see Nativity
Antioch, 53
Antiochus Epiphanes, 22, 33, 181
Antipas *see* Herod Antipas
Antonia fortress, 19, 111
Apocalypse, 180–1 *and see* End of the World; Synoptic Apocalypse
Apologists, 174, 175
Apostles, *59*, *90*, *133*, *221 and see* Disciples
Aramaic, 46–7, 173 *and see* Language
Archelaus, 24–5, 75
Architecture, 7, *11*, 19, *24*, *25*, 29, *123*
Archons, 177
Arianism, 175
Arius of Alexandria, 174, 175
Arrest of Jesus, 28, 29, 31, 41, *114*, 114–15, 118, *182*, 182, *185*, *212*
  and see Passion
Art, Christian, 198–221
  early, 198–9
  and see individual subjects
Ascension, *132*, 132–3, *133*
Asceticism, 82, 176
Astrology, 72
Athanasius, 174
Athenagoras of Athens, 174

Atonement, Day of (Yom Kippur), 170, 171
Augustine of Hippo, 174
Augustus, 60, 73

B

Banias (Paneas), 15, *107*, *168 and see* Caesarea Philippi
Bankers, 38 *and see* Moneychangers
Baptism, 84, *208*
  of Jesus, 14, *61*, 61, 84–5, *85*, 106, 166, 167
  and see John the Baptist
Baptist *see* John the Baptist
Barabbas, 26
Bar'am, *32*
Barnabas, 144
Bartholomew, 47, 91
Beatitudes, 149
Beelzebul (Beelzebub), 71, 87, 97, 101
  and see Devil; Satan
Belief, 154, 192 *and see* Faith
Benedictus, 67
Beth–Shean (Scythopolis), 14
Beth-zatha (Bethesda), 21
Bethany, 14, 93, 114, 115, *192*
Bethesda (Beth-zatha), 21
Bethlehem, 13, *63*, 64, *64*, 67, 70
Bethphage, 21
Bethsaida (Bethsaida-Julias), 16, 17, *25*, 95, *101*
Betrayal of Jesus, 114–15, *212*, 213
  and see Passion
Betrothal, 44, 69 *and see* Marriage
Bible *see* Gospels; Hebrew Bible; New Testament
Biography, 6–7, 50–51, 56

Birth of Jesus, 24, 60–61, 190 *and see* Nativity

Blasphemy, 119, 159

Book (codex), 51

Booths (Tabernacles), festival of, 33, *93*

Bridget of Sweden, Saint, 201

Bultmann, Rudolf, 193

Burials, 123, 127

C

Caesarea (coastal city), *24, 26, 26*

Caesarea Philippi (Paneas), 14–15, 25, 106, *107*, 107, *168*

Caiaphas (Joseph Caiaphas), 28, 29, 61, *117*, 119

Caligula, 24

Cana (Kafr Kanna, Khirbet Qana), 16, *44*, 79, *91, 93, 154*

Capernaum, 16, *17*, 17, 26, 32, *96, 96, 101, 142, 145*

Carpenters, 39, *80*, 81, 206, *207*

Carthage, *180*

Celibacy, 176

Censuses, 60–61

Centurions, 26, 27 *and see* Soldiers

Cerinthus, 69

Chalcedon, 175

Chalcedonian Definition, 175

Childbirth, 76

Chinnereth, Lake *see* Galilee, Sea of

Chorazin, 16, 32, *101*

Christianity, 176, 188–9, 191
    Gentile, 80, 172–3
    Jewish, 53, 58, 65, 80, 92, 172–3, 188 *and see* Christians; Church

Christians, 58, 170, 173, 198 *and see* Christianity; Church

Christology, 170

Christ's Table, Tabgha, *178*

Chronology

of Gospels, 52–3, 193

of Jesus' life, 60–1, 92, 93, 116

Church, the, 108–9, 131, 133, *157*, 170–1, 178–9, 188–9 *and see* Christianity; Coptic Church

Church Fathers, the, 58, 173, 174, 177

Circumcision, 76, 144, 173

Cleansing of the Temple, the, 18, 19, *103*, 103, *110*, 110–11, 183 *and see* Temple of Jerusalem

Clement of Alexandria, 174

Clement of Rome, 174

Climate of Palestine, 41

Codex (bound book), 51

Cognitive dissonance, 178

Coins, 29, *38*, 38–9, *45, 56, 105, 120*

Commandments, 36, 143, 145

Commitment, 152

Community, 108–9

Condemnation of Jesus, the, 26, 122–3 *and see* Trials of Jesus

Conflict stories, 100–3

Coptic Church, 175 *and see* Church

Creation myths, 176–7

Criticism, 50–1, 53, 193

Crucifixion, *47, 123*, 123, 124–7, *125, 156, 170*, 191, *196, 215*
    in art, 212–13, *213, 214*, 214, *215*, 216, *216, 217*
    burial of Jesus' body after, *127*, 127
    chronology of, 61, 112–13, 125
    and the Church, 171
    death by, 127
    drinks consumed at, 124, 126
    inscription on cross of, *47*, 120, *125, 165*, 183
    mockery at, 122–3, 124–5, 126, *213*
    other victims of, 26, 123, *124*, 125
    prayers from the cross at, 141, 147
    shame of, 171

soldiers at, 27, 122–3, 124, *213*
    symbolism of, 124, 127
    words from cross at, 46, 125–6, 166 *and see* Deposition

Crurifragium, 127

Curses, 17, *101*, 101

Cynics, 22

Cyprian of Carthage, 174

Cyrene, 123

Cyril of Alexandria, 174

D

Daughters of Jerusalem, 122

David, House of, 63, 64, 109, 165 *and see* Genealogies

David, King, 62, 64, 67, 70, 138, *165, 219*, 219

Dead Sea Scrolls, *37*, 37, 82, 141

Death
    by crucifixion, 127
    penalty of, 117, 119, 120
    and resurrection, 14, 95, 118, 159, 161, *192*

Decapolis, 13, 14, 25

Dedication (Hanukkah), 33, 77, 93 *and see* Festivals

Deists, 192

Demiurge, 176, 177

Demonic possession *see* Possession

Demons, 35, 87, 119, 133, 166, 167
    cast into herd of swine, 14, 96, *97*, 97, 158 *and see* Evil; Exorcism; Possession

Deposition, the, 127, 216 *and see* Entombment; Passion

Descent from the Cross *see* Deposition

Devil, 87, 97, *200 and see* Beelzebul; Satan

Diogenes, *22*, 22

Dionysius of Fourna, 209, 216

Disciples, *59*, 77, *90*, 90–91, *133*, 178, *209*, *221*
  commissioning of, 129, 130, 131
  desertion of, 114–15, 141
  and exorcism, 133
  and family, 101
  female, 77, 187
  of John the Baptist, 82, 83, 91
  power of, 133
  and the Resurrection, 129, 219
  symbols of, 77
  women as, 77, 187
Discourses, 92, 148–9, 152–3 *and see* Parables; Sermons
Divinity, 167, 175, 189, 190
Divorce, 35–6, 45, 73, 141, 143
Dove (symbol of Spirit of God), *65*, 84, *85*, *155*, 221, *221* *and see* Holy Spirit
Dreams, 64, 71, 73, 74 *and see* Prophecy
Dualism, 176

E

Earthquake, 124
Ebionites, 69, 173
Economy of Palestine, 38–43 *and see* Agriculture; Trade
Eden, 86
Edict of Toleration, 198
Education, 79
Egerton Gospel, *58* *and see* Gospels
Egypt, 73, 74–5, *148*
Egyptian, The, 161
Ein Karem, 66
Elijah, 35
  ascension of, 133
  and the Holy Spirit, 184
  and Jesus, 90, 95, 98, 105, 161
  and John the Baptist, 69, 105

and the Transfiguration, 106, *160*
Elisha, 90, 95, 133, 161
Elizabeth, 63, 66, 78, *82*, 207
Elymas, 71
Embalming, 127
Emmaus, 129, *131*, 160, *218*, 219
End of the World, 106, 165, 178 *and see* Apocalypse; Synoptic Apocalypse
Enoch, books of, 132, 168, 185
Entombment, *127*, 217 *and see* Deposition; Passion
Eons (Gnostic), 176, 177
Ephesus, *55*, 202
Eschatology *see* Apocalypse; End of the World; Synoptic Apocalypse
Esdras, 168
Essenes, the, 34, 37, 82, 82–3, 143 *and see* Judaism
Esther, 105
Eucharist, 112, 191, *221* *and see* Lord's Supper
Evangelists, 50, *51*, 52–5, *53*, *54*, *57*, 142, *146* *and see* Gospels
Eve, 68, *219*, 219
Evil, 87, 96–7, 98, 151, 176 *and see* Demons
Exorcism, 32, 83, 94, 96–7, 158–9, 166
  and disciples, 133
  and the Kingdom of God, 151
  and prophecy, 87, 97
  and see Demons; Healing; Magic; Miracles; Possession
Ezekiel, 138, 169, 184

F

Faith, 108, 144, 154 *and see* Belief
Family, 44–5, 90, 100–101, 153 *and see* Holy Family

Fasting, 37, 102
Feminist theory, 186–7
Fertility, 45
Festivals, 21, 32, 33, 77, 93, 99, 112–13
First Jewish War, 19, 28, 52
Fishing, 17, *29*, 43, 43, 98, *130*, *163*, *209*
Flogging, 7, 32, 120
Florus, Gessius, 28
Forgiveness, 109, 130, 146, 153, 159
Fourth Gospel (Gospel of John), 51, 154–5
  authorship of, 55, 57
  parables in, 137
  reliability of, 21, *192*, 193
  and see Evangelists; Gospels

G

Gabbatha, 21, 120
Gabriel, *65*, 66–7, 69, 73 *and see* Angels
Gadara, 14
Gadarene Swine, 14, *97*, 97, 158
Galatia, 172
Galileans, 16, 26, 37, 47, 103
Galilee, 16–17, 103, 130
  and Jesus' ministry, 16, 17, 83, 92, 101, 107
  Judaism in, 33
  and the Resurrection, 130
Galilee, Sea of, *10*, *16*, 16, *41*, 99
Gamala, 32
Genealogies, 62, 62–3, 64, 74, 78, 109, 165, 207
Gennesaret, 16
Gennesaret, Lake *see* Galilee, Sea of
Gentiles, 144–5 *and see* Christianity, Gentile
Gerasa (Jerash), 14

Gergesa, 14

Gerizim, Mount, 36

Gethsemane, 21, 42, 46, *114*, 114–15, *115*, *185*

Gnosticism, 58, 59, 173, 176–7, 186

God
  as Father, 46, 76, *146*, 146–7, 153, *155*, 155, *221*, 221
  of Israel, 146, 151
  and Jesus, 46, 76, 84, 87, 146–7, 170, 174
  Wisdom of, 174, 186
  and see Kingdom of God; Trinity

Golden Rule, 143

Golgotha, 46, *122*, *123*, 123

Good Samaritan *see* Parables

Gospel of Peter, 58

Gospel of Philip, 186

Gospel of Pseudo–Matthew, 191

Gospel of Thomas, *57*, 58, *59*, 138, 177, 186

Gospels, 7–8, 50–5
  accuracy of, 50, 192
  apocryphal, 58
  as biography, 50–1, 56
  chronology of, 52–3, 193
  Hellenistic influence on, 54, 55
  as history, 54, 56
  and language, 54, 65–6, 70, 168–9
  and Pharisees, 34
  in the Qur'an, 191
  synoptic, *57*, 92, 154–5
  teachings in, 92, 109
  and see Egerton Gospel; Evangelists; Fourth Gospel; Infancy Gospels; Luke; Mark; Matthew

Government, 24, 26–9, 111, 117, 120–1 *and see* Jewish law

Greco-Roman influences, *14*, 14, 18, *23*, 47, 198 *and see* Hellenism

Gregory Nazianzus, 174

Gregory of Nyssa, 174

H

Hadith, 191

Haggadah, 73

Halo, 208, *218*

Haman, 105

Harrowing of Hell, 218

Hasmonean rule, 22, 24, 28

Hazan, 33

Healing, 14, 32, 83, 94–5, 98, 144, 158–9, 191
  of blindness, 21, 92, *94*, *95*, 109, *158*, 158, *208*
  by disciples, 133
  of centurion's slave, 26
  of crippled people, 158, 186
  of deaf mute, 158
  of dropsy, 158
  of epilepsy, 108
  and faith, 158, 159
  of fever, *94*, 158
  of hemorrhaging, *94*, *95*, 158
  and language, 46, 95, 97, 159
  of leprosy, 31, 158
  of official's son, 158
  of paralysis, 21, 158, *159*, 159
  on the Sabbath, 32–3, 143
  and saliva, *94*, *95*, *208*
  of withered hand, 158
  of women, *94*, 158, 186
  and see Exorcism; Miracles

Heaven, 132, 185

Hebrew, *46*, 46

Hebrew Bible (Hebrew Scriptures), 30, 106, 140–1
  apocalyptic predictions in, 180
  and Christian art, 198
  and genealogy, 62
  and Gentiles, 145
  on God, 146
  and the Holy Spirit, 184
  influences of, 54, 101
  and the Kingdom of God, 151

  and the Nativity, 70
  and parables, 138
  and the people of Israel, 146, 167
  and Wisdom, 170, 186
  and see Mosaic law; Septuagint; Torah *and individual writings*

Hebrew Scriptures *see* Hebrew Bible (Hebrew Scriptures)

Hebrews, letter to the, 170

Hegesippus, 80

Hellenism, 16, 22–3, 46, 54, 55, 172 *and see* Greco-Roman influences

Heretics, 175, 189

Herod Agrippa I, 124

Herod Antipas (Antipas), 16, 24, 61
  coinage of, 38, *105*
  death of, 73
  and Jesus' ministry, 54, *107*
  and Jesus' trial, 24, *116*, 122
  and John the Baptist, 24, 103, 104
  marriage of, 45

Herod the Great, 16
  and Caesarea, *24*
  family tomb of, 72
  and government, 28
  and Hellenism, 22–3, 46
  and Jericho, 15
  and Jerusalem, 19, 23, *110*, *111*, *123*
  and Jesus' birth, 60
  and the Massacre of the Innocents, 72, 73

Herod Philip (Philip), 17, 24, 25, 38, *107*

Herodian dynasty, 24–5, 105

Herodians, 25, 34, 103 *and see* Judaism

Herodias, 24, 45, 105

Herodium, 32

Herodotus, 12

High Priest, 28–29 *and see* Annas; Caiaphas; Sadducees; Trials of Jesus

Hillel, 45, 143, 162

Holy Communion, 112 *and see* Eucharist

Holy Family, 67, 76, 78–81, *81*, *207*, 207

Holy Kinship, 207

Holy Spirit, *65*, 85, 133, *155*, 167, 173, 184, 190, *221*, 221 *and see* Annunciation; Spirit of God; Spirit of Truth; Trinity; Wisdom (Sophia)

Hosea, 74

I

Ignatius of Antioch, 69, 174

Illegitimacy, 68

Impurity, 36, 76

Incarnation, 175, 188

Incest, 45, 104

Infancy gospels, 58, 75, 78, *81*, 206 *and see* Gospels

Inheritance, 45

Inns, 38, *67*

Insanity, 116 *and see* Possession

Irenaeus, 52

Isaiah, 70, 82–3, 84–5, 132

Iscariot, 182 *and see* Judas Iscariot

Islam, 190–91

Israel, land of, 12 *and see* Palestine

Israel, people of, 74–5, 98, 144, 167
   and God, 86, 146, 151, 167
   in the wilderness, 86, 87
   Twelve Tribes of, 91, 98, 178

Israelites *see* Israel, people of

J

Jairus, 32, *95*

James (brother of Jesus), 80, 117, 172

James (disciple), 43, 91, 106, *160*, *185*

James, letter of, 173

Jehoash, 138

Jehoiachin, 63

Jehoiakim, 63

Jerash (Gerasa), 14

Jeremiah, 73, 75

Jericho, 14, 15, 27

Jerusalem, 13, 18–19, *19*, *20*, *21*, 21, 77, *123*, *132*, *170*, *215*
   architecture of, 7, *11*, 19, 29, *123*
   destruction of, 52, 54, 116, 122, 173
   Dome of the Rock, *19*
   el-Aqsa mosque, *111*
   entry into, 21, 27, 110, *118*, 118
   Essene Quarter, 112
   and Herod the Great, 19, 23, *110*, *111*, 123
   Jesus' journeys to, 14–15, 92–3, 108–9
   Roman siege of, 181
   and see Temple of Jerusalem; Temple Mount

Jesse, 62

Jesus, *2*, *51*, *90*, *102*, *116*, *150*, *159*, *220*
   appearance of, 198, 209, 214
   childhood of, 76–7, 80, *206*, 206–7, *207*
   chronology of life of, 60–1, 92, 93, 116
   death and prophecy, 29, 115, 124
   education of, 79
   and Elijah, 90, 95, 98, 105, 161
   and the family, 90, 100–1, 153
   family life of, 67, 76, 78–81, *81*, *207*, 207
   in Galilee, 16, 17, 83, 92, 101, 107
   genealogy of, 62–3, 64, 74, 78, 109, 165
   and Gentiles, 144
   and God, 46, 76, 84, 87, 146–7, 170, 174

historical reality of, 6–9, 192–5
   and Islam, 190–1
   and Jewish law, 30, 142–3
   Jewishness of, 92, 188
   and Jews, 92
   and John the Baptist, 82, 83, 85, 158
   as magician, 71, 86, 101
   names for, 65, 96, 162–3
   nature of, 174–5, 177
   and the Pharisees, 34–5, 101–3, *102*, *140*
   as Prophet, 160–1, 169, 190
   rejection of, 101, 114–15, 141
   and Samaritans, 36, 144
   sources for, 6–9, 58–9, 75, 78
   as teacher, *18*, 30, 35, 37, 76, *76*, 79, 141, 152–3, 162–3
   threat to, 24, 25, 101
   words of, 46–7, 92, 219
      at Crucifixion, 46, 125–6
      authenticity of, 8, 46, 56, 59, 141, 142, 166
      for healing, 46, 95
      about himself, 33, 163, 166–7, 168–9
      on Jewish law, 142–3
      at Last Supper, 112, 150
   and see Annunciation; Arrest; Ascension; Baptism; Betrayal; Birth; Condemnation; Crucifixion; Deposition of body; Entombment; Incarnation; Last Supper; Messiah; Ministry of Jesus; Mockery of Jesus; Nativity; Passion; Presentation in the Temple; Resurrection; Son of God; Temptation; Transfiguration; Trials of Jesus

Jesus Barabbas (Barabbas), 120

Jesus ben Ananias, 116

Jesus Seminar, 8–9, 56

Jewish Christianity *see* Christianity
Jewish law, 28, 30, 35–36, 37, 102,
   142–3
   and Christians, 172, 173
   and Jesus, 30, 142–3
   and Pharisees, 30, 35, 142, 143,
   162
   at Qumran, 83
   and Sadducees, 142
   and scribes, 30, 162
   and the Temple, 30–31
   and trials, 116–17, 119
   and see Government; Judaism;
   Mishnah; Sanhedrin; Talmud;
   Torah
Jews, 22–3, 28–9, 92, *144*, 145, 172
   and see Christianity, Jewish;
   Judaism; King of the Jews
Jezebel, 105
Joachim, *58*, 78, 207
John the Baptist, 37, *51*, 82–3, *83*,
   207, 219, *221*
   birth of, 61, 66–7, 190
   disciples of, 82, 83, 91
   and Elijah, 69, 105
   execution of, 24, 103, *104*, 104–5,
   105
   and fishing, 43
   forerunner of Messiah, 141, 161
   genealogy of, 63, 207
   and Herod Antipas, 45, 103, 104–5
   and Jesus, 82, 83, 85, 158, 207
   ministry of, 13, 14, 61
   as prophet, 161
   and the wilderness, 13–14
John Chrysostom, 174
John (disciple), 9, 91, *113*, *125*, 185
   and the crucifixion, 126, *127*, *215*,
   216, *217*
   and the Transfiguration, 106, *160*
   and see Fourth Gospel
John (Yehohanan), *124*

Jonah and the Whale, 198
Jordan River, *12*, 14, *84*
Joseph of Arimathea, 90, *127*, 127,
   216
Joseph Caiaphas (Yehoseph bar Qypa)
   see Caiaphas
Joseph of Nazareth, 39, 44, 64, 65,
   74–5, 76, *77*, 200, *201*
Joseph (patriarch), 64, 75
Joseph/Joses (brother of Jesus), 80
Josephus, Flavius, 76
   on crucifixions, 124
   on date of census, 61
   on high priests, 29
   on James (brother of Jesus), 80
   on Jesus, 58
   on John the Baptist, 82, 103, 104
   on kingship, 120
   on Pharisees, 34–5, 36–7
   on prophets, 161
   on Sadducees, 35
   on synagogues, 32
   on Temple of Jerusalem, 18, 19,
   110
   on trials, 19, 116
Judaism, 145, 162
   and Christianity, 188–9
   in Galilee, 33
   and Gentiles, 145
   and the Gospels, 55
   and Pontius Pilate, 23, 26
   sects within, 34–7
   and see Essenes; Herodians; Jewish
   law; Jews; Pharisees; Sadducees;
   Samaritans; Scribes
Judas the Galilean, 103, 182
Judas Iscariot, 87, 91, *113*, 114, 115,
   182, *185*
Judas Maccabeus, 22
Judas Thaddaeus/Jude (disciple), 91
Judas/Jude (brother of Jesus), 80, 91
Jude (disciple) *see* Judas Thaddaeus

Jude, letter of, 80
Judea, 24–5, 26, 83, 87, 93
Judgment Day, 9, 144, 147 *and see*
   Apocalypse; End of the World;
   Last Judgment
Julius Africanus, 63
Justin Martyr, 50, 174

K

Kerioth, 115
Ketubbah, 44
Kfar Kanna, *93 and see* Cana
Khirbet Qana, *91*, *93 and see* Cana
Kidron brook, 21
King of the Jews, 120, *125 and see*
   Crucifixion; Jews
Kingdom of God, 150–3, 154–5, 158,
   178 *and see* God
Kings at the Nativity, 70, *200*
Kiss, 114, *182*, 182

L

"L" (gospel source), 57
Lambs, sacrificial, *33*, 33, 112, 113,
   126, *201 and see* Passover;
   Sacrifices
Lamentation, 216–17 *and see* Passion
Language, 46–7, 50, 140, 162–3, 178
   accuracy of, 27, 29, 81, 136
   of the gospels, 54, 65–6, 70, 168–9
   and healing, 46, 95, 97, 159
   of Jesus, 46–7
   and see Aramaic; Greek;
   Hebrew; Jesus, words of
Last Judgment, 9, 153, *171 and see*
   Judgment Day
Last Supper, *33*, 33, 99, 112–13, *113*,
   135, 150–51, *178*, *179*, 179, 213

date of, 61, 112
Jesus' words at, 59, 150
Law *see* Jewish law
Laying on of hands, 95 *and see*
Healing
Lazarus, 21, 95, 118, *192*, 210, 210
Levi (disciple) *see* Matthew (disciple)
Levites, 31, 63
Liberation theology, 182
Lily, as symbol, *9*
Logos, 174–5, 220
Lord's Prayer, 56, *147*, 147, 150 *and*
see Prayers
Lord's Supper, 112, 179 *and see*
Eucharist
Love, 153, 154
Luke (evangelist), *51*, *54*, 54
Luke, Gospel of, 51, 53–5, 57
parables in, 55, 109, 136, 137, 138

M

"M" (gospel source), 57
Maccabean revolt, 22
Machaerus (Mukawir), 104
Madonna, *83*, *201*, *203*, 204, *205*
and see Mary (mother of Jesus)
Magdala *see* Mary Magdalene;
Migdal
Magi, *71*, 71, 72, 200 *and see*
Kings at the Nativity; Wise Men
Magic, 71, 86, 101, 119 *and see*
Exorcism
Magnificat, 67, 77
Man of Sorrows, 217
Mandylion of Edessa, *214*, 214
Marcion, 54, 69
Mark (John Mark) (evangelist), 51,
52, *52*, 57, *57*
Mark, Gospel of, *51*, *52*, 52–3, 57,
129 *and see* Gospels

Marriage, *44*, 44–5, 104, 143, 145
and see Betrothal
Martha (sister of Lazarus), 21, 45,
187, *210*
Mary Magdalene, *102*, *127*, 129, 130,
132, *186*, 187, *187*, *213*, 217
Mary (mother of Jesus), 9, 17, *44*, 62,
77, *221*
alleged adultery of, 68, 189
and the Ascension, *133*
birth of, 78–9
in Christian art, *201*, *202*, 202,
203, *204*, 204, *205*
and the Crucifixion, 45, *125*, 126,
127, *213*, *215*, 216, *217*
and Joseph, 44
and the Nativity, *65*, 66–7, *67*, *200*,
201
purification of, 31, 76–7
virginity of, *65*, 68–9, *69*, 81
Mary (sister of Lazarus), 21, 187, *210*
Masada, 32, *162*, *183*
Mashal, 136
Massacre of the Innocents, 24, 71, 72,
73, *73*
Matthew (disciple) (Levi), 27, *51*, *53*,
53, 91
Matthew, Gospel of, 51, 53, 57, 173,
193 *and see* Gospels
Melqart, 29
Messiah, 70, 164–5
acknowledgment of Jesus as, 14,
70, 107
belief in, 35, 62, 64, 84, 106–7,
172
claims to be, 33, 119, 120, *144*,
158, 164, 178, 183
and Judaism, 188
role of, 107
and see Son of God
Midrash, 140, 141
Migdal (Magdala), *186*

Ministry
of Jesus, 16, 17, 61, 83, 92–3,
100–101, 107, 208–11
of John the Baptist, 13, 14, 61
Miracles, 17, *154*, 154, 158, 166,
190, 191
and belief, 192
Clay Birds, *81*, 191, *207*
by disciples, 77
Feeding the Multitudes, *3*, *6*, 41,
43, 93, 98–9, 113, 161, 190, 209
Fish with Coin, *29*, 29, 98
fishing, 43, 98, *130*, *163*
"nature miracles," 98–9
raising the dead, 14, 95, 118, 159,
161, *192*, *210*
Stilling the Storm, *43*, 98
symbolism of, 92, 98, 154
Walking on Water, *43*, 98
Water turned to Wine, 44, *91*, 93,
154, 209
and see Exorcism; Healing
Mishnah, 30, 35, 36, 46, 116–17,
119, 162 *and see* Jewish law
Missionary work, 37, 54, 71, 130–31,
144–5, 172
Moneychangers, 38, 110
Monophysitism, 175
Morality, 62, 143
Mosaic law (law of Moses) *see*
Hebrew Bible (Hebrew Scriptures);
Jewish law; Mishnah; Talmud
Moses, 132, 190
and Egypt, 74–5
and the feeding miracles, 98, 99
parallels with, 72, 73, 75
Song of, 151
and the Transfiguration, 106, *160*,
167
Moses' seat, 32, 35
Motherhood, 45
Mount of the Beatitudes, *149*

Mount Carmel, 78

Mount Hermon, 14, *15*, *106*

Mount Horeb, 133

Mount of Olives (Mount Olivet), 19, 21, 42, *132*, *147*, *151*

Mount of the Precipitation (Mount of the Leap), 79

Mount Tabor, *106*

Mount of the Temptation, *86*

Muhammad, 190, 191

Muratorian Fragment, 51

Mysticism, 132, 184–5

N

Nag Hammadi, *59*, *177*, 177

Nain, 14, *95*, 95

Names, 46–7, 64–5, 76, 123, 182, 214

Nathan (prophet), 63, 138

Nathan (son of Solomon), 63

Nathanael, 16, 91

Nativity, *63*, 64–7, 70–71, 166, *190*, 190, *200*, 200–201 *and see* Annunciation; Birth of Jesus

Nazarenes (Jewish Christian sect), 173

Nazarenes (artists), 207

Nazareth, 17, 67, *74*, *75*, 79, *79*, 101, 159

"Nazorean," 74

Negev desert, 75

Nestorianism, 175

New Quest of the historical Jesus, 193

New Testament, 8, 58, 59, 139, 169, 176, 193–4 *and see individual writings*

New Year festival, 33, 93 *and see* Festivals

Nicea, *174*, 175

Nicene Creed, *174*, 175

Nicodemus, 90, 103, *127*, 127, 216

Nimrod, 72

Noah, 190

Noahide laws, 172

Nunc Dimittis, 77

O

Offerings, 18, 29, 36, 142 *and see* Sacrifices

Origen, 68, 174

Ossuary, *46*, *117*

P

Pagan beliefs, 29, 58, 68, 72

Palestine, 12–15, *13*, *25*, 26–7, *39*, 56 *and see* Israel, land of

Paneas *see* Banias

Pantera (Panthera/Pandera), 68

Pantocrator, *2*, *48*, *150*, *220*, 220–21

Papias, 52

Parables, 55, 59, 109, 136–8, 181, 186–7, 191

The Barren Fig Tree, 137

Choosing a Seat, 137, 138

The Creditor, 137

The Dishonest Manager, 38, 137

A Divided House, 137

The Eagle and the Vine, 138

The Evil Tenants, 40

The Faithful and Unfaithful Slaves, 137

The Fig Tree, 137

The Generous Employer, 41

The Good Samaritan, *36*, 36, 38, *109*, 109, *136*, 137, 138

The Good Shepherd, 137, *198*

The Great Net, *59*, 137, 151

The Growing Seed, 137, 141, 151

The Hidden Treasure, 137

Houses Built on Rock and Sand, 149

The Judgment of the Nations, 137

The Lost Coin, 137

The Lost Sheep, 137

The Mustard Seed, 137, 151

The Pearl, 137

The Pharisee and the Tax Collector, *31*, 31, 103, 109, 137

The Prodigal Son, 109, 136, 137, *138*, 138

The Rainstorm, 39

The Rich Fool, 137

The Rich Man, 109

The Rich Man and Lazarus, 109, 137

The Sower, 41, 137, 138, 191, *194*

The Sower of Weeds, 137, *139*, 151

The Talents or Pounds, 38, 39, 137

The Ten Bridesmaids (the Wise and Foolish Bridesmaids), 42, 45, *136*, 137, 191

The Two Builders, 137

The Two Sons, 137

The Unexpected Guest, 137

The Unforgiving Servant, 109, 137

The Unjust Steward, 41

The Vine and the Branches, *137*, 137

The Vineyard Laborers, 109, 137

The Wedding Banquet, 137

The Wicked Tenants, 118, 137, 138, 166–7

The Widow and Unjust Judge, 137

The Wise and Foolish Bridesmaids *see* The Ten Bridesmaids

The Yeast, 137, 151

and see Discourses; Sermons

Parousia (Second Coming of Christ), 171, 178, 181

paschal lambs, *see* lambs, sacrificial

Passion, 107, 108, 116, 212–17 *and*

see Arrest of Jesus; Crucifixion; Deposition of body; Entombment; Lamentation; Last Supper; Trials of Jesus

Passover (Pesah), festival of, 33, 93, 99, 112–13 *and see* Festivals

Patristic Period, 174–5, 192 *and see* Church Fathers

Paul, *50, 55, 90,* 161, *176, 221*
  and the Ascension, *133*
  and the early Church, 144, 171, 172–3, 189, 195
  and Gentile mission, 144, 172–3
  letters of, *55,* 69, 112, 131, 172, *176,* 176
  and Luke, 54
  and mysticism, 185
  and the Resurrection, 131, 170
  teaching of, 142, 172, 188–9
  and the universal gospel, 145

Pella, 173

Pentateuch, 30, *35 and see* Hebrew Bible (Hebrew Scriptures); Jewish law

Pentecost, 33, 93 *and see* Festivals

Peoples of the Book, 190

Perea, 14, 93

Pesah *see* Passover

Pesher, 141

Peter (Cephas, Simon, Simon Peter), 17, 43, *52, 52,* 91, *157, 176, 210, 221*
  calling of, 98, *209*
  confession of, 106–7, 160, 164, *168*
  denial of Jesus by, 115, *119*
  and Jesus' arrest, 107, 182, 185, 212
  and Mark, 52
  and the Resurrection, 130, 131
  and the Transfiguration, 106, *160*

Pharisees, 23, 30, *31, 102,* 162

  and divorce, 45, 141
  and exorcism, 96
  and Galileans, 16
  and the gospels, 34, 53
  and Jesus, 34–5, 98, 101–103, *140,* 141
  and Jewish law, 28, 30, 35, 142, 143
  and Judaism, 34–7
  and the synagogue, 32
  and see Judaism

Philip (tetrarch) *see* Herod Philip

Philip (disciple), 47, 91, *144,* 172

Philistines, 12

Philo, 29, 71, 123

Physicians, 94

Pietà, 196, 216, 217

Pilate *see* Pontius Pilate

Pilate Stone, *26*

Pleroma, 177

Political unrest, 58, 120, 182–3
  and the Cleansing of the Temple, 111
  and false prophets, 161
  in Galilee, 16, 103
  and Hellenism, 23
  and Jesus' arrest and trial, 26, 118, 120, 121
  and Roman rule, 28, 61, 111
  see also First Jewish War; Second Jewish War

Polycarp of Smyrna, 174

Pontius Pilate
  coins, 38, *120*
  and Jesus' death, 61, 120–21, *121,* 125, 127
  and Jesus' trial, 19, 24, 116, *121,* 183, 213
  and Judaism, 23, 26
  and the Temple of Jerusalem, 26

Populations, 14, 16, 17, 21

Possession, 27, 36, 96, 96–7, 101, 184

and see Demons; Exorcism; Insanity

Poverty, 77

Praetorium, 18

Prayer of Nabonidus, 159

Prayers, 141, 147, 184–5 *and see* Lord's Prayer

Presentation in the Temple, 76, 77, 77, *195*

Priestly lineage, 63 *and see* Genealogies

Priests, 31, 63, 102 *and see* High Priest

Prophecy, 65, 73, 141, 160–1
  of betrayal, 115
  and exorcism, 87, 97
  of desertion of disciples, 141
  of destruction of Jerusalem, 54, 116, 122
  of Jesus' death, 29, 115, 124
  and John the Baptist, 141
  and Judas Iscariot, 115
  of Last Judgment, 82
  of Nativity, 66, 71
  and the Resurrection, 129, 131
  of Second Coming, 181
  of Simeon, 77
  and the Temple, 110, 116, 118, 180
  and see Angels; Dreams; Prophets

Prophets, 160–61, 169, 190 *and see* Prophecy

Prophets (section of the Hebrew Bible), 30, *35 and see* Hebrew Bible (Hebrew Scriptures)

Prostitutes, 186

Protevangelium of James, 58, 78, 201

Psalms, 30, 70, 84–5, 126

Pseudepigrapha, 132

Purification, ritual, 31, 76–7, 83, 111, 141

Q

"Q" (gospel source), 47, 57
Qatzrin, *78*
Quirinius, 61
Qumran, *37, 37*, 82–3, 112, *141*
    sect of, 112, 141, 151, 179, 195
    writings of (Dead Sea Scrolls),
    46, 55, 71, 72
Qur'an, 190–1

R

Rabbis, 79, 162–3 *and see* Teaching
Rahab, 62
Rasul, 190
Redemption, *134*, 177
Reliquary, *172*
Repentance, 153
Resurrection, 35, 95, 101, 141, *151,
    171*
    chronology of, 130–31
    and the Church, 131, 170–71
    and the disciples, 129, 219
    of Jesus, 111, 128–31, *129,
    218–19, 219*
    and women, 128–9
Revelation, book of, 173, 180, 181,
    221
Roads, 26, 38, *108 and see* Trade
Roman rule, 24, 26–7, 28, *60*, 60–61,
    117
    and Jesus' arrest, 115
    and Jesus' trial, 120–1
    and persecution of Christians, 198
    and political unrest, 28, 61, 111
Rufus of Cyrene, 123
Ruth, 62

S

Sabbath, 32–3, 35–6, 103, 143
Sacrifices, 18, 36, 111, 173, 179
    and Atonement, 170, 171
    Passover, 112
    and Purification, 31, 77
    and sin, 171
    and see Lambs, sacrificial;
    Offerings
Sadducees, 28, 34, 35, 141, 142 *and
    see* High Priest; Judaism
Salim, 14
Saliva, and healing, 94, 95, *208*
Salome, *105*, 105
Samaria, 36, 93, *144*
Samaritans, 34, *36, 36, 144*, 144–5
    and see Judaism
Samson, 66, 74
Samuel, 77
Sanhedrin, 28, 30, 32, 35, 117
    and Jesus' trial, 28, 116, 118, 119,
    183
and see Jewish law; Scribes
Satan, *86, 86, 87, 87,* 97 *and see*
    Beelzebul; Devil
Schweitzer, Albert, 193
Scribes, 28, 30, 32, 34, 53, 101, 141,
    162 *and see* Jewish law; Judaism;
    Pharisees; Sanhedrin
Scripture, 30, 33, 51, 140–1, 174
    and see Hebrew Bible (Hebrew
    Scriptures); New Testament
    and individual writings
Scythopolis (Beth-Shean), *14*
Second Coming (Parousia), 171, 178,
    181
Second Jewish War, 71, 188
Seder, 112 *and see* Last Supper
Seleucid empire, 22
Sepphoris, 16, 17, *23, 23,* 24, *64,* 79,
    103
Septuagint, 66, 67, 74, 136, 140

and see Hebrew Bible (Hebrew
    Scriptures)
Sermons of Jesus, 148–9, 152–3
    on the Mount, 53, 56, 130, 143,
    148, *149,* 149, 153
    on the Plain, *56,* 148, 149
    and see Discourses; Parables
Settlements, 14, 17, 29, *78,* 79
Seven Last Words, 126
Shabbetai Zvi, 188
Shammai, 45, 162
Shekinah, 68
Shem, Treatise of, 72
Shepherds at the Nativity, 70, *201,
    201*
Shrouds, *126, 126,* 127, *214*
Sidon, 12, 15
Siloam, Pool of, 21, *158, 208*
Simeon, 66, 77
Similitudes of Enoch, 168
Simon bar Kokhba (Simon bar
    Kosiba), 71, 188
Simon of Cyrene, 27, 123
Simon Peter *see* Peter
Simon Iscariot, 115
Simon the magician (Simon magus),
    68, 71
Simon the Zealot (disciple), 91, 182
Simon (Simeon) (brother of Jesus), 80
Sin, and sacrifice, 171
Slaves/servants, 41
Soldiers, 26, 27, 122–3, 124, *213*
Solomon, *219*
Son of God, 63, 119, *155, 155,*
    166–7, 174 *and see* Messiah;
    Trinity
Son of Man, 155, 168–9, 178, 181
Song of Moses, 151
"Sons of Thunder" *see* James *and*
    John (disciples)
Sophia (Wisdom), 173, 186 *and see*
    Wisdom of God

Sparrow, *81*, 191, *207*

Spirit of God, 84 *and see* Holy Spirit

Spirit of Truth, 154 *and see* Holy
  Spirit

Star, at the Nativity, 71, 72

Stations of the Cross, 214

Stephen, 117, *172*

Stoning, 100, 117, 172

Strauss, D.F., 192–3

Suetonius, *56*, 58, 73

Suffering Servant, 171

Sun, eclipse of, 124

Swine *see* Gadarene swine

Sword, *9*, *182*, 182

Symbolism
  of agriculture, 40
  of Ascension, 133
  of casting out demons, 97
  in Christian art, 198, 201, 202,
    204, 208, 210, 218, 220
  and the Crucifixion, 124, 127
  of destruction of the Temple, 111,
    124
  of disciples, 77
  of dove, *65*, 84, *85*, *155*, *221*, 221
  of evangelists, *51*, *53*, *54*, *57*, *146*
  of fishing, 43
  of lily, *9*
  of miracles, 92, 154
  of Nativity gifts, 70
  of sword, *9*
  of Trinity, *167*
  of virginity, 204
  of wilderness, 86

Synagogue, 14, *32*, 32–3, 47, 92, *96*,
  101, 162, 188

Syncretism, 22

Synoptic Apocalypse, 111, 178, 180,
  181 *and see* End of the World

Synoptic Gospels, 57, 92, 154–5 *and
  see* individual gospels

Syria, 53

T

Tabernacles (Booths), festival of, 33,
  93 *and see* Festivals

Tabgha, *3*, *99*, *178*

Tacitus, *56*, 58

Talmud, 30, 68, 124, 162, 189 *and
  see* Jewish law

Tamar, 62

Targums, 140

Taxation, 26, 27, 28–9, *29*, *31*, 38–9,
  43, 103

Teacher of Righteousness, 37, 141,
  195

Teaching, 31, 162–3
  in the Gospels, 92, 109
  of Jesus, *18*, 30, 35, 37, *76*, 76, 79,
    118, 135–155, *141*, 152–3
  of Paul, 142, 172, 188–9

Temple of Jerusalem, *31*, *35*
  construction of, 19, 23
  desecration of, 22, 33
  destruction of, 111, 118, 124, 162,
    180
  Jesus and the teachers in, 67, *76*,
    76, 79–80
  and Jewish law, 30–1
  offerings to, 18, 29, 36, 142
  personnel of, 28, 29, 31
  and Pontius Pilate, 26
  Presentation in, *76*, 77, *77*, *195*
  prophecies concerning, 110, 116,
    118, 180
  and taxation, 28, *29*, 29, 38–9, 43
  Treasury, 18, 28–9
  wealth of, 28–9, 38
  and see Cleansing of the Temple;
    Dedication; Presentation;
    Temple Mount

Temple Mount, *18*, 18, *19*, 19, *103*,
  111 *and see* Jerusalem; Temple
  of Jerusalem

Temptation, 13, *86*, 86–7, *87*, 166

Ten Commandments, 143 *and see*
  Commandments

Thaddaeus (Lebbaeus), 47, 91

Theotokos, 202 *and see* Mary (mother
  of Jesus)

Theudas, 161

Thomas Didymus, *59*, 91, 155

Tiberias, 16, 24

Tiberias, Lake of *see* Galilee, Sea of

Tiberius, *56*, 56, 61

Tithes, 36, 102 *and see* Taxation

Titulus, 47, *125*, 165, 183

Tombs, 72, 123, *127*, 127, *128*, 131,
  192, *210*

Torah, 30, *142*, 142–3, 172 *and see*
  Hebrew Bible (Hebrew Scriptures);
  Jewish law

Touching, 95 *and see* Healing

Tower of flocks, 70

Trade, 38–9, *39*, 70, 81 *and see*
  Economy; Roads

Transfiguration, 14, *15*, 106, 132,
  160, *167*, 167, *193*

Transjordan, 14, 173

Transport, 38

Trials of Jesus, *116*, 116–21, *119*,
  121, 161, *164*, 164–5, 213
  and Jewish Law, 116–17, 119, 161
  and political unrest, 26, 118, 120,
    121
  and Pontius Pilate, 19, 24, 116,
    121, 183, 213
  and Sanhedrin, 28, 116, 118, 119,
    183
  and see Condemnation of Jesus

Trinity, 190, 220–21, *167* *and see*
  God as Father; Holy Spirit;
  Son of God

Turin Shroud, *126*, 126, 214 *and see*
  Shrouds

Twelve, 91, 178 *and see* Disciples

Twelve tribes of Israel, 91, 98, 178

and see Israel, people of

Two-Document hypothesis, 57

Two-Gospel hypothesis, 57

Tyre, 12, 15, 38

U

Universalism, *55*, 63, 77, 145, 146

Universal gospel, 145

Unleavened Bread, feast of, 12 *and see*
    Passover (Pesah)

Usury, 38

V

Vera icon, 214

Via Dolorosa, *122*, 214

Via Maris, 17

Virgin birth, *65*, 68–9, *69*, 81, 173,
    189, 190, 200, *204*, 204

Virgin Mary *see* Mary (mother
    of Jesus)

Visions, 185, 201

W

Wadi Qelt, *108*

Wadi Ze'elim, *82*

War, First Jewish, 19, 28, 52

War, Second Jewish, 71, 188

Washing, 37, 83, *102*

Water, 41, *43*

Weddings, *45*, 45

Weeks, festival of, *see* Pentecost

Widows, 45, 187

Wilderness, 13–14, 86, *87*, 87, 184

Wine, 40, *40*

Wisdom of God, 174, 186 *and see*
    God; Wisdom (Sophia)

Wisdom (Sophia), 173, 186 *and see*
    Wisdom of God

Wise men, 38, 67, 70, 71 *and see* Magi

Woes, 101, 149

Women
    Daughters of Jerusalem, 122
    as disciples, 77, 187
    exclusion of, 186
    and feminist theory, 186–7
    and the Gospel, 186–7
    and Gnosticism, 186

    healing of, 186

    legal rights of, 45

    role of, 62

    and the Resurrection, 128–9

Writings (section of the Hebrew
    Bible), 30, 35 *and see* Hebrew Bible
    (Hebrew Scriptures)

Y

Yeast, as metaphor, 98

Yom Kippur (Day of Atonement),
    170, 171

Z

Zacchaeus, 15, *27*, 27

Zachariah, 78

Zadok, 35

Zadokites, 35

Zealots, 182, 183, *183*

Zebedee, 91

Zechariah, 31, *82*, 122

PICTURE CREDITS

1 Sant' Apollinare in Classe, Ravenna, Italy/ET
2 Hagia Sophia, Istanbul/ET
3 ES/Axiom*
6 Sant' Apollinare Nuovo, Ravenna, Italy/ET
7 Tom Ang/RHPL
9 Museo de Zaragoza, Spain/ET
10 AF Kersting, London
11 ES/Axiom
12 ES/Axiom
14 ES/Axiom
15 ES/Axiom
16 ES/Axiom*
17 Chris Bradley/Axiom
18 ZR
19 ES/Axiom
21 AF Kersting, London
22 Museo Nazionale, Rome/ET
23 ES/Axiom
24 ES/Axiom*
26tl ES/Axiom

26bl Erich Lessing/AKG London
27 Bobrinskoy Collection/Michael Holford, London
29 Superstock, London
31tr Erich Lessing/AKG London
31bl Sant' Apollinare Nuovo, Ravenna, Italy/ET
32 ES/Axiom
33 Superstock, London
34 Basilica Sant' Angelo in Formis, Capua, Italy/ET
35 ZR
36 Caylus Anticuario, Madrid/BAL
37 Sonia Halliday Photographs, Weston Turville, Bucks, England
38 ZR
40 ZR
41 ES/Axiom*
42tl ES/Axiom*
42tr ES/Axiom
43 Musée d'Art et d'Histoire, Geneva/BAL
44 Musée du Louvre, Paris/ET
45 Erich Lessing/AKG London
46 Erich Lessing/AKG London
47 Musée du Louvre, Paris/BAL
48 Kariye Camii, Istanbul/ET
50 Bibliothèque Nationale, Paris/BAL
51 Basilica Sant' Angelo in Formis, Capua, Italy/ET
52 James Morris/Axiom
53 British Library, London/BAL
54 Lambeth Palace Library, London/BAL
55 F.H.C. Birch/Sonia Halliday Photographs
56 ZR
57 Bibliothèque Nationale, Paris/BAL
58 Ashmolean Museum, Oxford/BAL
59 Museo de Santa Cruz, Toledo, Spain/BAL
61 Museo di San Marco dell'Angelico, Florence/BAL
62 Richardson and Kailas Icons, London/BAL
63 ES/Axiom
64 ES/Axiom*
65 Museo Nacional del Prado, Madrid/BAL
66 ES/Axiom
67 National Gallery, London/ET
69 Noortman (London) Ltd/BAL
70 Victoria and Albert Museum, London/BAL
71 Sant' Apollinare Nuovo, Ravenna, Italy/ET
72 ES/Axiom*

73 Museo di San Marco dell'Angelico, Florence/BAL
74 ES/Axiom*
75 Chris Bradley/Axiom
76 Scrovegni Chapel, Padua, Italy/Superstock, London
77 Galleria Querini-Stampalia, Venice/BAL
78 ZR
79 ES/Axiom*
80 British Museum, London
81 Museo Nacional del Prado, Madrid/ET
82 ES/Axiom
83 Musée du Louvre, Paris/PW/BAL
84 Sonia Halliday Photographs, Weston Turville, Bucks, England
85 Baptistery of the Arians, Ravenna, Italy/ET
86 ES/Axiom*
87 Fitzwilliam Museum, University of Cambridge/BAL
88-89 ES/Axiom
90 Museo de Arte de Catalunya, Barcelona/BAL
91 ES/Axiom*
92 Keble College, Oxford/BAL
93 ES/Axiom*
94 Musée du Louvre, Paris/Giraudon/BAL
95 ES/Axiom*
96 ES/Axiom*
97 Sant' Apollinare Nuovo, Ravenna, Italy/ET
99 ES/Axiom
100 Roudnice Lobkowicz Collection, Nelahozeves Castle, Czech Republic/BAL
101 ES/Axiom*
102 Musée Condé, Chantilly, France/Giraudon/BAL
103 ES/Axiom*
104 Museo Nacional del Prado, Madrid/BAL
105t ZR
105b Kunsthistorisches Museum, Vienna/BAL
106 ES/Axiom*
107 ES/Axiom*
108 ES/Axiom
109 Hermitage, St Petersburg/BAL
110 Scrovegni Chapel, Padua, Italy/ET
111 ES/Axiom*
113 Museo di San Marco dell'Angelico, Florence/BAL
114 Museo Nacional del Prado,

Illustrations on pages 1–3:

Page 1: A *6th-century mosaic in the apse of the church of Sant' Apollinare Nuovo, Ravenna, Italy.*

Page 2: Christ Pantocrator, *a 12th-century mosaic in the church of Hagia Sophia, Istanbul (formerly Constantinople).*

Page 3: *A 5th-century mosaic in the Church of the Multiplication of the Loaves and Fishes at Tabgha in Galilee (see also p.99).*

Jacket illustrations: *See pp.197, 214.*